7. 1. 20

D0997364

THE WIND BENEATH
MY WINGS

Sylvia Gallimore

THE WIND BENEATH MY WINGS
Copyright © Sylvie Gallimore 2005

All Rights Reserved

No part of this book may be reproduced in any form
by photocopying or by any electronic or mechanical means,
including information storage or retrieval systems,
without permission in writing from both the copyright
owner and the publisher of this book.

ISBN 0-9548516-1-7

First published in 2005
Gale's Publications,
Marian Cottage, Harry Stoke Road, Bristol. BS34 8QH

I would like to dedicate the following pages to my eldest sons Adam and Joseph, my wonderful grandsons Dave and Rick and to my husband Richard, who shared both terrible and good experiences described in this book. Without 'my boys' I doubt that I would have remained sane enough to write The Wind Beneath My Wings.

I would also like to thank Piers Morgan, Sue Carroll and the then Mirror team for their kindness to my family, David Blunkett for his encouragement as well as Lisa Webb (nee. Potts), Jules Barrington, Chris Evans, Sherry Eugene and Paul Burrell, among others, for making life worthwhile after all. The Bristol Evening Post and Western Daily Press for their continued support. Our wonderful solicitor Hector Stamboulieh and the legal team he gathered together to help us. Dr. Richard Spence for his care and continued kindness. My thanks also to anyone else who has helped my youngest son Daniel overcome a horrendous setback in life, allowing him to keep his sense of humour.

A special thanks also to Jim McKay for making life easier at the beginning, Geoff Warnock for putting his head on the block for us, and Kate for just being there.

Introduction

This is a story that I felt had to be written. It is about a young man who struggled with ill health from the age of eight and every time he took one step forwards, life kicked him two steps back. It is irrelevant that the young man in question is my son. Anyone would be proud to know Daniel. I was just the one who was lucky enough to have produced him and therefore shared his life closely. He was always a young man with outstanding strength of character and perseverance. Knock backs became a challenge to Daniel and he faced them all head on. I watched as all the things he really enjoyed were taken out of his grasp. As his illness progressed he had to stop playing energetic sports, which he enjoyed and was once very good at, such as football, ice-skating, street hockey, ice-hockey. So he turned to snooker and pool, winning cups at that. Knowing he had an incurable, chronic, debilitating illness, he chose a career he could do sitting down and, despite being dyslexic, got all the qualifications needed. Then the worst blow of all came when in 1996 in a senseless act of unprovoked violence our lives were changed for ever. So this story tells why he is my hero and in the words of that beautiful song sang by Bette Midler – 'The Wind Beneath My Wings'.

The Early Years

I married Richard, a childhood friend, in 1969 and we were blessed with three fine sons, all very close in age. I have always had a philosophical attitude to life that made me believe that everything that happened in life has a plus side. Looking back I wonder why I every had this attitude at all but I did. My youngest son developed this optimistic trait, and he was the least likely. As his story unfolds I am sure you will agree with the idea that optimism is the best defence and I believe it was always my youngest son's saving grace.

I always wanted sons. My father was of the attitude that women were second-class citizens and only put here to produce males to run the world. He had been terribly disappointed when I was born, five years after my sister and was the 'wrong sex'. So I suppose in a way my wanting sons was a result of brainwashing. I guess that I wanted them to be accepted by him, and to an extent, myself at last, because of them. Luck or fate and a splattering of the right chromosomes, whatever, gave me three sons. I particularly wanted three sons. You would have to be a certain age to understanding the reasoning behind wanting three sons, and then I doubt very much if anyone but me would really understand. My favourite programme as a girl was *Bonanza*. This was the ongoing story of a large ranch owner Ben Cartwright and his three sons. It went on for donkey's years. The young men in this programme all had the same father but different mothers who had either died in childbirth or soon after. Why anyone would get involved with Ben Cartwright played by Lorne Greene with his track record, I will never know.

The three Cartwright sons were all very different but very close and protective of each other, what I saw as a perfect family. Adam was the eldest and smartest and had a French mother. Then came Hoss a sort of gentle giant. I am sure he had a real name but he was always Hoss in the series. Hoss was played by the late Dan Blocker. He was a loveable but not too lucky in life and love character. Then there was my favourite, the youngest, Joseph, known as Little Joe (even when he was going grey) and played by Michael Langdon. Far too good-looking and not given to taking life too seriously.

Because I didn't have a particularly happy childhood and no strong bond with my sister or brother I had this strange notion that if I named my sons after this ideal family who would die for each other, they would be close. Strange idea or no, it worked. My boys have always been good friends and allies, and strangely enough I named them in perfect order for the characters. I didn't think I had until they grew up but I know I have now. Also I should mention that I have formed a closeness to my sister now in later years that I never imagined would happen, due to the events mentioned in the forthcoming pages.

My eldest son was born in 1971 and I called him Joseph. I didn't name the boys in the correct character order just in case I didn't have all three. So I named them in character preference. As Little Joe was my favourite, I called my firstborn Joseph. You never have to ask Joe twice to help you with anything; he's always laughing, never takes life too seriously and is a very talented pianist. (I don't think Little Joe had that trait.)

My second son is Adam, was born in 1973 and is much more sensible than the other two. Very intelligent, totally reliable and organised, knows what he is capable of achieving and where he is going in life. He is kind and caring and has a very strong sense of right and wrong, maybe takes life a bit too seriously sometimes, though he does have a wicked sense of humour. Adam would always know exactly how to behave in every situation, when to be sensible and when to let himself go. I would describe Adam as totally dependable and someone who would never let himself or anyone else down.

Then we had Daniel, who was born in 1974. Daniel is Hoss, though not in stature. Dan grew to be taller than the other two boys with very pale skin and very blue eyes. Good-natured, easygoing, amazingly laid back to almost comatose proportions, always smiling and thinking the best of everyone. I could hardly have called the lad Hoss so I named him after the actor, Dan Blocker. And it is my youngest son that this book is about.

I needed to write and tell the world about my youngest son who, in my mind, is a hero. Bette Midler's *Wind Beneath My Wings* expresses my thoughts on my son Daniel perfectly. He has lived with a rare, chronic, progressively debilitating illness called Behçets Disease since the age of eight, and dyslexia, without a single complaint. Every obstacle was met head on with a positive attitude. Knowing he had Behçets and the possibility of ending up in a wheelchair didn't hold any fears for Daniel, not that the world ever saw anyway. He considered his options and decided to head for a career that he could manage to continue with throughout his life. Danny went for computer servicing and maintenance, a job he could do sitting down. This task was not made any easier by the fact that Daniel is dyslexic. He had to work twice as hard as the next person to get the qualifications he needed. Even though the practical side came naturally to him it was the written exams that caused the problems. He did get his City and Guilds in Computer Maintenance and Servicing and, in the spare time he had at college, took a communications course, which he also completed successfully.

Daniel did, however, have far more challenging life changes to overcome than these now trivial ones. The following chapters go on to tell you all about these events.

The First Brush with Death

Dan was a normal, healthy eight-year-old in 1983 when we moved into a large house in Cotham, a district in the centre of Bristol. We had moved house so that my boys could go to what I considered to be the best school in Bristol at that time, Cotham Grammar School. One bright sunny day, Dan and his brother Adam, who was then just ten, went to the local park. I crossed with them over the road and left them for a short time. Adam was soon back with his nose bleeding profusely yelling that Dan had been hurt. I rushed across to the park to find Dan lying on the floor clutching his side and back. Apparently, some delightful boys of around fifteen or sixteen in the company of a youngster I knew, who was just one year older than Dan, had decided to steal Dan's ball and give him a kicking as well. The older boys tripped Dan up and the younger one, who was unfortunately the son of a friend of mine, was edged on to kick Dan several times whilst he was on the floor. This was done to riotous applause apparently and the younger boy was wearing Doctor Martin's boots which can be quite lethal weapons, in the wrong hands, or on the wrong feet. Adam had obviously gone to rescue Dan, and an older boy bloodied Adam's nose for interfering.

I carried Dan home and called the doctor. His kidneys had been bruised and the doctor thought it best to send him to hospital. Whilst in the Children's Hospital, whatever they gave him, medicine wise, to combat the damage, started a strange reaction. Dan was very soon covered in ulcers right down though his mucus glands and erupting on the skin. The inside of his mouth was so full of ulcers that they all blended into one. His lips were bloody and almost raw. Terrible temperatures, so high that they had to pack the boy in ice to try to bring them down. He looked as if he was rotting away. I had never seen anyone look so absolutely dreadful in my life and couldn't imagine that anyone could look so bad and still be alive. The worst part was the poor little soul's genitals, they were so swollen and blistered, with ulcers appearing from the tip. My father came to visit Dan and ignoring the barrier nursing signs, as he would, walked straight in, without mask or gown, took one look at Dan, felt so bad he was actually sick all over the bed. You can imagine how all hell let loose and Dad was banned from ever coming again. But I did know how he felt.

Richard discovered that the boys responsible for Daniel's injuries were from a halfway house for juvenile delinquents, in Somerset Street, near our home. It is a home that they enter after leaving borstal and where they are helped to prepare for the outside world. Needless to say, nothing whatsoever was done about these boys. However, as we knew the younger boy and his parents, Richard went round to see them and told them what had happened. The mother, who is now a social worker, would not allow Richard to take her son to see Dan, in case it upset him as he was, and I quote, 'a sensitive lad'. Richard would like to have dragged him screaming to the hospital but there was nothing he could do without the parents' consent, so he too went unpunished, and needless to say, we did not continue with any friendship with that family.

The doctors decided that Daniel had contracted the Stevens-Johnson Syndrome, a rare skin condition characterised by severe blisters and bleeding in the mucous membranes of the lips, eyes, mouth, nasal passage and, of course, genitals. Stevens-Johnson Syndrome is a life-threatening form of erythema multiforme, and is believed to be caused by a drug reaction. We were told that if Dan survived this very severe attack, he would be fine as it does not reoccur. Daniel's body did not, however, agree with this verdict and he spent the next couple of years with almost permanent mouth ulcers. If you have ever had a mouth ulcer you will know how painful they are. Daniel's ulcers were so numerous that the whole of the inside of his mouth looked white and he could not swallow properly. His tongue would swell and we used to have to feed him a liquid diet, usually something like the build-up drinks used in hospitals. The first major attack kept Dan in hospital for five weeks under the care of Dr Carswell. I got to know the Children's Hospital very well. When he came home, he looked like someone on their way to hospital rather than returning. Luckily our general practitioner, Dr Spence, is a wonderfully caring man who visited regularly.

Several months later Dan told me that when I first brought him home from the park after the attack, Abdul, a Libyan student from the Abon Language School, who was staying with us, had given him a tablet for the pain. What it was I will never know, but chances are it could have been the very drug that started the chain reaction. I am sure Abdul had meant well as he appeared to be very fond of my sons. We had two Libyan language students at this time, Saleh, who was with us for a long time and Abdul, who was only really passing through looking for a flat to rent. Saleh was a sullen-looking individual, only seventeen when he first moved in with us and twenty-one when he went home to Libya. I often wonder if he settled back home easily after living in the corrupt West.

When Dan was in hospital Saleh phoned his father in Libya and asked him to send over some cotton pyjamas as he was concerned that Daniel's were nylon. Two days later Saleh went up to Heathrow to meet a package off a plane containing pairs of beautiful fine cotton Arab-style pyjamas. They had long overshirt-style tops with a long opening up each side and long deep slit pockets. The bottoms had the traditional long crutch that reached to the knees. They were beautifully made and you couldn't fault the sentiment behind the gesture. I never realised until then that the reason for this long crutch was because of the belief that the next Allah would be born to a man and this sack-like effect in the trousers was to catch the baby – or so Saleh told me.

Behçets Syndrome

Dan had his next really serious attack of the Stevens-Johnston Syndrome, when he was ten and spent a month in the Children's Hospital. Once again we were assured that this condition would disappear and that he would get better and be well again.

By the time Daniel was sixteen, he had been in and out of hospital several times and although the medical profession seemed puzzled as to why the Stevens-Johnston Syndrome seemed firmly established in Daniel's body mechanism, no reason for this was ever given.

In 1991, having had regular attacks of the so called S-JS and in the midst of yet another serious one, he was admitted to an adult hospital for the first time. And also for the first time, a doctor looked at Dan and said, 'Hold on, I don't think that Dan has Stevens-Johnson's.' The trouble is, once someone has decided that a person has a certain ailment, whenever a similar attack occurs they go into hospital with the words, 'It's the boy with Stevens-Johnston's.' No one wonders if maybe it is something else. But now at last, whilst in K Ward of Southmead Hospital, an isolation ward used mainly for tropical diseases brought back into this country, Dr Glover was interested enough to ask questions and not just save Dan's life.

It took a few years of tests before it was decided that Dan definitely had, as far as they could tell, Behçets Disease. We were given a full explanation of the meaning of Behçets. It is a rare disorder in which the main symptoms are recurrent mouth ulcers, genital ulceration, and inflammation of the mucus glands. There may also be rashes, arthritis, and venous thrombosis (abnormal clot formation in the veins). Less common features are intestinal ulcers, arterial disease, epididymis, and neuropsychiatric symptoms. Daniel had to, of course, have some, if not all of the less common features. An attack always brought with it a form of meningitis. His body would stiffen and the headaches were unbelievably painful. Every time the hospital always insisted on doing a lumbar puncture.

13

This was the only time I ever saw Daniel cry. This procedure is very painful and totally pointless in Daniel's case because it is part of having Behçets. Behçets affects the brain stem, which causes the headaches. It is a rare disorder, the cause being unknown but, like most dramatic syndromes, it can be triggered by trauma. The diagnosis relies on one or more of the three main symptoms being present. It is classed as a chronic debilitating illness.

Once we knew what we were dealing with, life became a little easier for Dan. It was whilst under Dr Glover at Southmead Hospital that Dan was first introduced to steroids as a antidote to Behçets. Dan learnt to anticipate an attack and know when to take the steroids and how to wean himself off them as the attack subsided. He also took Colchicine, a drug usually used to combat gout, to help fight the mouth ulcers.

By this age Daniel was walking with a slight limp due to arthritis in his left hip, and he was getting to the stage when playing football was becoming difficult due to both the hip problem and lack of stamina.

Dan had been signed to a model agency in London for the past year but obviously a limp made this a no-go area as well now.

Life Goes On

Daniel was keen to earn a little money in his spare time so his father bought him a scrambling-style motorbike which he rode everywhere and he worked evenings for Sprint Pizza delivering food parcels, which he loved. The bike was stolen several times, which was annoying but the bike was finally shelved when Daniel had an accident on a roundabout in the centre of Bristol. He was out riding with his friend Justin Lawrence when a foreign lady driver got confused on the Bristol Broadmead roundabout and decided to turn left off the road with out signalling, straight into Daniel. His bike got well and truly lodged under the car and Dan was very lucky to escape with only severe bruising and grazes. The bike was a write-off. Justin luckily kept calm and took care of Daniel until help came. We then decided that maybe a car would be safer and Dan started driving lessons. He was a natural and it took very few lessons before he passed his test and we bought him a little car when he was seventeen.

Life for my other sons went on. Joseph got married in 1991, whilst only nineteen. David, my eldest grandson, was born in June of the same year.

Despite dyslexia, Dan stayed on at school and took a CPVE Business Course after his O Levels. In 1992 Dan wrote to several computer firms and eventually one such firm gave him a chance to work for them on a Youth Opportunities Scheme, with day release at Brunel Technical College in Bristol where he took his City and Guilds in Electronic Servicing and Electronic Systems Servicing and Mechanics. He also took City of Guilds in Telecommunications. The practical side of the course was easy to Daniel but the written work took real concentration, but this he overcame and passed with flying colours on all courses taken.

I have never really liked these Youth Opportunity Schemes. They seem a bit like slave labour to me but he needed a foot in the door of the computer world and a firm in Nailsea offered him all the training needed to get on and start a career. Dan, however, found a thirty-nine-hour week too much and had a lot of time off sick, sometimes with simple fatigue due to the Behçets which is a very tiring ailment. I managed to get his employment taken over by the Social Services who run a scheme for disabled employees. They pay a percentage of the person's wages when well, and all when they are sick. It is calculated by simply ascertaining how much the employee would be worth to the firm if he or she could guarantee a full week's work each week, then extracting what the employee was actually worth to the firm with a bad health record, and an agreement is reached as to what percentage the Social Services will pay of the difference. So, in fact, the firm get a qualified, disabled member of staff for next to nothing and it keeps that person in work. It is a brilliant scheme.

Daniel got engaged when he was eighteen to a lovely girl called Ann-Marie. She was willowy, with long blond hair. When she used to visit Dan in hospital she was usually mistaken for his sister, they looked that much alike. Annie came over as a caring person and had spent a lot of her young years in and out of different foster homes; and all she seemed to want out of life was a steady life with children and Daniel. I felt that Annie would look after Dan, though I thought they were a little young to be committed.

Ann-Marie longed to trace her father who she had not seen or heard from since he split up with her mother several years ago. I think she had a rosy view of this man, thinking he would be thrilled to see her and there must be some really good reason why he had left her and not kept in touch. Annie knew that her father, Derek, known as Dell, was supposed to be in Portugal. I decided to try to find Dell and wrote to the British embassy in Portugal who had never heard of him and gave me no hope of finding him. Then just by chance I was speaking to a friend of mine who was about to go to Madeira on holiday and she just slipped into the conversation that Madeira was part of Portugal. So I wrote to the capital of Madeira, Funchal. I had an amazing reply from the powers that be in Funchal. Not only did Derek live and work there but he was known to members of the embassy and they could give me his full address. Obviously I wrote to Derek before telling Annie in case he didn't want to see her. Derek was thrilled to hear from me and asked me to arrange for Annie and Dan to go out and see him, promising to refund any expenses. So I took out a bank loan and booked tickets on a flight to Madeira that Christmas for Ann-Marie and Daniel. They had a wonderful time, staying with friends of Derek's, who treated them very well. They spent Christmas in a large hotel on the island but strangely enough saw very little of Annie's father. He, it appears, had a very young girlfriend who was jealous of Ann-Marie. Although a good time was had by all, I do not think that Annie was in any hurry to return and she certainly seemed cured of any romantic notions about her father who appeared to be a bit of a crook, according to Dan's analysis. He made no attempt to refund me any money so I believe Daniel's idea to be correct. I was glad Dan had seen Madeira though he found it far too hilly to be comfortable.

Not long after the trip to Madeira, Ann-Marie went to Butlin's holiday camp on a weekend trip with a group of mentally disabled youngsters as part of a care course she was attending at college. Whilst there she met a soldier and everything went pear-shaped romance wise for Daniel. They are still friends and probably always will be and I know that Dan still holds fond memories of his time with Annie, but que sera sera. She is now married to a lovely young man, not the soldier, and they have three little ones and I still love her to bits.

Obviously, having lost his girlfriend, Dan was a little depressed so he decided to go with a couple of friends on a drive down through France, with a tent, in his Fiesta. He went with two brothers, Chris and Danny Ryall. Chris is the same age as our Dan and Danny a couple of years older. This was July 1994.

The boys had been away on their adventure for almost a week when I had a rather worrying phone call from Montpellier in southern France. Apparently, the boys had gone for a swim, having locked everything in the car, including money and clothes. When they went back to the car they discovered that someone had broken into the car and stolen the contents. Luckily the passports were at the campsite where they had left the tent and bedding, and the rest of their clothes. So now they were in Montpellier, no petrol in the car and not a half-penny between them. Naturally being young they had not considered insurance before setting out and they were well and truly stuck.

It was a Thursday late in the afternoon. Chris had phoned his boss at work who said he could send money but couldn't guarantee its arrival until Monday or Tuesday. This would have meant that they couldn't even get back to the campsite for three or four days.

Why they allowed the petrol to get so low, I will never know. Daniel had told his friends that I would be able to sort things out. I am not sure what sort of miracle worker he thinks I am, but amazingly enough fate stepped in and I didn't let them down. I told Dan to hover round and phone me back within the hour and I would let him know what I had discovered. I rather assumed that all I had to do was phone the British embassy and they would rescue the boys. No chance. The nearest embassy was over eighty miles away and they would have to go there themselves – not possible, no petrol.

I went into work to find Richard. Both he and I were working at Cotham Grammar School at this time, and I told him what had happened. One of the French teachers was there, Sylvia Aldis. She is a bubbly blonde whom Daniel was very fond of at school. This encounter with Sylvia Aldis proved to be most opportune as she had a French friend living in Bristol, who had a friend who lived in Montpellier. The chances of Sylvia being at work that afternoon and her knowing someone from this part of the world have got to be a million to one. I would say that was fate! She immediately phoned her friend, who likewise phoned France and told her friend Robert Clot in Montpellier the story and where the boys were. The outcome was that Robert promised to go to the boys and give them any assistance they needed. This was remarkable as I did not know any of the people concerned, and they did not know us. I went home and waited for Dan to phone. Even he was amazed when I told him to stay put because a gentleman would arrive and sort them out. Later that evening Daniel phoned me from Robert's home to say that this wonderful gentleman had taken them to the campsite, paid the money they owed there, and had then insisted that they went home with him to stay for a couple of days. Daniel said they were treated like royalty. When Robert and his wife decided to go to their chateau in the mountains they asked the two Dans and Chris to go with them. It was an experience of a lifetime. They dug a ditch for Robert whilst at the chateau, as a kind of thank you, hardly adequate for what this man had done for the boys but there was nothing they could have done that would have been enough. My faith in mankind increased one hundred per cent because of Robert Clot. His kindness didn't stop there. He lent the boys enough money to get themselves home and they arrived back in Dover on the Tuesday. Obviously we repaid the debt owed to these wonderful people, money wise, but it would have been impossible to repay them properly. We have kept in touch ever since. Chris told me later that Daniel had jokingly said, 'Mum probably knows someone living close by', but was rather taken aback when a rescuer actually did arrive and within two hours of Daniel's phone call home.

Dan went round to the French lady in Bristol who organised the rescue and took her a huge bunch of flowers. I felt humbled by the whole event.

I think that holiday took a lot out of Daniel as he became unwell shortly after returning. On 24 August Dan was admitted to hospital for a couple of days but managed to get out in time to attend a rather subdued gathering to celebrate Richard and my silver wedding anniversary. We had originally planned a very large party to be shared by Richard's parents who celebrated their golden wedding anniversary at much the same time. Unfortunately, Richard's mother Marion, who had been seriously ill on and off for several years, died just days before the planned event, so we cancelled the celebration. Marion's death hit the family very hard. She was very much loved by us all. Also my cousin, Stephen, had lost his baby son on 21 August so although we went ahead with a sort of anniversary party our hearts were not really in it.

Daniel's health continued to ring a few alarm bells for the rest of the year and then on 5 December he went to a nightclub called Odysseys with the same boys he went to Montpellier with, walked in through the door and was almost immediately floored by the strobe lighting. (This was a later analysis of the event.)

I got the proverbial phone call about midnight from Chris saying that Dan was unconscious in the Bristol Royal Infirmary. Richard and I arrived to find that the nursing staff were most disinterested. They had jumped to the conclusion that Daniel had taken some form of drugs. This attitude really annoys me, tarring every youngster with the same brush. They hadn't even opened Daniel's SOS bracelet. It wasn't until I told the nursing staff that Daniel had Behçets that they started to worry about his condition. He was unconscious for fourteen hours, but he only stayed in hospital for four days as everything settled down again once he regained consciousness. Daniel struggled back to work for Christmas week.

1995

1995 proved to be a very bad year for Daniel health wise, as I could not get him well for any length of time. He fell sick on 1 January, and although we involved the doctor, after two weeks Daniel decided that he should try to get back to work. When he arrived at work he was given the most incredible letter I have ever read. It was a formal warning telling Daniel that if he did not show an improvement in his health and subsequent time off work, he would have his job terminated. How Daniel's health was suppose to improve just because he received a letter, I do not know. I cannot imagine how these people thought that a piece of paper would suddenly act like a visit to Lourdes and make Daniel free of Behçets overnight. Daniel managed to stay fairly well until 7 March, then he was unwell for another two weeks. He went back to work, still shaky on his feet and ended up back in hospital with Behçets and pneumonia. Dan came home on 6 April and insisted on going back to work just two days later. He was so unwell. I was very worried about him as his legs would hardly carry him along. The hospital arranged an MRI scan for 21 April and the firm Dan worked for very begrudgingly allowed him to attend this appointment.

Magnetic Resources Imaging (MRI) is a way of looking inside the body without using X-rays. It uses a large circular magnet, large enough to surround a patient, radio waves and a computer. It is considered to be completely safe, but it is necessary to remove any metallic objects such as watches and jewellery. The radiographer discussed the scan with Dan before making him comfortable lying down on the scanner bed. The table then moves into the magnet, like slipping a torpedo into the firing mechanism. Daniel could still speak to the radiographer and was advised to bring a tape with him that he could listen to, to help him to relax as you have to keep perfectly still throughout your time inside the machine. When the scanner starts there is a knocking noise as the machine collects information – it is all very strange and takes about an hour.

I could tell that it was the end of the line for Dan's job and, quite frankly, I also felt it would be for the best as they were quite obviously not a caring group of employers.

Dan remained well for a couple of weeks and then unwell again; he had another short spell in hospital and several weeks just too unwell to do anything at all. Unfortunately, the firm Daniel worked for were not as understanding as they could have been and despite the disabled placement cover terminated his employment in July. It was probably for the best. He was always tired and they paid him an insulting amount of money. Dan had worked for this firm for three years and, although in the last year he was qualified and no longer held by the Youth Opportunity Scheme, they did not increase his wages. Having his position terminated by the firm he had trained with hit him very hard. He was very upset which was unusual for philosophical Daniel. We, at first, decided to take the firm to the Industrial Tribunal for unfair dismissal but decided that the stress probably wasn't worth the effort.

Dan was actually financially better off out of work but actually wanted to be employed regardless of finances. Dan was nearly twenty-one, had his own flat at this time, and had done so for eighteen months. He could manage quite well when he felt well and only came home when he really felt too unwell to cope. He needed to have a little independence before Behçets made it impossible for him. Dan's father and I made sure he always had plenty of food in the fridge and money in the electric meter, so his independence was only superficial as it is with most youngsters starting out.

July was quite an eventful month for me as well. I had a poetry book published in America, called *The Lives and Rhymes of an Ordinary Housewife* and the launch was in July 1995.

Dan was due to be twenty-one in September and wanted to try to drive across France again. I think the fact that he seemed to be particularly unwell more often than he was well that year made him think that maybe Behçets was starting to take over his life. After a stress-free month out of work, he seemed quite well again so Richard and I funded his trip to France. This time Dan had full insurance cover and the holiday proved fairly successful, though he intended on the off to be away two weeks but only stayed just over a week as he started to feel unwell and decided it might be safer to get himself home.

We did have another bright spot in 1995. We all, Joe and his then wife Emma, Daniel, my husband and I, went on an organised trip with friends to Paris by coach. It was on this trip that I saw my youngest son in a new light. Joe had been able to find someone to look after the two children for a few days so that he and Emma could both come. I love being with my family and was only sorry that Adam could not have joined us. My sister, her husband and daughter came as well so it was a very family-orientated few days away. I love Paris. If I won the lottery I would buy a flat in the Latin Quarter.

We got on the coach literally outside our front door, drove to Portsmouth for the crossing. The ferry over is the high spot for my sons and this overnight crossing was no exception. We did all have cabins but I do not think many of us saw them that trip, certainly not the youngsters anyway. The coach load of us gathered in the bar and cabaret area, sitting round the edge of the dance floor. The first part of the evening began with a down tempo disco, plenty of flashing lights but very middle of the road music. This was followed by what could only loosely be called a cabaret. It took the shape of a duo, a man with a guitar and a rather overweight female in far too short a skirt, singing to a background tape. It was really low budget stuff. The female wiggled and twisted about, vaguely in time to the music and the man just stood with a sickly grin on his face. They were pretty dire. They attacked Van Halen's 'Jump' with the energy and enthusiasm of a dead frog and then went on to murder Spandau Ballet's 'True'. At this point Joe and Danny could stand it no longer and they sprung to their feet and did an impromptu dance routine that took up the whole of the dance floor. They mimed as they dance to 'True', using the most outrageous gestures to express the lyrics of the song, falling on their knees from time to time with hands on heart. Until this moment in time I had actually believed my youngest son to be a shy and quietly reserved type. Well, how wrong can one be. I always knew that Joe was an extrovert. He was like this continuously but Dan was definitely a dark horse. We were all in hysterics. Dan and Joe entertained everyone for quite some time and then the 'cabaret', knowing they were beaten, went off and Joe took over. There was a grand piano in the corner and he sat and played until five o'clock in the morning. Richard went to bed at about three and I went down at about four. I didn't actually sleep and came up again just after five in the morning. It seemed that everyone on the ferry now knew Joe and Dan. I walked into the bar area again to be greeted by total strangers asking me if I was looking for my sons. They were still drinking. Where they put all that liquid, I cannot imagine.

We went on to Paris, had two days there in a small hotel near Notre-Dame. The last evening we all went out for a meal in a recommended restaurant. It was a very large cellar-style set-up. There was a large basket of raw vegetables on the table, which was the starter. It consisted of radishes, carrots, celery, cucumber, cauliflower, fennel, turnips – none of which were trimmed or appeared to have been washed. A very strange idea. The next course was a help yourself from the salad and cold meat section, all you could eat. There were dozens of different sausages that you just had to cut slices from and several tubs containing different pickles and bean-style salads. Then there was a meat course that was barbecued near the table, followed, finally by several types of cheeses. Through out this meal there were several jugs of red wine on the table that were never allowed to empty. The meal was a set price and the wine was free. As you can imagine, the majority of the customers leaving that restaurant were rather merry. Strangely enough, and this was something that struck me in Paris, we never saw crowds of loud drunk youngsters as you do here. I think that the Parisians probably just drink as much as they actually want and it is only the tourists that get drunk at these as much wine as you can drink restaurants, to get their money's worth. Anyway, our party was definitely keeping up the British tradition of getting their money's worth. Joe and Danny were well oiled. We came out of the restaurant and Danny insisted that he knew a quicker way back to the hotel and started at a fair lick off in the wrong direction. He took a lot of persuasion to come back and go the way everyone else was going. All the way Dan kept saying we were going the wrong way. He wouldn't shut up until we were actually standing outside the hotel entrance. From then on Dan was referred to as the intrepid explorer.

Our trip being over, back home we came, stopping en route for the customary hypermarket duty free shopping, this time on a daytime ferry, not half as much fun.

I will always treasure that short break and when I close my eyes I see Daniel and Joe dancing round the floor, so full of life and fun. This was something that I would never see again and would give my right arm to be able to.

Starting Work at Cotham

I was working in Cotham Grammar School in Bristol in 1995 and had been for about six years. The head teacher at the time, Jim McKay, was the one who first made me aware of the Social Services Placement for Disabled Employees Scheme. Daniel had been a student at Cotham Grammar School and Jim had always been interested in how he was doing, being aware of Daniel's health problems. When the firm Dan worked for started to get heavy about his sickness record I had spoken to Mr McKay and he advised me to put Daniel's name down to join the Placement Scheme. Apparently we had a teacher with MS who was employed under the scheme so Mr McKay's knowledge of the arrangements was quite up to date. I followed up this line of enquiries at that time and the person running the scheme sent a representative out to Dan's firm to explain the help they offered. After negotiations, Daniel joined the scheme, not that at the end of the day it really made that much difference, the firm still sacked him. The point is that this scheme is not the employer's scheme but the employee's and, as such, transferable.

At this time Cotham Grammar School was desperate for an assistant to help their computer engineer keep the complex computer systems throughout the school running and also to offer a little in class support, but as usual finances were against employing anyone. Mr McKay spoke to the governors about Dan and the Placement Scheme and as our ratio of disabled staff was practically nil, one part-timer to be exact who had MS, the school decided to offer Daniel a position as a computer technician. So Daniel started working at Cotham Grammar School in October 1995, despite the fact that he was financially better off not working and claiming incapacity benefit. Daniel actually wanted to work, just twenty-five hours a week, which he could manage. He was a great success, the kids liked him and he is a good computer mechanic. It looked like Daniel's life had turned a positive corner at last. The following February, the school had a special post box for Valentines Day cards and Daniel had a large pile of them addressed to him from students. He found that quite amusing. Yes, life for Dan had really turned a corner, how right we were, but it was the wrong corner.

1996 had started so promisingly. Richard's father, who was a widower, remarried on 2 March. The wedding itself took place in the registry office in Bristol town shopping centre. The guests then walked or took the minibus provided to Jurys, a rather smart hotel just off the centre of Bristol by the marina. It was rather pleasant to see relatives and friends gathered together for a happy event. These days it always seemed that we only got together at funerals. I went to the wedding with mixed feelings. It seemed such a short time since my mother-in-law had died though it was actually nineteen months. I loved my mother-in-law as if she was my own mother and will always miss her. It was very hard to see her replaced and yet I would not have wanted my father-in-law to spend the rest of his days alone.

It was a strange day. I think a lot of us found it difficult to imagine someone in Marion's, but Father looked so happy and who would begrudge him that! It was a pleasant day and everything went well. I took a very amateur video film of the occasion, mostly centred round my sons and their partners. I was very glad I had done this as the year unfolded.

March went on being the best month of 1996. My eldest son, Joe, plays the piano and was in a rather good blues-style band at the time called Desire. Having sent off several tapes, the band was invited to play at the London Marquee Club. Unfortunately, the venue had to be changed at the very last moment due to a fire and the event was rearranged at the London Astoria on 24 March as part of a package to promote new bands. We got a coach load of supporters and went up to watch. I may be biased but they were definitely the best there. I had bought a video camera especially to film Joe but wasn't allowed to take it into the show. Desire went on at about six in the evening for an hour and came off to a very good response. When the participating groups arrived their names were literally put into a hat and the order of appearance decided that way. Six o'clock was not an ideal time but that was the luck of the draw. We also did not know what time to tell the coach driver to pick us all up as we had no advance knowledge of the time of the event, so we had arranged to stay in London until eleven o'clock, which was a long time in the cold on a Sunday though it would have been great in the warm.

Joe was on a high that day as you can imagine. He had, however, problems waiting for him back at home that the rest of us knew nothing about. His wife wanted to leave the family home. They had been married since 1991. Emma had started work again and realised what she had missed by having children so young and I believe she just wanted to reclaim a slice of her youth that she felt she had lost. Apparently, unknown to us, the couple had reached this point in the previous year but decided to give their marriage another try. It seems that they were only putting off the inevitable and, having reviewed the situation at the beginning of 1996, Emma decided that she actually wanted to go this time. So Joe had this to go home to. No wonder he wanted to make the most of his success in London. He had kept all the dramas to himself as he believed that his father and I had enough to worry about with Daniel's continued ill health. I had no idea when we all went to Paris that Joe and Emma were having any problems at all.

It was a freezing cold evening. We older 'fans' went in search of a warm restaurant after the gig, whereas the youngsters, who included my other two sons, Adam and Dan, went on a binge. My husband, friends and I were just changing pubs casually when a frantic Joseph came rushing up to his father and dragged him off muttering something about a spot of bother. I could not imagine what sort of bother this group of rather pleasant youngsters could be in. We, the adult fans, all hurried after Joe and Richard, who led us to a pizza parlour. Inside the pizza parlour were all the youngsters drinking tea and several of them, Daniel included, were soaking wet having been thrown or jumped in the fountains. We were dangerously close to Trafalgar Square. Apparently when it was Dan's turn to get a drenching he hyperventilated and an ambulance was sent for. The paramedics had sorted Dan out in the back of the ambulance and had wanted to take him to hospital to be on the safe side but Dan didn't want to go. He was worried about being stuck up in London on his own, not as if we would have left him alone. Anyway, the ambulance went on its way and now everyone was trying to warm Dan up. The other wet people had waded in to get Dan out of the water when they saw he was in trouble. So we had soggy youngsters and two hours to wait in the cold for the coach to take us home and a further two-hour journey to look forward to. I suppose I should have realised at that point that 1996 was not going to be a good year after all. This was the first time I had met this bunch of youngsters but they were, in the majority, to play a large part in my life over the next couple of years.

Danny went to Paris in April to see Oasis with the same crowd of youngsters. I knew he would be in safe hands this time as they all had London very much in the back of their minds and were now aware that Dan had a health problem, something he did not advertise. Happily he had a great time and as the year progressed I has very glad that he got to see his heroes.

Joe's marriage had ended; his wife left and she didn't take the children which was a blessing for me at least. I would have hated to lose them. Joe felt as though his wife was making a big mistake. All the danger signs were there and Emma drifted about from relative to bed sit for a while before getting settled again. I do not think other people were anything to do with the real problem. I think they just grew apart, they were two very different people.

Still Joe now had a lot on his young hands, twenty-four and a lone parent with two little boys aged four and five!

When we returned from London I found that my mother was suffering from cancer and she was admitted to Frenchay Hospital in Bristol, where she died on 10 April. I could not spend as much time as I would have wished at her bedside. She was bright yellow having been taken in with jaundice but it was her liver. She had suffered from. Alzheimer's for a number of years and had not known who I was for a long time, or in fact who she was herself. She usually thought I was her sister, Evelyn, and that we were teenagers. It was painful to see her so frail and not having the slightest notion of what was happening to her or who we were as we visited.

A strange thing happened as she lay dying in Frenchay Hospital; she looked up at me one day and said my name. It was quite a shock and a very emotional moment. Even though this frail little yellow lady was no longer the mother I knew, I was deeply effected by her plight. My father had died two years previously, so this was then the end of an era. I was sorry that I was not close by when she finally died. My sister and I had stayed until quite late on the evening of 9 April and Mother seemed to be breathing very shallowly. I went back again for a while. I am not sure what drew me there but I left again just after two in the morning of the 10th. It had just turned five when the hospital phoned to say she was going. We rushed back but were too late. A familiar story, no doubt. I never liked the idea that she was actually alone when she died.

On 17 April we held the funeral. All the relatives came and I was now starting on another stage of my life as virtually the matriarch of the family now. My sister and I were now speeding towards being branded as those old relatives that are only visited under sufferance.

Dan was unwell at the end of April and wasn't really fit again until 23 May. He had probably done too much in the past couple of months and it was all catching up with him.

One light spot that was quickly overshadowed was a wedding I attended on 11 May. A long-term friend of mine, Sima, an American Jew I had known since the early seventies, lived in a flat below a woman called Jude for many years and they were good friends. Jude was getting married and Sima was bridesmaid. I had to see this and took my new video camera with me, and my ordinary still camera. The service was in the modern Catholic Church in Clifton, Bristol. I was impressed. I had never been inside that church before and it is very unusual. The church is in a round. The centre of the open plan building is the altar with triangularly placed chairs coming away from it, forming a wheel-like pattern. Round the outside of the chair formation is a wide walkway and tables are set against the walls covered in candles, some lit, some not. The walls are made up mainly of huge abstract stained-glass windows. The building has a feeling of light airiness.

Even though a wedding was taking place people still came in and out walked round the outer walkway, lit candles, knelt and prayed in other sections of the church as if nothing was going on. It seemed strange to me.

I filmed the wedding, which was a colourful affair; the men wore kilts. Sima looked wonderful. She wore a black crushed silk effect fitted jacket and quite full skirt, the skirt a cream colour. It was an unusual choice of colour scheme for a bridesmaid but Sima having very dark hair and a good colour seemed to compliment the clothes she was wearing.

I took a whole still film of the wedding as well as the video. It was the first time I have not gone straight home and removed a full film from the camera straight away. I am a keen photographer and I usually replace films in cameras immediately. I very much regret not following my usual trend that day. I was due to go out early that evening so I put the film changing on hold. I obviously regret this action now, as this pleasant day wedding watching was followed by a burglary. My new still camera and video camera (complete with films of course) and jewellery were all taken, amongst other things.

It is a very strange feeling, being burgled. Richard and I realised it had happened as soon as we pulled up on our drive. We had been to friends in Kingswood, a suburb of Bristol, playing cards until about one in the morning. As we pulled up on the drive, the house was obviously illuminated and we knew we had not left that many lights on. We had two little dogs at this time, a Pekinese and a Lhasa Apso. I had the desire that evening to swap them for a couple of Rottweilers, but knowing my luck they would be burglar's friends as well.

You step in through the front door and the place is strewn with the contents of bags, draws and cupboards. It is a very uncomfortable feeling. Happily these burglars did not actually break anything or do any of the disgusting things that I have heard about from other victims. It amazes me that people could actually break into strangers' homes and rummage through their belongings. I cannot imagine the mentality of these people. I can only hope that they experience the effects of burglaries themselves one day. I had worked voluntarily in Horfield Prison, our local prison, for eighteen years but never imagined, even though I spent a lot of time with criminals of all types, that I would ever be a burglar's target. I rather felt I had a guardian angel – wrong!

We walked through to the kitchen and could see that the perpetrators had gained access through the back door. They had actually come in through the dog flap, which was a very small one, used my husband's tools once inside to prize the seal off the double glazed unit at the bottom of the back door and taken that panel out. All very neat and apparently quite a common practice.

I phoned the police straight away and they said they would send someone from SOCO (Forensics) round some time in the morning. They could not give a definite time. So Richard and I left everything strewn all over the bed and slept in the spare room.

The police arrived at about ten in the morning and dusted everywhere. They lifted a few possible prints from the back door area and told us that there had been an epidemic of burglaries in the area lately. I spent the rest of the day clearing up the mess.

Richard and I decided that we could do with a break. We decided to go to Jersey for a few days, it was half term coming up. We booked the flight to go out of Bristol Airport on Saturday 25 May, returning on the Wednesday. We decided just to fly there and find bed and breakfast ourselves. I had wanted to go to Jersey for some time as my family originates from St Helier and I was tracing the family tree. My mother dying seemed to make it more important.

Daniel and his girlfriend, Sarah, drove Richard and I to the airport in Bristol, despite Dan not having been very well for the few weeks before. He brought our grandchildren with him and he had quite a time persuading them to go back home afterwards, as they really wanted to come with us on the plane. I had never flown before but wasn't worried about this new experience. I was right not to worry. It was a very tiny plane but the weather was good and the flight very smooth. I enjoyed the view from the window. It is a very short trip, less than an hour, not long enough to get bored.

It was easy finding bed and breakfast accommodation. We settled for a family-run small hotel with a bar. The owners were from Bristol as it happens, all be it twenty odd years ago, and were friendly.

We were very quickly struck by the politeness of drivers. They actually stop for you and let you cross the road. In Bristol even at the crossings the drivers seem to try to knock you down if possible.

The weather, after the first day, was awful but I had great success with my project. The records office in St Helier is very organised. The gentleman in charge there couldn't have been more helpful so I spent the majority of our stay in Jersey quite happily in the records office family tree tracing. I found that my family was very easy to trace as generation after generation had lived, married and died in St Helier. We descended from one of the oldest families in Jersey and could be traced back to the 1200s. I did not want to go that far. I think I probably bored Richard to death but he didn't complain as I dragged him from one grave-yard to another in the rain.

We returned on the Wednesday and Daniel was there to meet us off the plane, our grandchildren in tow, complete with pyjamas in anticipation of them spending the remainder of the week with Richard and me. We are lucky enough to have two beautiful grandsons, David and Richard (Ricky). Every Friday night since they were born they had stayed with Richard and I. Because Joe was so young when he married, we always thought it was important that he and his wife had at least one night a week to be young and without children. Now that Joe was alone with the kids, Friday nights seemed even more important. I wanted to keep the stability and regularity in the little ones' lives. Anyway, I would probably get withdrawal symptoms if I didn't spend at least one evening a week with the youngsters. We were happy to have the little boys stay on from Wednesday night to Saturday morning. I always try to have the grandchildren for part of any holiday.

That Friday, 31 May 1996, started like any ordinary Friday. Joe was going out that evening with several friends, including Danny whose flat was quite near to Joe's house. Joe and Danny often went out together. They usually started in the Somerville Club, which is a gentleman's snooker club in St Andrews, a Victorian district of Bristol, then they moved on to The Showboat pub on the Gloucester Road. The Showboat was a pub that had changed its name several times. It was called The Anchor when my husband and I had our wedding reception there in 1969, later changing its name to The Big Apple, which I believe was what it was called when Joseph had his wedding reception there. (We believe in keeping things in the family!) At this time in 1996 the pub was called The Showboat. It has, however, since changed its name again to Bar Oz and now back to The Anchor.

In fact Joe and Dan met up with several friends at the Somerville Club and they did go on as planned to The Showboat, a move that we all have lived to regret. Richard was in the Somerville Club early on in the evening and had a drink and game of snooker with his sons. The boys were both in very boisterous moods and taking the mickey out of their dad as usual, in a light-hearted way. Joe and Dan even kissed Richard goodbye when he left, something quite unprecedented but something that played on Richard's mind greatly over the coming months, the reasons for this will become clear later in the story.

Richard and I always had a problem getting the elder of the two grandchildren to go to bed so he usually ended up with us until he dropped to sleep. We went to bed at about ten o'clock, and Ricky was already fast asleep in the spare room, Dave was, however, firmly established right in the centre of our bed. We sat in bed reading to David for a while. He then settled down a little but he was not asleep as yet. Richard and I continued reading our individual books, when at about 11.15 the phone rang. When the phone rings at that time of night, it is never good news. It was a breathless, almost frantic young voice on the other end that told me that Danny had been knocked down on the Gloucester Road, outside The Showboat pub. I asked how bad it was and the voice said that Dan was unconscious and they were waiting for an ambulance. Naturally I got dressed immediately. Richard couldn't come, as one of us had to stay with the grandchildren and I decided that someone was Richard.

The Scene

Friday Evening – 31 May 1996

I was outside The Showboat by 11.30, to find two ambulances and a police car at the scene. It was then that I discovered that Danny had not been knocked down by a vehicle, but by a man – more precisely – two men. The area was swarming with youngsters all in different degrees of hysteria, my eldest son Joe being the worst. Joe was covered in blood, talking incoherently and shaking like a leaf. Dan was already in one of the ambulances, unconscious. I imagined that there must have been a violent fight and assumed that Joe was also involved, looking at the state he was in. However, as the story unfolded I discovered that the blood that appeared to be well soaked into Joe's clothing was not actually his own, it was Daniel's.

People kept pulling me to show me where Dan had fallen, there was a large pool of blood in the gutter and on the curb of the pavement where he had hit his head. I naturally felt quite sick. Everything seemed like a dream. It was a very strange feeling. I looked about at all the youngsters to see if any others were hurt. Another lad, who I now know to be Wayne, was semi-conscious in the second ambulance. There was a short girl with dark hair with what looked like a black eye and a red-headed girl called Kate, whom I remembered from the trip to the London Astoria, with a very swollen face. Daniel's girlfriend, Sarah, a young lady who was studying at Bristol University of the West of England at this time and was lodging in a friend's house, looked shocked. I could not get a lot of sense out of anyone or real information as to what exactly had happened.

Someone told me that Joe had been sitting in the gutter with Dan's head in his lap telling everyone to keep away from his brother, which is why he was in such a mess. I told Joe to get in the ambulance with the two injured girls. Joe seemed in a worse state than they were. He was crying and shaking, obviously in serious shock, and I could get no coherent information out of him at all, not that I tried very hard in the circumstances. He just kept saying, 'How's Danny, How's Danny?' The answer I did not know. I spoke to the paramedics on board the ambulance and they said he was stable. I do not know why but I really wasn't that worried. I, and I suppose most people feel the same, could not imagine anything terrible happening to any of my sons. All three are decent young men and things like this only happens to yobs, not so I'm afraid! Also, I believe Daniel's medical history kept me calm. Dan had been through a great deal already in his life and always came out the other side smiling. Why should today be any different? The paramedics had not attempted to open Dan's SOS bracelet so I told them that Dan suffered from Behçets and that a blow on the head was probably the very worst thing that could happen to him. There didn't appear to be any sense of urgency or panic on their part so I once again assumed all would be fine.

I then spoke to the police who were standing about speaking to the youngsters. They did not seem to have a clear idea to what had happened, nor did they seem very interested either. They just said it was a fight. I knew that this was unlikely. My son, Daniel, is not someone inclined towards fighting in the slightest, nor would he have the build or stamina for such an occupation. The police did not have any details of who was involved, or what the whole episode had been about. They rather gave me the impression that to them it was just another boring Friday night fight and that if I didn't push in any way, nothing further would happen. A young man I did not know who was called Michael was there with his fiancée and gave the police his name and address as a possible witness to the incident, though, as it happened they didn't contact Michael until nearly two weeks later.

There were a few faces I recognised. One being Isabelle, who used to serve behind the bar in The Showboat and was a good friend of Dan's. A lad called Jason whom I had met round at Joseph's once or twice, Kate known as Babe, who had come to London with us in March. There were a lot of other youngsters who I do not believe I had ever seen before that evening, several were sitting on the pavement heads in hands, others just walking about looking dazed.

I didn't learn the whole story until the following November at the Magistrates' Court. Until that time I was too busy watching Dan's life hanging by a thread and wondering if it might snap to be desirous of the why and wherefores of how he got in that state. Though I was aware that we were dealing with seriously disturbed people as we had so many silent phone calls. Strange that someone phoning and not actually speaking can be menacing, but that added to the fact that the men involved in injuring Daniel were actually harassing witnesses. We understood the message being sent to us.

Not knowing too many details at our lowest moments was probably my saving grace because I think if I had been in receipt of all the facts I might have gone out looking to seriously injure the perpetrators of the deed.

The Incident

Having sat through two court cases connected to my son's assault, I have a fairly clear idea of what happened on the evening of 31 May 1996. I do not intend to go into too many details as they will be repeated further on and in full in this book at the chapter relating to the Magistrates' Court.

It appears that the evening of Friday 31 May started the same as most Fridays. I had the grandchildren and Richard went out for a quick drink at the Somerville Club returning home at around 8 p.m. with a Chinese takeaway. This was our usual Friday evening, we are rather creatures of habit, I am afraid. Richard had apparently met up with two of our three sons, Joe and Dan, along with several of their friends in the Somerville Club. Dan and Joe were usually together. I think it would be reasonable to say that they were always the best of friends.

The Somerville Club is an old style gentleman's club. It has been established for one hundred years and has no political affiliation. It is situated behind the façade of a pair of large Victorian semi-detached houses. If you were not told of its existence you would not be aware of the secrets hidden behind the front door. Part of the houses form an upstairs flat for the steward of the club, the bottom floors of both houses contain two snooker tables, a dance area, a very large bar and a sitting room for watching television or meetings.

My sons are also creatures of habit and usually went to the club on Friday evenings en route to anywhere else they decide to go. The club is a cheap watering hole and the two full-size snooker tables are a great attraction.

Because it is a members' only club there is never any trouble; everyone knows each other and there is a good age mix. My boys had never been very keen on nightclubs or going downtown much at the weekends.

Richard came home as usual at about 8.30, leaving his sons still in the club. Both the boys kissed their father goodbye. It was not a serious sign of affection, and they are not usually so demonstrative, but Joe and Dan were on a sort of high that evening for some reason. This action played on Richard's mind a lot over the next few weeks.

The boys went on from the Somerville Club about 10.15 p.m. to The Showboat pub on the Gloucester Road, the main road that runs through Bristol. Daniel had only had one drink so he drove his girlfriend Sarah and a couple of other friends to the pub. When they arrived The Showboat was extremely full and very smoky so Dan decided not to stay inside for very long as his eyes have always been very sensitive to smoke, probably due to Behçets. Dan went outside to wait for Sarah to join him.

Next to The Showboat is a large Lloyds Bank. To the right of the bank there is a very wide strip of pavement forming the corner of Dongola Avenue and Gloucester Road; there is a cash point in the wall there. On the opposite side of Dongola Avenue, across from the bank is a branch of Tileflare. Tileflare also has a wide pavement on the Dongola Avenue side, this strip is tiled elaborately next to the shop and has a link rail round the floor tiles with metal upright pillars just the right height to sit on supporting the chain fencing.

Daniel perched himself on one of the metal uprights outside Tileflare and was joined very quickly by a friend of his called Jason, a lad who was on leave from Leeds University. Jason is a slightly built lad of mixed parenthood and he, too, was waiting for his girlfriend to come out of the pub. The spot they were sitting in is very well lit. There are lights positioned high round Tileflare and the opposite corner is lit because of the cash point. The view of The Showboat is obscured by Lloyds Bank because the pub is set well back off the road. It was a dry night, not terribly warm but quite pleasant for late May. Jason and Dan were chatting nonchalantly. As they spoke a situation started to take place before their eyes.

People started to slowly come out of The Showboat. Slightly to the front of these revellers was a lad of eighteen called Wayne. Daniel was not actually a friend of Wayne as such, though they had several mutual acquaintances. Joe knew him better as he sang and played guitar from time to time in a band that performed occasionally in The Showboat. As Wayne approached the corner of Dongola Avenue on the pavement opposite where Dan and Jason were sitting, he was stopped in his tracks by three older-looking

37

young men. Two were about five foot ten inches and of stocky build and the third was leaner and taller, around six foot two inches. All three men were dressed alike and all three had skinhead hairstyles and goatee beards. The taller of the men shouted something at Wayne about him not getting a good enough beating before, and at that point Daniel noticed that Wayne was sporting a black eye and showed signs of having been in some sort of scuffle previously. We learnt later that these 'men' had cornered Wayne earlier, at around 9 p.m. and that he had been slapped around a bit by the taller of the group then, causing the black eye and slightly swollen face that could clearly be seen at this time.

The taller man, who I will refer to as MB, who was obviously known to Wayne, was shouting something about Wayne having shared a taxi with his girlfriend. Wayne appeared to proclaim his innocence and made very little attempt to protect himself except by trying to talk his way out of the situation as he was set upon by MB. Several blows were rained upon Wayne by at least two of the assailants and he fell to his knees. Daniel and Jason were both alarmed by what they were watching. Dan shouted to the assailants to stop. Obviously this cry was ignored and the beating continued. Dan was not a friend of Wayne but regardless of this he was not prepared to sit and watch as the lad was pummelled mercilessly in front of his eyes. Jason warned Dan 'to stay out of it' as he was aware of these thugs' reputation. Ignoring the warning, Dan got up and went over to the group. A crowd of people who had just left the pub were now heading down the Gloucester Road and were starting to gather behind the incident. Daniel approached and told MB and his friends that Wayne had had enough and tried to help the young man to his feet. I cannot imagine what made Daniel think that because he was not involved he would be safe from these louts. Without warning, Dan was knocked down. Dan must have got back to his feet because he was reported to be staggering in a stunned way and was then pushed over the railing round the corner of Tileflare. Daniel appeared to make no attempt at retaliation. Jason, meanwhile, had got to his feet and went over to Wayne who looked like he was in a bad way. Jason knew MB from school where they had both been educated as had Wayne and several of the later witnesses and the other assailants. MB and crew had been in a higher year than everyone else and were well known as undesirables.

MB grabbed Jason and had him in a stranglehold up against the wall of Tileflare. Jason was trying to use the fact that they had been to the same school to secure his release from MB's grip, but it fell on deaf ears.

Meanwhile, one of the thugs struck Daniel again whilst he was in a muddled state and he was now unconscious in the gutter, having cracked his skull from ear to ear on the edge of the curb. Joseph had now appeared on the scene, having hurried towards the commotion and intending to rescue Jason, unaware that his brother was unconscious close by. As Joe got close to MB, MB released Jason and turned towards Joe. Joe stepped back and tripped over the curb falling backwards. MB stood towering above him in a menacing stance. Katie, seeing what was occurring, rushed over thinking MB might kick out at Joe whilst he was down. Pandemonium had broken out and all three of the thugs had wild expressions and were shouting and threatening everyone in sight.

Kate stood in front of MB. He called her a 'stupid bitch' or some similar pleasantry. She slapped him and knelt down by Joe to help him up. MB, out of his mind with uncontrollable anger, took the opportunity to kick Kate in the face; her head shot back on impact. Possibly the blow was meant for Joe but we will never know. Joe, meanwhile, had glanced to his right and spotted Daniel lying in a pool of blood in the gutter. He struggled to his feet and rushed to Dan's side, his mind now empty of any other events around him taking place. Jason's girlfriend, Rachel, a girl with a strong Birmingham accent who was at this time attending the University of the West of England with Sarah, rushed towards Jason. MB and his cronies started to push their way through the crowd, walking up the Gloucester Road in the opposite direction to which the majority of people where originally heading. Rachel grabbed MB's arm and said something like 'How can you walk away, you...' and several swear words and was punched in the face by MB for her outburst. Another girl, Babe, was pushed across the bonnet of a car and landed in the road.

Isabel, a young lady who lived and worked in The Showboat, had seen the tail end of the drama and ran back into the pub to phone for the police and an ambulance. The landlord and one of the bouncers came out just in time to see the thugs walking up the road.

We were later told that MB and his delightful friends had gone downtown where they saw Wayne's older brother and bragged to him how they had given Wayne a good hiding and also knocked down another lad who had gone down like a skittle. It appears that Dan must have been unconscious before he hit the ground as he made no attempt to stop his fall.

Katie, now nursing a fast swelling face, went over to Daniel and with Sarah's help put him into the recovery position following instructions from another young lady. They had to persuade Joseph to move first as he was now sitting in the road with Daniel's head in his lap in a very distressed condition. The whole scene was one of disbelief. Those who had not actually been injured were all very shocked.

The police and ambulance arrived shortly and one of the group phoned me at home on Sarah's instructions to tell me what had happened. When I was told Dan had been knocked down I assumed it was by a car. I never imagined a human being would have injured him so badly. It was the start of a long running nightmare.

The First Hospital

There was a lot of confusion as to who was going in the ambulances and who wasn't. I decided to follow the one containing Daniel to Southmead Hospital which was a very short distance away. Sarah came in my car with me and we actually arrived at the hospital before Daniel. I went straight to the reception and told them Daniel was on his way and gave them his details. The ambulance arrived at about 11.50.

Daniel was put into a cubicle immediately and Wayne was in the one next to him. Someone phoned Wayne's mother and one of the young men went to fetch her. Wayne's mother is a widow with four sons so everyone was a little reluctant to worry her. The young man who had phoned me made himself known to me. He was a nice-looking lad called Brian of around eighteen or nineteen with a pronounced stutter.

Wayne looked like he had just done six rounds with Mohammed Ali but had regained consciousness and was talking endlessly in a gabbling nervous fashion, so I felt sure he would be fine. Daniel, however, was still unconscious.

The youngsters from outside The Showboat all seemed to arrive in batches. I was not quite sure how they all got there. Joe had come in the ambulance with Danny, so also had red-headed Kate. Kate registered her arrival and also waited to be seen by a doctor. Joe was pacing about, still completely covered in blood. It was all down his front and as it was all over his hands he went off to wash his hands.

I tried to find out what had happened that evening. Everyone seemed confused as to the details. I asked if anyone knew who had hit Daniel and that was the first time I ever heard the name's of Dan's assailants. They had all been barred from The Showboat, so everyone knew their names. The leader, MB, was described to me as about six foot two inches and of slim build. At this time, I had never heard of him or seen him. It was all very alien to me. I had worked for eighteen years voluntarily in Horfield Prison before I started paid work, and the only way I had any contact with thugs was there.

We waited just over an hour for the doctor; she arrived to look at Daniel at about 1.15. I always thought head injuries were treated with a degree of urgency, but apparently not that night. I do think that if a member of the police force had accompanied the ambulance we might have got better service. The nurses had looked in on Dan, taken his blood pressure and checked his other vital signs. Every now and again he seemed to be coming round and was either sick, or mumbled something before blacking out again. I was beginning to suspect that we had a real problem but never dreamt for one moment how much of a problem we were going to face.

By now Wayne was sitting on the edge of the couch in the next cubicle with his mother, raring to go home.

The doctor seemed very young; she was tall and thin with dark hair. She looked at Daniel briefly and went off to order X-rays for all and sundry. Apparently there was no radiographer on site so they had to call one out. The doctor returned and started to examine Daniel. She seemed very interested in how much he had drunk. Sarah had been with Daniel since 6.30 so she was in a good position to give an account of this and she said, 'Very little.' Regardless of this, the doctor had it in her head that Daniel had drunk some amazing amount of alcohol. I explained that Dan had Behçets Disease and because of this he did not drink a lot as a rule. As the doctor had never heard of Behçets, she did not see the connection. I did try to explain a little about the disease and how it effects the brain stem, which is why I was concerned about the knock on the head. I noticed that still no one had bothered to examine Dan's SOS bracelet. I was beginning to wonder why I always insisted that Dan wore it when he went out.

At around two o'clock the radiographer arrived and everyone who needed to be X-rayed was. Luckily, at this time the only customers in casualty were The Showboat crowd so it didn't take too long.

God knows what they X-rayed because the doctor came back to tell Sarah and I that Dan only had a broken nose and a chipped tooth. There was no fracture. Sarah and I made a joke about checking Dan's nails to make sure he hadn't chipped a nail as well. On the strength of the X-rays, the doctor stapled the large cut at the back of Dan's head. As it turned out later Dan did not have a broken nose or in fact a chipped tooth. He did, in fact, have a compound fracture to the base of the skull that stretched from ear to ear and this doctor had stapled the cut at that point. He also had a hairline fracture of the neck. These points were not discovered for several hours. I will never know whose X-rays they were, they obviously were not Dan's. As Wayne was the only other male who had been hit about the head I would assume they were his although he was told he had sustained no broken bones, just bruises and lacerations.

No one seemed concerned about the effects of shock on any of the youngsters gathered in the Accident and Emergency Department. In fact there appeared to be no signs of urgency about anything or anyone whatsoever. Kate's face, although swollen, we were assured was not seriously damaged, neither apparently was the girl Rachel with the black eye.

Every half hour or so I phoned Richard at home, not that there was much to relate to him. There was an endless trail of young people in various degrees of distress coming in and out of the cubicle to see how Dan was. I would have liked them all to disappear at this point. Still I did not think anything was too worrying. After all, we had all been told that there was no skull fracture, the bleeding had stopped, and apparently Dan only had a broken nose! The doctor advised me to take Dan to the dentist on Monday to have his teeth examined. If only things had turned out to be that simple.

By four o'clock, most of the youngsters had gone home. Joe, Kate, Wayne and Sarah were still there. Someone had taken Wayne's mum home. She had wanted to stay but I insisted she went home and didn't worry. The doctor returned, looked at Dan and decided that maybe he wasn't going to come round to any degree and maybe she should transfer him to Frenchay Head Injuries Unit to be on the safe side. This seemed like a good idea to me and I phoned Richard to let him know that the doctor was phoning for an ambulance to take Dan to Frenchay. Daniel kept drifting in and out of consciousness, throwing up what looked like blood. He had a steady trickle of blood coming from his nose and ear which I was assured was the result of the broken nose as was the blood Dan was bringing up. We were told that obviously he had swallowed copious amounts of blood from his nose. This didn't really make sense to me as I knew Dan had fallen backwards and struck his head; also his nose didn't appear to be marked. There was a bruise appearing on the right side of Dan's chin and another on his forehead, but no black eyes as you would expect from a heavy punch on the nose. I had studied first aid as a member of the Woman's Royal Voluntary Service Emergency Team, and knew enough to wonder.

I decided to nip home and get some paper work on Behçets just in case Frenchay hadn't heard of it either. I rushed off, leaving Dan with Sarah, half expecting them to be en route to Frenchay when I got back. I was only gone for half an hour. I need not have hurried. Everything was as I had left it, only by now Wayne had also gone home. I gave a copy of details about Behçets to the nursing staff for future reference.

An ambulance arrived with a heart attack victim who strangely enough had his sister with him whom I have known for a number of years. The lady lived at the sheltered accommodation where my elderly aunt lived, and had also been a lifelong friend of my mother-in-law. Small world.

The ambulance we were waiting for arrived at six o'clock. We had now been at Southmead Hospital for six hours. I now know that head injuries are not treated as seriously as one would expect.

I persuaded Joe and Kate to go home, promising to phone them as soon as I had any news. There was, however, no budging Sarah; she was clearly going wherever Daniel was going and nowhere else. Sarah's landlady's son, James, had looked into the Accident and Emergency wing of Southmead, so he could report back as to where Sarah was at this unearthly hour.

At last we were about to go to Frenchay and maybe get something actually done about Daniel, or so we believed.

Frenchay Hospital

Saturday, 1 June 1996

We were about to cross town to Frenchay Hospital which has a good reputation for dealing with head injuries. Sarah went in the ambulance with Dan and I followed in the car bringing the X-rays with me. When I arrived I booked Dan in at the reception expecting him to go straight to a ward. Wrong again. Daniel was wheeled into another cubicle and placed on the bed. A nurse trotted in and took his blood pressure and temperature. After about half an hour a very young tall blond registrar arrived. He asked Sarah and I to leave the cubicle whilst he examined Dan. We could hear him shouting at Dan to wake up. I was starting to get a little frustrated at this point but stayed quiet and calm. Both Sarah and I were very tired. It was nearly seven o'clock and I had now been up since 7.30 the morning before, twenty-four hours previously.

The young doctor emerged from the cubicle and asked us to join him and answer some questions. He wanted to know how much Dan had drunk. Sarah said, 'About two pints', to which he replied, 'A young man on a Friday night, you can't expect me to believe that.' I told him Dan had Behçets, to which he replied, 'What has that got to do with anything?' I explained the problems with Behçets and told him how Dan had passed out under strobe lights at a disco a few months previously and had not regained consciousness for fourteen hours. He could check the Bristol Royal Infirmary records. Dan was a patient of Doctor Kirwan there and he had Dan's full medical history. This doctor as good as called me a liar and said the only thing that would cause such an effect was if Dan took drugs. He said he thought there was very little wrong with Daniel. I asked why he was not waking up and the good doctor said it was because he was drunk and after he had slept it off, we could take him home. Both Sarah and I were absolutely flabbergasted. I couldn't believe how rude this young man had been. I had a son who had suffered some dreadful injury at the hands of thugs and according to the registrar he was merely drunk. (I would be fascinated to know exactly what the doctor at Southmead told the registrar at Frenchay when she said she was sending Dan to him. I doubt that a transcript of that conversation would ever be made public.) I, of course, wish the young doctor had been right and Dan had been drunk! I mentioned that the X-rays showed Dan had a broken nose at least. This delightful young man went on to explain that they didn't set broken noses and they did not waste X-rays on drunks. To say I was amazed would be an understatement. The doctor was immovable; in his opinion Dan was drunk and he would come back in an hour so we could take him home. Off he went. Sarah and I just looked at each other. If it hadn't been so serious we would have laughed. Sarah and I were beginning to wonder if we were the only sane ones around.

True to his word the doctor did not reappear for over an hour. We could hear a real drunk in the cubicle next to us being treated with a lot more respect that my son had been. I could not understand what was happening. Daniel is a very respectable and personable-looking young man. He doesn't have studs in his ears or nose, no nipple rings, no tattoos. Dan isn't a skinhead and doesn't have love and hate inked on his fingers. If he had any of these possibly offensive acquisitions I might have understood the doctor's attitude but he hasn't. He is a particularly nice, squeaky clean looking lad with fair hair and blue eyes, dressed smartly, slightly blooded of course. What was this doctor's problem? I can only assume that so many drunken young louts do come into Frenchay A & E wasting doctors valuable time that they have become hardened to the sight of semi-conscious youngsters and are slightly blinkered.

Eventually the doctor deemed to return. He had another go at shouting at Daniel to no avail. He said he still thought he was drunk and maybe he would need a little longer to recover. I could not get through to this young man that as Dan had been knocked out at 11.15 or thereabouts, and would have had his last drink some half hour before that at least, which was now nine hours ago. Even a hardened drinker would have sobering up in that time if in fact he had ever been drunk in the first place.

It was now gone eight o'clock, we had been trying to get some real attention for more than eight hours and I was starting to get a little peeved. I insisted that the registrar phone someone senior and get them to look at Daniel. I said I wanted a proper doctor. The young registrar did not take too kindly to my comments and kept telling me he was a 'proper doctor'. 'Well, I want another one,' I replied. He went off muttering.

At around 10.30 another doctor arrived, an obviously senior one. Apparently the registrar had phoned him at home whilst he was off duty. After Dr. Younge had hung up he had thought about the matter for an hour and something in the back of his mind made him decide to see this problem patient for himself. Sarah and I explained what had happened and I said that we had come to Frenchay in good faith, expecting Daniel to be admitted at least for observation. We told him word for word what the young registrar had said. 'He said what!' was the reply. Then we told him how long we had been waiting for proper medical help – almost eleven hours by now. 'How long!' Both these comments soon became catchphrases. For a while Sarah and I were collecting them.

Dr. Younge gave Dan a thorough examination and decided that things did not look too good. I told him Dan had Behçets, which seemed to ring alarm bells. Thank goodness, someone had heard of it. Things started to happen at last. Dr. Younge went off to arrange a series of tests, including a CT scan. We seemed to be waiting another age when an orderly came to take Dan off for these tests. Our saviour, Dr. Younge, returned and told us to go to the visitors' waiting room and he would come and see us soon. Dan vanished into the distance. Sarah and I made our way to the other waiting room. I phoned Richard, Joe and my middle son, Adam, to let them all know the score. Sarah phoned her landlady to let her know she was still at Frenchay Hospital.

My middle son, Adam, and his then girlfriend, Marie, arrived first. Joe had phoned him on the evening when we were first in Southmead but Adam did not realise then that there was a serious problem so he hadn't come immediately. (Marie is a very striking-looking girl, slim, with very dark long straight hair and had met Adam a few years previously when Dan was going out with Ann-Marie. Ann-Marie and Marie were on the same course at college.)

Richard and Joe were not long behind. A doctor came out to speak to us telling us that Dan was going for a CT scan and, depending on the results, he would either be on a ward, where exactly he would tell us later, or in Ward 2 which was an

47

emergency ward.

A CT scan is a computerised X-ray. The equipment records the images not onto a film but electronically. In most cases the amount of radiation used in a CT scan is greater than used for an ordinary X-ray. For some kinds of investigation, the information that comes from the X-rays as they pass through the body is recorded in a series of cross-section pictures or scans that can even be built up into three-dimensional images of a particular organ in the body, in this case the brain. CT scans are used to diagnose tumours, abscesses and haemorrhages in the brain, as well as stroke and head injuries.

As everyone was assembled and it was apparent that we had a long wait, I decided that I would go to Southmead police station to make sure that the police were actually following up the disturbance that resulted in Daniel's injuries.

I drove off to Southmead Road alone. I spoke to the duty officer who did not seem aware of what I was talking about. I gave him all the details I had, explained that my son appeared to be seriously injured, and assured him that I wanted this followed up. The duty officer told me that unless there is a serious injury these assaults were very rarely followed up because they were so commonplace on a Friday and Saturday night. The thought that total morons could leave my son for dead in the gutter and the police would have just ignored the incident amazed me, to say the least. I came away wondering what sort of world we were all living in. I made it quite clear that I would be back the next day and this would not be swept under the carpet. I wanted charges brought against these creatures.

I drove straight back to Frenchay. By now I think I must have been on overdrive as I didn't even feel tired despite the fact that I had not been to bed for thirty hours or more.

It was now 1.45 on the afternoon of 1 June, nearly fourteen hours after arriving at Southmead by ambulance, and we still did not know what was wrong with Daniel.

At last, a very serious-looking doctor came to speak to us all. Daniel had been taken to the Emergency Head Injuries Ward, Ward 2. It would take them a while to settle him in and then we could see him. We were told that Daniel had a compound fracture to the base of the skull that stretched from ear to ear and a hairline fracture of the neck, bruising to the frontal lobes of the brain and a small haemorrhage on the left side at the back of the brain, positively no broken nose. Daniel still had not regained full consciousness. We all just looked at each other in amazement. Sarah was obviously distressed but at least we now felt that something would be done to help Daniel. I wanted to march back into the Accident and Emergency and punch that registrar on the nose but managed to restrain myself, although I planned to write an official complaint the next day.

For the rest of the day, Adam, Marie, Sarah, Richard and I were continuously at Dan's side. We went off occasionally in pairs to get cups of tea and so on. Joe had gone home to his children but luckily managed to get a babysitter and came in later in the evening.

We all went home about eleven o'clock with a promise that we would be phoned by the hospital if there was any change. I was absolutely worn out. I couldn't sleep regardless and just wanted to get back to the hospital to check on Danny.

The following week was a very strange one for us all. Dan remained in a state of semi-consciousness, occasionally lucid but more often talking as though he was trapped in a computer game. He kept asking people to bring in the manual as he couldn't get off level two.

The nursing staff walked about shouting very loudly at the patients who I assume were all head injury patients. These angels kept asking the same questions over and over again to each patient in each bed. It actually started to get on your nerves. 'What is your name?' 'What is your date of birth?' 'Who is Prime Minister?' 'What is the date?' Dan gave some very strange answers. Occasionally he knew his name, not very often though. He said that the prime minister was a short fat man in a Mac and that it was 1939. Still we didn't realise how serious things were and we all laughed at Dan's strange replies. Occasionally Dan knew who we all were, but as quickly as he recollected us, he forgot us again.

Joe had friends almost permanently babysitting for him. Sarah and I hardly left Dan's side all that week. Adam took the week off work as did Marie. Dan obviously was suffering a lot of discomfort from the head wound, which was continuously weeping and he obviously had dreadful headaches. Dan kept crying out when his head hurt a lot and he was not one to make a fuss so it had to be bad. The family were continuously around and friends of ours who were actually Sarah's landlady and landlord, Keith and Sandra, popped in and out most of the week for a while. We sometimes went home for tea and returned in the evening, or maybe just went to the canteen for a snack instead. Frenchay canteen became a very familiar sight to us all and it was a very cheap watering hole. The meals were quite good as well.

I was beginning to feel that I knew Frenchay Hospital very well, having only the previous month been visiting my mother there for the six weeks before she died. I was rather hoping not to ever see that place again, let alone so soon.

Dan used to twitch violently occasionally, almost bouncing up and down in the bed. He was lucid enough from time to time to want to use a bottle to spend a penny. One of us would help him if the nurses were busy, very often Sarah volunteered. I felt that this was taking togetherness a bit too far but I didn't interfere. One day we laughed our heads off as Dan managed to miss the bottle and drown Sarah, it was all over her. She didn't seem the least bit perturbed. We are breeding a tougher type of young women these days!

Dan had not eaten since 31 May but had been taking small drops of water so by now he was having difficulty swallowing. I thought that the side of his face looked a little strange but could not quite put my finger on the problem.

On the Thursday Dan asked Sarah to marry him on 26 July. Now I knew he wasn't well!

Odd friends of Dan also dropped in along with red-headed Kate.

I popped into work on the Thursday to report how Dan was. Everyone seemed to think that it was a bit of an exaggerated drama. Keith, who also worked at Cotham, had told everyone that Dan had recognised Sandra, so he must be fine. I was a little annoyed, but didn't say anything as Keith is a bit of a joker.

On the Friday morning Dan was still complaining of headaches but I was told that he was a lot better. He answered some of the usual questions correctly so I was beginning to think that maybe the doctors were right and things were improving. Richard came in and Dan was in the computer game again by then. He looked up and asked Richard where his alien life force was. Very strange! Because Dan had not eaten anything since admittance the nurses kept talking about having to correct this. He was still struggling to swallow the sips of water offered to him.

I went home Friday feeling a little more confidant that Dan would soon start to improve. I was very wrong. I would have to say that Dan did not actually look or seem any better to me but we all put our faith in doctors.

Having spoken to the nursing staff Sarah felt so much better about Dan that she decided to go home to her parents in Kings Winford near Birmingham for the weekend to get a well-earned rest and a little pampering. I promised to phone if there was any changes worth reporting and told her that she was to go home and have a good weekend.

On the morning of Saturday, 8 June 1996, the real nightmare started. I had decided to go in quite early that morning and then intended to go on to the market in the grounds of Southmead Hospital for provisions, returning a little later. This did not happen.

I arrived at the hospital just after eight o'clock. I had to use the entrance that looked like an old air-raid shelter. There was a covered outer passage with ugly pillars that were suffering from concrete cancer that supported a corrugated iron canopy, leading to double doors that took you into the main hospital. The hospital has had a lot of cosmetic improvements since 1996 but at that time Frenchay consisted of lots of primitive looking out buildings that were used by troop during the war and an unattractive main building.

I walked in the entrance to the very long corridor that faces you on arrival. Ward 2 is the second door on the right. I started to walk that way but was aware of alarms going off and the crash team tearing like maniacs down the corridor towards me. It was as if I had stepped into a film set, quite unbelievable. I literally stopped in my tracks to let them get to wherever they were going. They, too, were going into Ward 2. I followed. They were at Dan's bedside in seconds. There were nurses everywhere, two of which were performing cardiopulmonary resuscitation (I had played at this for my St John's Ambulance First Aid Badge for work, but had never seen anyone actually doing it on a person in earnest until then). As soon as they arrived at the bedside, the crash team took over and went to work. It was as if I was in a dream or an episode of *Casualty*. There were all these people shouting at Dan or about Dan. Then I watched as they picked up what looked like large rubber pads connected to wires and a electronic machine placed one either side of Dan's chest and shocked him. I was only a few feet away and could see his body rise and fall with the treatment. Suddenly it occurred to me that I was watching my precious son die. A nurse shouted, 'We are losing him!', several other things were shouted out such as we have no input, we have lost the pulse but I wasn't really taking it all in. Then a nurse turned and looked at me, she recognised me and came over, pulling me roughly away. 'Don't worry, everything is going to be all right!' she said. I just smiled at her and replied matter-of-factly, 'Don't be silly, is he going to die?' 'Not if we can help it,' she replied. She tried to make me leave but I wouldn't, I just told her to get on with her job. Mine was to be with my son. I think she realised that to insist would be a waste of time so she walked back towards the crowd round the bed. I just watched in total bewilderment as the oxygen mask was fitted and various gadgets appeared and were used. A man in a white coat picked up the round shock treatment gadgets. Then they shocked Dan again and someone gave a cry of delight that I took to mean that they had found a spark of life. It didn't seem real. I was just standing on my own wondering if there was anything I should be doing but I was transfixed and my feet wouldn't move.

I stood for a few minutes and then someone shouted, 'Let's get him into crash!' The whole party started to move, bed and all; I jumped out the way. Dan was rushed past me out of Ward 2 and into a door almost opposite where I was not allowed to enter. I just stood in the silence looking at the door, wondering what I should do, wishing that Richard was there. The nurse I had spoken to earlier came out; she told me to wait a moment and disappeared back inside again. After a few minutes a man came out. To this day I cannot remember what he looked like but he was wearing what looked like a surgical robe and took his mask off to speak to me. He spoke in a low, gentle voice and he put his hand on my shoulder as he did so. I felt my legs turn to jelly, my chest felt tight as I fought to stay calm, feeling sure he was going to say that Dan was dead but he didn't exactly. He spoke very slowly and clearly. He advised me to get my family together immediately as he did not think that Dan was going to make it. Furthermore, he explained that Dan had woken in the morning with an absolutely terrible headache that had made him scream out. The nursing staff had called a doctor immediately but Dan had a fit and arrested before the doctor got there. The nurses had managed to keep Dan's vital signs going until the crash team arrived but with difficulty. Dan had suffered a stroke due to what this man thought would turn out to be abnormal brain swell. I was advised not to waste too much time, but to make the calls needed.

I was flabbergasted but moved like a robot as instructed. I hurried up the corridor to the phone. First I phoned Adam and told him to come immediately. I didn't give out too many details as I was frightened that he would drive too fast and come to grief himself. Then I phoned Joe who had Dan's mobile. I didn't tell him too much either for the same reasons. Joe was still in bed but seemed to wake up immediately when he heard what I had to say. Joe had friends staying round his house so he had built-in babysitters, which was a blessing. I was worried about Richard because I had the car and he had to open up the school for Saturday school at 10.30 that morning. I needed someone to fetch Richard for me. I cannot understand why I didn't just ask Adam or Joe to go get Richard, but I didn't. I phoned a friend who was also a nurse so I thought she would have a clear understanding of the drama unfolding. I explained very clearly what was going on, I told her Dan had arrested and was probably not going to make it. Wrongly I assumed that she would grasp the seriousness of the situation and just follow orders. I asked her to get her husband to fetch Richard and bring him to Frenchay to join me. I told her to hurry and please not to come, I just needed Richard here as I thought Dan might die. I then phoned Richard and told him what had occurred and that a lift was on the way to bring him to Frenchay Hospital.

I made my way to the front of the hospital to wait for my sons. I was amazed how quickly Joe got there. He could see that things were serious. We hugged and I told him exactly what had happened. Joe was very calm. The next person to arrive was the friend I had phoned to fetch Richard. She parked quite a way from Joe and me and was alone in her car. I was amazed. I thought my instructions had been clear. She certainly appeared to understand them. I just didn't want to see anyone other than Richard and couldn't imagine why she had come and why she didn't have Richard with her. For some reason this small incident really tipped me over the edge. I felt I wanted to explode. I asked Joe to go and tell her to please go away and that I would phone her later. Joe did as asked and I believe he was polite. I watched as she drove away and Joe decided to go fetch his dad himself. As Joe pulled away, Adam and Marie pulled up. I hurried over to Adam to tell him what had happened and we waited together for Joe and Richard. Adam decided that maybe he should phone Sarah, and he wondered off to do so. Marie and I waited by the entrance.

Richard and Joe arrived at the hospital. The friend's husband had not shown himself, so I assume that if Joe hadn't had gone Richard would still be at home waiting for a lift. We all made our way into the hospital.

We went up to the crash door and I knocked. It seemed like an age before someone came out. They said they were not ready to let us in yet. They were still battling to get Dan stable. Some time later a doctor in a white coat came out and said we could just come in for a couple of minutes. We all trailed in after the doctor, in silence. He took us to a very small cubicle which contained Dan wired up like Spaghetti Junction to several monitors that were soon to became very familiar to us all. The man explained that it was very early days. He repeated to the assembled group what I had been told, how Dan had fitted and arrested but they had managed to get him stable but it was a long haul and Dan had a long way to go before he would be out of danger. We were told that the next forty-eight hours were vital. (That seems to be the usual phrase.) Apparently, Dan had not behaved in a familiar manner. Usually head injury patients fit and get severe brain swell in the first forty-eight hours. It is very unusual for a patient to go a whole week before such an occurrence so it had caught everyone unprepared. He said he thought that Dan only had a very slim chance of surviving. We went up one by one. Both Dan's brothers touched his hand for a second. I felt they were saying goodbye just in case. We were all calm at this time and I think we were all probably slightly in shock. We were only allowed to stay for a couple of minutes before being ushered back out into the corridor.

Very shortly after seeing Dan in crash, he was transferred to ICU (Intensive Care Unit). We couldn't go in for at least an hour as it would take that long to get him settled in ICU.

At about 10.30, Sarah and her mum and dad arrived. We all went off for a cup of tea and explained to Sarah what had happened. Obviously she was very upset and her little face crumbled and tears poured down her cheeks. I had tried so hard to think positively and not cry for my other two boys' sake, but seeing Sarah so distressed made that impossible for me to continue.

As soon as we were able, we went into ICU to see Dan. This place is your worst nightmare, it is indescribable.

There are double doors at the entrance and an entrance phone.

You have to buzz and say who you are and who you wish to see. Only relatives or people appointed by the family can go in. You go through the doors and in front of you is a pillar with a shelf on it containing a bottle of antiseptic which every visitor must rub into their hands before approaching the bed. The pillar obscures your view of the room. You walk round the pillar and look down a room of people in beds, each attached to high-tech equipment. It is like something out of a space movie; each patient looks like they are attached to an aeroplane cockpit, there are so many dials and screens. Dan was at the far end of the room so we had to walk past a lot of barely alive-looking people before we reached his bed. We went in two at a time. I went in first. When you first see someone you love wired up in this way you have to catch your breath for a moment, but it is amazing how quickly you adjust.

Daniel was in a deep coma from which there was a very strong possibility he would not recover. It is your very worst nightmare to see your child in such a state. His fate is out of your hands. Dan and I had always been very close. As I have mentioned several times already, Daniel has suffered from Behçets Disease since the age of eight, so we had spent many hours in hospitals; in fact, Frenchay is the only hospital Dan had not previously been a patient at in Bristol. He had even been an outpatient at Hammersmith, London, at one time. Although I had always known the seriousness and possible repercussions of Behçets it was nothing compared to this. I realised that having Behçets was going to go against his recovery from this head injury. Behçets affects the brain stem, causes severe headaches, high temperatures and a form of meningitis. All these points do not help when you are fighting serious head injuries. In fact, if these 'men' who attacked Daniel were looking for the most vulnerable person to attack and damage the back of head of, they made the right choice.

In twos, we all went into the ICU to put our minds at rest that Dan was actually alive. Sarah went in with her mother, Andrene. Her father had recently lost his mother. She had been in ICU in Birmingham and he didn't feel he could cope with seeing someone else in such a situation so soon, which was fair enough.

Each came out visibly shocked and upset by Dan's situation. We just clung to each other in the corridor, unaware of anyone else who might or might not have been around. It had to be the worst day of my life, in fact all the members of my family's lives.

I couldn't help thinking about how much Dan had been through already in his life. How we nearly lost him originally when he was eight and then again a year later, to what we then thought to be the Steven-Johnston Syndrome. I thought about the endless tests performed by Doctor Kirwan at the BRI (Bristol Royal Infirmary) to confirm that Dan had Behçets. And now my son was fighting for his life as a result of human intervention, if you can class such people as human, and not the disease as I had often half expected might claim him. To say life isn't fair would be an understatement!

How we all got through that first day, I will never know. We were certainly drained by the evening.

Sarah's father, Pete, decided to go home and Andrene wanted to stay with Sarah. I offered to put them both up as Sandra was out of town. I think under normal circumstances Andrene might have stayed with Sarah's landlady and landlord, Sandra and Keith. We didn't leave the hospital until after midnight. We only left then because they had taken Dan to theatre to put a monitor in his head to keep track of the pressure inside the skull and a drain to remove any fluid build-up. Both pupils were equal, non-reactive. His heart rate was 80/110 and his blood pressure altered from 110/135 to 75/85. His chest appeared to rattle. Things did not look very hopeful. The nursing staff promised to ring if there was any change at all, whatever the time, so we all wove our weary way home to bed; none of us were very keen to leave or expected to sleep that night. Adam and Joe went to their own homes, very tired and emotional.

Andrene and Sarah had to share the bedroom usually reserved for my two young grandchildren. It wasn't exactly the Ritz but I think we were all too tired to worry about details. I had never met Sarah's parents before that day; it was a strange time to meet and quite difficult having a total stranger in your house at such a personal, private family time, but I could understand why Andrene would want to stay and keep an eye on Sarah. I would have wanted to have done the same if she was my daughter.

Coma

We all had a rather restless night and breakfast did not appeal to any of us. When we had left the previous evening, Dan had been on his way down to theatre to have monitors fitted into his head to measure the pressure on the brain and to have drains put into his head to remove fluid building up. It was all very high-tech and beyond my powers of understanding.

It was no wonder we all felt drained; we had left Dan in the hands of strangers, in a deep coma. Seeing someone on life support in Intensive Care for the first time is quite mind-blowing, especially when it is someone you love. I had just spent six weeks watching my mother die in this very hospital but it had nothing on this. No one wants to lose their mother but it is the natural progression of life that this must happen, but we should never have to bury our children. I felt like I was a total emotional wreck and, looking around at everyone else gathered in my little house, I could see that we were all in the same state, trying desperately to hold each other up. It was still very early and no one seemed worried about their appearance. We just wanted to get back to the hospital and Daniel, as soon as possible. I assumed that things would be unchanged when we arrived as the nursing staff had promised to phone me at any time if there was the slightest improvement or drama to report.

We, Richard, Sarah, Andrene and I, arrived at Frenchay Hospital by 8.30 in the morning. It is a strange feeling entering that hospital in these circumstances. Although Frenchay is surrounded by greenery, part of the building is very drab. You could still see clearly how the hospital had been used during the war; it had a barracks-style approach, very dreary and not at all welcoming. Not as if you would expect a hospital to exactly beckon you.

We entered the hospital through the electronic doors, into the main corridor and started the long walk towards the Intensive Care Unit. It is strange how long that corridor seems to be at a time like this. We were each dreading reaching the entrance of the ICU, remembering the sight we had left. I had gone to bed last night hoping to wake up and it all had been a bad dream. Unfortunately, it was now the morning and the dream was in fact reality.

I rang the bell on the wall with trepidation and a voice from inside asked who I was. I just said I was Dan's mother and I was told I must wait for a few moments in the room provided. We all trailed into the ICU waiting room. On a table in the waiting room was a china tea service; it didn't have any significance at the time but as time went on it began to figure quite heavily in our lives.

Adam, Marie, Joe and Kate soon joined us and we all stayed close by Dan's bed, in shifts that day. We couldn't move Sarah, so it limited who else could sit with Dan which became a bit annoying as the days, then weeks dragged on. Dan's brother actually wanted to spend time alone with him, even though he was in a coma and obviously oblivious as to who was there anyway. Sarah was, after all, just a girlfriend, and not a very long standing one either. Knowing Dan's track record, he would probably wake up and not fancy her any more, whereas his brothers would always be there for him. The poor girl did seem determined to be with Dan, and Andrene kept referring to herself as Dan's future mother-in-law when asked who she was by nurses.

It was difficult trying to keep up conversations with people we hardly knew at a time like this. Because Daniel was not living at home at the time of the incident, I did not know Sarah very well and had only met her mother the day before. The truth was that I didn't really want these outsiders there at all, even though they were terribly nice people. It respected Andrene's thoughts that she didn't want her daughter so far from home and alone in a situation where her boyfriend might die any minute, as would be the reaction of any sensible mother.

When the staff were running tests we took advantage of the moment to grab a coffee at the restaurant. However, I could never sit still for long and returned before the others, impatient to just see Daniel and put my mind at rest that he was actually still alive.

Only relatives of the patient or special people, listed by close relatives, can enter the ICU. I was happy about this as I didn't want people coming just for the spectacle, not that I could imagine anyone wanting to do this but according to the staff it does happen. Once I had told the ICU staff who I was, via the intercom system, I was told to enter. I was expecting to be told to wait in the side room. There is another larger waiting room but it is very public so the small one is preferred; also the intercom system is connected to this room and they inform you when you can go in. But on this occasion I could go straight in. I wasn't alone with Dan for long. Intensive Care means exactly what it sounds as though it means. Every patient has a nurse attached to them all through the day and they never leave the patient's side even for a moment. When they have lunch or a coffee break, someone takes their place. Everyday the nurse is changed so they do not get too emotionally involved with the person they attend. If you visit someone in Intensive Care long enough you get to know the nurses very well as there is only limited staff so you get a reoccurrence of carer and they do get involved despite the great plan; they wouldn't be human otherwise.

These are a group of specially trained nurses, both male and female and they are really dedicated. They were the most gentle and wonderful people I have ever met, and I became very fond of a couple of them in particular. There are agency nurses occasionally as well, but even those you meet again, if you are there long enough. I felt that if this group could not get my lad back on his feet, then no one could.

I always approached Daniel's bed with trepidation, wondering what I might find. The first visit sends you a bit wobbly. Because Dan had head injuries, he had probes in his head, an oxygen mask that was changed to a tracheotomy tube after a few days (this happens if the oxygen will be needed long term), catheter, heart monitor, pulse monitor, blood pressure monitor, temperature probe, feeding tube down the nose, taps in hands for taking blood and giving of drugs. All these objects were wired up to a huge television screen that monitored everything as well as inner cranial pressure. Sarah and I got quite well informed about these devices very quickly, and we could see all the danger signs in Dan and other patients. The oxygen levels were monitored on a different machine. Dan was absolutely still, not an eyelash flickered. His pupils were equal at this time but non reactive. His eyes were wide open so a jelly like pad was placed over his eye to prevent them from drying out. He looked for all intents and purposes as if he was dead, except that he was very highly coloured and ran a continuous temperature.

From day one, one of us was either with Dan or in the waiting room continuously. We only went to the canteen when they performed physio on him. This was horrendous to watch as it looked like these women were beating him up whilst he was unconscious. Also they had to take the patient off the oxygen supply and bag him whilst moving him about, and this looks dreadful. They use a hand oxygen pump and it all looks very dramatic. It is amazing how much thick liquid they were getting out of the chest in such a short time, using suction. Obviously they were trying to prevent pneumonia setting in. I could not begin to describe the sheer horror you feel when you think that without all those wires and the physio the patient would be long gone. We saw so many people die whilst in Intensive Care it was mind blowing. Sarah and I got to spot the telltale signs, we watched the blood pressure and cranial pressure and realised when it was dangerous for the patient. There would be a lot of activity then the curtains would suddenly go round a bed then we would all have our curtains pulled round tightly. A few moments later you would hear a rattling sound, which was a huge tin box on wheels that took the bodies away. When you went back to the waiting room there would be signs that a china tea pot and cups and saucers had been brought out for the loved ones. We all quickly decided that if we were ever offered a cup of tea in that delicate china, we would refuse it. What is it about tea and the English? Do we really believe that a cup of tea kills all emotional pain? I think not.

The ICU is a strangely binding place. You find yourself rooting for total strangers and their families for you. For example, there was a young man in the bed opposite Dan's who had already been in ICU for five weeks when we arrived. His name was Peter and he was twenty-four. He had been in a motorbike accident and his main problem was his lungs, which would not operate without assistance. He was in a drug-induced coma, which he was taken out of every now and again to check on his other impulses. His fiancée was there every day, as was his mother. They were obviously not keen on each other and they never sat at Peter's bedside together. I ascertained from the cleaning staff that his mum blamed the girl because she and Peter had bought a house together, and if he had still been at home this would not have happened. He was an only child so it was really tragic all round. The father arrived from time to time. He had a very red face and seemed quite unpleasant. Sue, the fiancée, was a lovely girl, and she and Sarah spoke quite often. Sue and Pete had booked to marry just a couple of weeks after the accident so Peter was brought round just long enough for the chaplain to perform a blessing-style ceremony. Not an actual wedding ceremony, of course. There wasn't a dry eye in the place. Pete was on the latest high-tech bed, it all looked very out of this world. Everyone hoped that Peter would make it, although we quickly learnt that the longer you spend in the ICU the less likely you are to come out. The longer machines do the work for you, i.e. breathe, the less likely you are to get your body to do this function for itself, the body just becomes reliant on the machine. The function of the ICU is to get people off life support as quickly as possible. The ICU is run by anaesthetists, I always thought they were a long way down the scale of medical expertise until now, but they actually totally sustain life, not just during operations, but in the ICU as well.

Dan was in a coma – self-induced, caused by brain swelling beyond the space allowed in the skull. Because the skull is solid, when the brain swells it has no where to go so it closes in on itself, causing damage and closing down vital functions, stopping the victim breathing and so on. That is a coma.

On the Sunday afternoon – day two Intensive Care – we were called to a meeting with Doctor Chris Chandler as promised, to give us an update on Daniel's condition. Dr Chandler is a very likeable, good-looking, young American neurosurgeon. He took us to the waiting room where no one other than our party was allowed in for the duration of the meeting. He spoke softly and clearly, answered all questions openly and fully explained everything as much as was possible to lay-people like us. We were shown the scans, X-rays and results of all tests taken so far. We could clearly see the huge fracture across the base of the skull. Several blood clots could be identified. There was an enormous blood clot than ran from the brain stem to a great distance down Dan's spine. All these horrendous-looking things did not count, according to Dr Chandler. It was the brain swell that was doing the most damage and it was this that would kill Daniel if anything was going to. He explained that he could not afford for the brain to swell much more and if in fact it did, the ICU monitor fitted in Dan's head would tell him at which point something had to be done, or Dan would surely die. Dr Chandler explained how he intended, with our permission, to remove a small portion of the front of Dan's brain – a partial prefrontal lobotomy. Apparently this would allow enough room for the brain to swell a little more and we can operate without this section of the brain although it can cause personality changes. This form of operation was used in the forties and fifties on serious psychiatric disorders to change their personality for the better. Obviously if you do not have this mental problem in the first place, it can have the opposite effect. Not a very comforting thought – we did not ooze with enthusiasm at the thought of this option and, thank goodness, we never had to make that choice in the end. We asked the obvious question, 'What were Dan's chances?' To be told that the doctor would be very surprised if Daniel survived the injuries he had sustained. The odds were very much against this happening. We were grateful for his honesty but devastated. I think Sunday, 9 June would now have to go down as the absolute worst day of my life, on a par with day one. My son was likely to die at any moment, I cannot imagine how any day would ever touch this one for total despair and inner pain. I have always been someone who is devoted to my children. I know we often wonder how much we would sacrifice for our children in certain circumstances but I know without putting it to the test that I would die in my sons' places because I know I could not live without them. I knew that if Daniel died part of me would as well and that I would find it very difficult to continue.

Our little group left the room each wrapped in our own thoughts and stood in the corridor for what seemed like an age just hugging each other. There was nothing to say. The good doctor had said it all. We must have looked like a family who had just lost a member because the vicar hurried down the corridor towards us. I caught a glimpse of her out the corner of my eye and thought, out loud I'm afraid, 'Oh, bloody hell, we are going to have to put up with patronising platitudes from the bloody vicar.' We were greeted with an invitation to a service in the chapel and a load of rubbish about Dan being in God's hands. I was very rude, I am afraid, but I just couldn't cope with that; religion has always been way out of my remit. I could never understand why people could not just behave in a civilised way without a threat of heaven or hell to guide them. I have always thought that the Commandments as a whole are a pretty good set of rules to follow especially the do unto others bit, without the trappings that go with it. Another day and I would have been polite as it is not my usual nature to shout at vicars but this day I definitely shouted at her to get away from me. I think Richard was quite embarrassed. I did think later that maybe I would seek her out and apologise but I never did.

Adam, Marie, Joe and Kate all went to their homes, and Andrene, Sarah, Richard and I went to ours. I don't think any of us slept that night. I know for certain that Richard and I didn't. I sat at my computer and planned Dan's funeral. It sounds pretty creepy but I knew that when the time came I would be unable to do it, so I was writing a speech for Adam to say to all the youngsters I would expect to attend. Telling them not to fill their hearts with hate as Dan would not have wanted this and to think about my precious son from time to time and smile when they remembered him. It was all very strange. I wanted everyone to feel sorry for the sort of people who could do such a terrible thing to another human being without even knowing him. And I wanted my lad remembered for his continuous good humour, despite having a harrowing illness that would have broken the spirit of a lesser person. I wanted everyone to pity the families of the perpetrators of the crime, as they would have a lifetime of wondering how they could have produced such monsters. A somewhat naive outlook on life altered forever once I was face to face with the animals who had hurt my son. In court I realised that they were not people in the sense that I understand people to be. They were creatures without conscience and without morals or backbone and not worthy to even breathe the same air as any of my sons.

I even chose the songs we would play at the funeral. It would be a totally non-religious ceremony – no mention of hymns or prayers. I was going to get friends and relatives to relate their memories of Dan. I wanted to come into, 'He Ain't Heavy, He's my Brother' by the Hollies. Joe wrote a beautiful ballad for Dan called 'My Baby Blue-Eyed Friend' (Dan has incredible blue eyes). This had to be included along with Dan's favourite, Michael Jackson's 'You are Not Alone', finishing with 'Daniel' by Elton John. It was all very morbid and even I find it hard to believe that I actually sat for several hours planning my son's funeral at that time.

The Continued Nightmare

Monday 10 June

We all spent the day in a kind of daze, unable to be less than a few yards from the ICU in case something dreadful happened. It was made quite clear to us all that Daniel's life was hanging literally by the thinnest of threads and I for one had no intention of allowing my son to be alone for even a few moments in case I was to lose him. I held him when he was born and I intended to do the same if he was going to die.

Dan was now on a Nimbus Mattress – a special mattress with a rippled effect that enables the patient to lie still without having to be turned so often. It also prevents bed sores which occur if you lie still for too long. Moving Dan caused his blood pressure and ICP (inner cranial pressure) to hit the roof. His blood pressure was 120/125 and heart rate was 110/115. His temperature caused continuous concern. Sarah and I watched the nurses do every observation. These consisted of shining a torch in Dan's eyes to see if the pupils reacted to light; they did not. I found myself wondering if this process of shining the light in an unconscious person's eyes laid the foundations for the near-death experiences so often read about with the light at the end of the tunnel and if the subconscious put that thought into the patient's mind. Also we watched as they tested for life signs by inflicting what they called deep pain. They pinched Dan's nails at the base and his chest. This makes the arms or legs twitch slightly, as even people in a deep coma react to deep pain. It was unbearable to watch but I could understand the significance of this action. If Dan did not react to deep pain then there was nothing going on in his brain and the damage was definitely irreversible. Dr Moncra, who was in charge of the ICU at Frenchay, was a very blunt man. He made it very clear from the start that he felt that they were only going through the motions and that Dan was not saveable. This did not mean that he was not prepared to pull out all the stops to prove his own diagnosis wrong.

We all, that is, Adam, Marie, Joe, Sarah, Kate, Richard and I (and for a couple of days, Andrene) took it in turns sitting by Dan's side willing him to live.

Detective Constable Phil Rodda, the police office in charge of the 'incident', arrived with a companion to see how Dan was. I believe he was quite shocked when he was told of Daniel's injuries and could see that he had a possible murder inquiry on his hands. Apparently, he was about to arrest two of the men involved. One of them, the one I believe inflicted the main damage, who I will refer to as H, had fled. He had obviously heard that Dan was in a serious way. Funny to remember that H had only been bragging a week earlier, downtown straight after the assault, how he had floored a young man who went down like a skittle. Now here he was hiding like a scared rabbit. The police didn't stay long.

At this time I was not very interested in the men concerned. I could only think about Daniel and I was still naive enough to believe that these 'men' had not meant to hurt Dan so badly and that they were probably feeling inconsolable about what had happened. What an idiot I was! I had worked for so many years in Horfield Prison and still always thought the best of people. I always thought that there were reasons why people behaved so badly – accident of birth, lack of education, lack of love, of self-esteem, lack of paternal care and guidance. When it is your child who suffers at the hands of another person the excuses count for nothing and all high ideals go out of the window. I have now learnt that some people have no conscience, are a waste of space, and are just pure evil. If someone had taken that angle before Dan's attack I would have felt sorry for his or her negative attitude. Now I know for certain that there is a 'them and us' situation out there and I regret every year that I wasted slogging myself to death trying to give the prison inmates I came in contact with the benefit of the doubt. I really thought that if I taught these inmates to read and write they would raise their game and now I felt a failure. Hopefully the feeling will pass and it was just a rush of frustration and anger. I felt as though a piece of me was dead already.

I heard on the grapevine that the three men, who were involved in the assault on Dan, MB, H and G, had been charged with attempted murder. Then I further heard that G, for some reason that escaped me then, and still does, had been released and all charges dropped though it was clear from witnesses that he was there egging the other two on and made no attempt to prevent the damage done to any of the victims that evening. This, in my mind, made him as guilty as the other two. Releasing G proved to be a fatal error that cast a shadow over the whole legal system and allowed a great miscarriage of justice to take place.

That first week went on, every day much the same as the last. My extended family and I were at the hospital almost continuously. When tests were being carried out on Dan or the doctors were on their rounds and we could not go into the Intensive Care Unit, we would gather outside the visitors' room window on a very small area of grass, deep in despair. I badly needed to hug my other two boys on a regular basis, which led to floods of tears from us all. None of us had ever cried so much and we were emotionally drained.

We were starting to get worried about Dan's left lung as he appeared to find it harder to breathe, even on the ventilator if he was placed slightly on that side. Dan's temperature was very high indeed and ice packs were applied to try to bring it down. Dan developed the hiccups, very strange when he was completely out of it. Every time he hiccupped his blood pressure shot up. One pupil appeared to be slightly larger that the other and his eyes remained wide open and covered in the jelly compound to prevent them from drying out and keep the dust out. They started to give Dan Chlorpromazine as a sedative to treat any brain disturbances. Although Dan was in a deep coma the idea was to give the brain nothing at all to do, not even try to bring Dan round. The hope was that this would give Dan's brain time to calm down and stop swelling.

Andrene went home on Wednesday and Sarah returned to her lodgings and her own bed that night. It was quite a relief to go home to our own home alone and not have to be polite to strangers at a time when all Richard and I really wanted to do was get through each day with as little to worry about outside of the ICU than necessary.

By Thursday, 13 June, we were all getting quite used to the layout at Frenchay. There was a sale every day in Ward 9, clothes one day, china or plants another. It was somewhere to go when Dan was having treatment, other than the canteen.

I had phoned Dan's GP on Monday and told him the worst. He

was genuinely very upset and he immediately visited Dan and gave me a sick note for six weeks. This brought me up to the summer holidays so I didn't have to worry about going into work, not as if I intended to go anyway. I was lucky in a way because I worked at Cotham Grammar School at the time and the head teacher, Jim McKay, was a family man and understood my despair and was prepared to cover my job for as long as it took. Knowing that the head was there for me made life a lot easier and gave me one less thing to have to worry about, something I will always be grateful for.

Thursday Dan went for another CT scan and his ICP monitor fell out.

CT Scan – Conventional X-rays are essentially shadow photographs, but CT (Computer Tomography) scanning uses X-rays in a completely different way. Multiple beams of X-rays are passed through the body, and their degree of absorption is recorded by sensors. The scanner moves around the patient, emitting and recording X-ray beams from every point. The resulting data is then analysed by a computer, which uses the variations in absorption of the X-rays to construct cross-sectional 'slices' through the body.

CT images are more detailed than those produced by conventional X-ray techniques. A further advantage of CT scanning is that images can be manipulated by the computer to obtain a better view of the area under study, or to produce a three-dimensional image. CT scanning was first used in the early seventies for studying the brain. The technique quickly became the first-line test in the investigation not only of brain disorders but also of symptoms affecting virtually every other part of the body.

Friday, 14 June – the neurosurgeons decided to replace the ICP monitor a little deeper this time. They replaced it at 7 p.m. They also decided that it was time to put in a tracheotomy tube and this was done in situ. This is a normal procedure when a patient is expected to require ventilation for a long time as it is easier for the patient.

Tracheotomy – this operation requires surgery to make an opening in the trachea (windpipe) and the insertion of a tube to maintain an effective airway. Tracheotomy is often performed to treat an emergency such as a obstruction of the airway. A planned tracheotomy is most often performed on a person who has lost the ability to breathe naturally and is undergoing long-term ventilation (the pumping of air into the lungs by machine) or who has lost the ability to keep saliva and other secretions out of the windpipe due to coma or a specific airway or swallowing problem. In such cases, tracheotomy is performed after passing an endotracheal tube through the nose or mouth and into the trachea. Sometimes patients are incubated in this way prior to a coma state to give extra oxygen to brain swell patients and prevent such things as blindness.

The operation is carried out under local or general anaesthetic. An incision is made in the skin overlying the trachea, between the Adam's apple and the clavicles (collarbones). The neck muscles are pulled apart, and the thyroid gland, which surrounds the trachea is usually severed. A small vertical incision (called a window) is made in the trachea so that a metal or plastic tube can be inserted. If the patient cannot breathe unaided, the tube is then obviously connected to a ventilator. Air from the ventilator is humidified before it passes into the tube. Any excessive mucus that accumulates in the airway can then be sucked up through a catheter inserted into the tube.

While the tube is in place, obviously the patient is unable to speak. Sometimes it takes a considerable time after removal for a person to get the power of speech back after a tracheotomy tube has been in for a long time. When the tube is removed as the patient starts to recover, the hole will grow over eventually, leaving a round scar. I was given the full details before the operation.

We did not see Dan much that day although we all hung about the hospital, afraid to leave in case something terrible happened and we were not all there.

Saturday, 15 June – they started to use suction through the trachea hole. They lowered a thin tube down the hole and a machine sucked out any fluid. It obviously caused a great deal of discomfort and caused Dan to cough. Even though you are in a coma you still feel these discomforts and it is very distressing to watch someone in this helpless position having such treatment performed on them, although it is obviously a necessity. After every suction it took Dan's vital signs a long time to settle down again. His temperature was very high, 38.3 to 39 all day despite Paracetamol. Pupils still non-reactive and blood pressure erratic, sluggish reactions to deep pain, heart rate 80/90 and, what's more, he wasn't absorbing the food being pumped into him. They tested the amount of food absorbed at a certain time each day, noting the amount of food that had been pumped down the tube in his nose. This directly passed down into the stomach, and then withdrew what lay in his stomach back out to see how much actually was absorbed. Dan was losing weight fast and the poor soul also had diarrhoea.

Andrene and Pete had arrived from Birmingham and they wanted to take us all out to the nearby pub on Frenchay Common for a meal. We were reluctant to go but decided that maybe a break was needed and it was nearby so we could return to Dan before we went home that night for a final check on him. Joe had to decline to come as he was already using every favour he was ever owed by anyone to gather babysitters for his youngsters so he could be at the hospital as often as possible. Adam and Marie came.

We actually had a very good evening despite the dramas at the back of our minds. Andrene and Pete were very likeable people.

Sunday, 16 June – this was Adam's birthday but he decided to cancel it this year. Dan's temperature was very high again despite ice packs and fans. Dan had a very high white blood count and I kept explaining that because he had Behçets, this was usual for him but they were convinced he had an infection regardless. Today he was neurologically unresponsive. This was bad and Dr Moncra was convinced that Dan was nearing the end.

A very large man was admitted into the bed next to Dan. He was a heavy drinker and had collapsed at work. I went into the waiting room for a short time whilst Dan was having a bout of physiotherapy which happened at least twice a day to keep his lungs clear. The china tea service was in situ and I knew that this meant that someone was going to be given really bad news. Selfishly I hoped that it would be someone other than myself. This was not a pleasant feeling but I think an understandable one. Shortly after I was back with Dan and the curtains were pulled round the beds, followed by the rumble of the tin box on wheels arriving and leaving. The first time this happens you image that you are in a dream and will wake up but, strangely enough, after a very short time you get used to this procedure and just pray that you will not be the next to get the 'tea service treatment'. When the curtains opened again we realised we had lost our new neighbour.

Marie and I spent a little time alone with Dan whilst Richard and Adam went for a drink at the pub on Frenchay Common, literally five minutes walk away. Joe was at home with the boys. It was a rare occasion that we did not have Sarah's company. It was quite pleasant to spend a few minutes with Marie as we had not really spoken to each other since the dramas started. Marie had always had an inclination to be a nurse and I think that the experiences at Frenchay finally convinced her that it was right for her. She had a quiet calm that is needed in such a career. We were getting very clever at detecting problems by the readings on the monitors. You seemed to get almost hypnotised by all the gadgets. We read the charts every morning on entering the ICU and compared them to the day before. We were probably getting too knowledgeable for our own good; I think that what they say about a little knowledge might be true.

Suddenly as Marie and I sat by Dan everything started to go haywire. Daniel's temperature seemed to shoot through the roof; his inner cranial pressure was erratic as was his heart rate. The nurse who was caring for Dan this day very quickly raised the alarm. It seemed that Dan had a small stroke and for a moment I thought I was going to watch him die for a second time in two weeks. Marie and I were moved away and the curtains drawn. Quite quickly we were reassured that Dan was still alive; it wasn't good but they were beginning to stabilise him again, though they were not sure how much more damage had been done. Dr Moncra took me aside and said he wanted us to be prepared for the possibility of having to turn off the life support. He said we wouldn't have to decide for a week or two but felt we should discuss the possibilities.

Marie and I walked swiftly across to the pub to see Richard and Adam. We were both trying desperately not to show the anguish we were feeling.

Frenchay is set in a rather pretty part of Bristol, surrounded by green. We left the hospital grounds and crossed the road on to Frenchay Common. The common is always full of people and activity. There is a very picturesque church with a high tower. Next to the church is a small infants school.

Cottage-style houses surround three sides of the common and in the far corner is a very large and popular pub. Marie and I had to pick our way through groups of picnickers, cricket matches, small football games and dog walkers to reach the pub. Adam and Richard were sitting outside at the front of the pub on a bench seat and table. Adam saw us coming and I could tell that he realised straight away that all was not well. I told them both what had happened and what the doctor had said. We all walked back in a sober fashion. As we got closer to the hospital Adam speeded up and all of a sudden rushed off at a high speed heading for Intensive Care.

Adam was coming back out of the ICU when we all arrived and for a moment, looking at his face, I thought that the worst had happened but Dan was still with us, only just but he was hanging in there. Adam had hurried ahead because he had a premonition of pending doom that turned out to be a little premature, thank goodness. Adam had got himself a little worked up and upset and had actually shaken Dan, shouting at him not to go. The nurses were very understanding and had gently led him out of the ICU. Marie tried to comfort Adam who was inconsolable and didn't want anyone near him for a moment whilst he composed himself. I understood how he felt. Sometimes you just want to stand-alone and try to get your head round the situation. I decided that Richard and I could do with just a few moments on our own. We walked slowly up the corridor away from the ICU. It was the first time that I began to actually believe that Dan really would leave us.

By the end of the day Daniel seemed stable again; the immediate danger was over and we all went home absolutely exhausted with a promise of a phone call if there was the slightest development.

Monday and Tuesday Daniel showed no improvement and these two days were busy with tests to establish if any permanent damage had been done on Sunday.

Wednesday, 19 June – he was coughing very strongly. His whole body jumped when he coughed and it looked like he was having a fit. There was a lot of muck coming out of the trachea tube with suction. His breathing was definitely more laboured on his left side. The renal probe was removed because of diarrhoea. It was a strange dream-like time. Everyone visiting people in the ICU were living the same hellish existence. We knew by now that the longer you stay in the ICU the less likely you were to come out. As we arrived at Frenchay each day our ICU comrades would ask after Dan and we would enquire after whoever they were visiting. A strange bond formed between us all.

Thursday – copious amounts of thick, creamy, bloodstained secretions were removed. We are all on first name terms with everyone by now. Sarah seemed to have knowledge of every other visitor's life story, which amused me. Dan's temperature was the highest yet, forty plus in the afternoon but there was still no change neurologically. Dr Moncra, the anaesthetist who ran the ICU, spoke to me briefly and repeated that he was not very hopeful about Dan's outcome. He tried to press the point that we would have to make a decision soon as to whether to switch off the life support machine as nothing was happening neurologically. Dan's arterial tube was removed as the site was starting to track, his veins were starting to break down. His right hand was now very swollen and red and there were large red areas appearing on his chest.

I was beginning to understand comas. Dr Moncra was a very up front person and I liked that. I do not like having the facts glossed over, I need to know how the land really lies. He didn't treat us like children. He told us the facts as he saw them and explained quite comprehensively the pros and cons of certain actions. You did feel as though you were actually included in the happenings of the ICU. Dr Moncra explained how important it was to get Dan off the ventilator and how just coming out of a coma was not the full story. You can come out of a coma but that does not mean you are on the mend – it is just one possible step forward. The longer you stay on the ventilator, the harder it is to get a patient off. The body gets used to being helped and soon stops trying to do things for itself. If Dan came out of the coma and was still unable to breathe for himself we would not be allowed to make a decision as to whether to turn off the life support machine. If Dan proved to be a cabbage if and when he started to wake we would at this point have to obtain a court order to withhold drugs and stop food and liquid being administered. Whilst he remained in a coma the decision to switch off the machines that were actually his life lines could be made. I had already decided that there was no way I was ever going to consent to my son's life being ended by the flick of a switch, whether the time dragged on into years I would change my mind, who knows. It is a decision no parents should ever have to face and my heart goes out to anyone on this earth who ever had to make it.

I received a reply from a letter of complaint I had placed in the complaints box in the corridor at Frenchay, regarding the registrar that we had met whilst trying to get Dan admitted. The reply was from Mary Adams, the patients' representative, and said she was looking into things. I had also written to Southmead Hospital complaining about the six hours we spent there and the X-ray mix-up. I had not received any acknowledgement of that as yet.

Another quickly followed the Frenchay letter, this time from Ann LLoyd, chief executive, apologising for distress caused to my family and me. I also received, on the same day, a letter from G Wadey, senior nurse/quality adviser at Southmead, saying he was looking into my complaint.

Friday, 21 June – these terrible temperatures continued so Dan was taken for another scan to compare it to the previous ones and see if there was any activity, which was making the temperature rise so high. Dan was looking visibly weaker and thinner. We spoke to the doctors after their rounds and they said that as Dan had made no attempt to wake, in their opinion it was very unlikely that Dan would survive. So it seemed that this was a unanimous thought. We decided not to tell Sarah what was said. The latest scan did, however, encourage us all a little as it showed that there was a slight improvement in the swelling of the brain.

All the while dramas were unfolding around us. People, young and old, were admitted, some left in boxes and some were only passing through having been stabilised and returned to a normal ward. A lady who had been a bed away from Dan in Ward 2 and seemed to be improving was brought into the ICU having had a relapse. Richard got quite friendly with the husband and son of that person and every morning they exchanged progress notes.

I felt like I was living in a nightmare. Nothing seemed real any more. Every day was spent in a kind of daze. Every day you hope to wake up and find everything was as before but we all knew that nothing would ever be quite the same again. The sights we had all seen, the smell of death, the feeling of hopeless despair were bound to leave their mark. I went to bed each night and spent a fitful night unable to actually sleep deeply. Something told me that if I slept deeply so would Dan; only he wouldn't wake up again. Every morning I hurried to the hospital to face more horrors. Richard tried to do a certain amount of work but obviously his mind was not focused. He hates hospitals with a passion. It is almost a phobia and he always avoids them where possible. Lately he has been overdosing on them. He sat for hours when his dear mother struggled and finally died and swore he would never set foot in a hospital again. Unfortunately, life does not always afford us choices and we have to confront our phobias at times.

Often I would find that my sister was at the hospital before I even got there and I got there very early. My sister is the headmistress of an infant school and she used to go to the hospital to see how Dan was before going to school. I developed a great respect for my sister over those terrible weeks. When young I always thought her to be quite a cold person but having cried with her over Dan I felt a warmth that I never imagined and I formed a bond with my sister that I wish I had formed years ago. It has struck me that real dramas either bring out the best or the very worst in people – there is no in between.

Sometimes I would spend a couple of hours totally alone with Dan before anyone else arrived. Sarah was trying to continue her course under these terrible circumstances. Obviously the university was aware of her commitments outside the complex and were very supportive. Adam tried to go to work most days, as did Richard. Joe had his boys to worry about but all managed to come in at some point each day. My mind seemed to be working overtime. I would sit by Dan and just think quietly to myself. It is strange how the mind works and what you think about at times like this. I did wonder quite frequently how it was that Dan was allowed to arrest in Ward 2 and why they didn't realise that he was in danger before June 8. I would also sit, look about and just marvel at the technology in the ICU. It would not have been very many years before that that Dan would have had no hope at all of living but at least here, under Dr Moncra's care, if it could be done I felt he would be saved.

Saturday, 22 June – another really bad day. Dan's temperature hovered round forty plus, he had diarrhoea and didn't seem able to breathe without sounding very laboured, even with the help of the respirator. I spoke to Dr Moncra again begging him to be honest with me as usual. He explained that his job was to get Dan off the life support machine and able to sustain life on his own and at this time he could not see that it would be possible to get Dan off the respirator as he was making no attempt to breathe for himself. Every time he tried to turn down the respiratory support, Dan coughed violently and this was not good. He said that despite the brain swell being now controlled, he felt that there was little hope of survival and he felt that there would be very limited lifestyle expectancy if Dan, did in fact, against all odds, survive. Unfortunately Sarah had also listened to the conversation and we went outside for a chat about it on our own. I told her that I thought she should go home and meet a nice lad from the Midlands and invite us to her wedding. Her eyes were open wide in an almost wild expression and total devastation and disbelief was edged on her pale little face. I was glad that Andrene and Pete were due to arrive that day.

When Pete and Andrene arrived, Richard had a word with Pete. We didn't want a young eighteen-year-old girl to be here when the worst nightmare yet occurred and it seemed that the general opinion was that there was no hope for Dan. We decided to go out for a meal again this evening, this time to Frampton Cottrell, and the Golden Lion. We went into say goodnight to Dan and a strange thing happened. The nurse told Dan to stick out his tongue if he could hear her, and he did. It was a very slow, very laborious event but we were elated – we took this to mean that something was happening, there was a spark of life inside that shell after all. Did he subconsciously hear Dr Moncra's words or was it just a coincidence that Dan chose that moment to show us that he was still here?

We all went off happily for that evening meal and were probably overexcited about the whole event.

Time to Make Decisions

Sunday, 23 June

Adam, Marie, Sarah, Richard and I all went in early, hoping for another breakthrough after yesterday but we were greeted by the opposite from what we expected. Dan's temperature was forty plus again – how much can a body take? He was gasping for breath and looked dreadful. I couldn't understand why they hadn't phoned us. I had asked to be kept informed of any changes. I could tell just by looking at the faces of the staff around that there was genuine concern today for Dan and that they felt we would soon have to face the fact that all the wishing, hoping and technology in the world might just not be enough. His blood pressure was erratic and they decided to X-ray his chest to see if maybe pneumonia was setting in.

They allowed us all to go in together. I felt this was an ominous sign of pending doom. Richard could not bear to look any longer at his son struggling and decided to go outside in the fresh air. Adam went with him mainly because he felt that moral support might be needed. Sarah and Marie sat on either side of Dan's bed and I stood at the foot of the bed looking at the girls. It was like looking at a negative. Sarah was as fair as it was possible to be, with long straight hair and a very pale complexion and the biggest bluest eyes imaginable whilst Marie had long very dark hair and an olive complexion. Both were very striking-looking girls and quite alike in lots of ways. They were both sitting there, each holding one of Dan's hands, very composed and serene-looking. I actually caught myself smiling for a second thinking that Dan must have something going for him to inspire such loyalty.

The X-ray apparatus arrived and Marie and I decided to leave. Sarah asked if she could stay and that was fine. The rest of us all wondered across to the common, aimlessly wasting time waiting to see how the day developed. The morning was spent in and out of the ICU waiting for the X-ray results. When the results finally arrived it confirmed our worst fears: Dan had a spot of pneumonia.

The morning was an endless stream of medical experts looking at Dan and tests being done. We spent more time in the waiting room than we did in the ICU. The men decided that maybe the pub was a good place to wander over to whilst tests were carried out. Once again Sarah decided to stay. The men had a pint but Marie and I could not settle and quickly walked back. We spoke to Dr Moncra again. He said there were definite signs of pneumonia and he felt that this would mean the end for Dan. All Dan's life signs were fading and whilst Marie, Sarah and I were there he arrested yet again. We were quickly evicted from the ICU, the curtains went round the bed and we were outside trembling with fear and each with a desperate feeling of hopelessness and helplessness. We went into the little ICU waiting room. I said something flippant about if we are offered a cup of tea to refuse it. Suddenly a voice came over the speaker telling us to come back in. We wondered what we would find when we returned but happily once again these angels had managed to bring Dan back from the brink.

Sarah just stood and cried. We were told, however, that there was a good chance that this was going to be the last day of Dan's life. Marie and I decided to walk back to the pub and tell the boys about the state of play. I also thought that as it looked as though this was going to be the last day of Dan's life, I should fetch Joe as well. We spoke to Adam and Richard and then left them in an obvious state of disbelief and grief whilst Marie and I went to fetch Joe.

Kate was at Joe's, so she came too and luckily the boys were with their mother for a few hours. We all met up at the pub and sat to talk for a few moments before walking back across to the hospital. Once again Adam hurried on ahead. He had rushed into the Intensive Care Ward absolutely beside himself and shouted at Dan. He had to be restrained and asked to leave the ICU to calm down. It quite frightened Sarah. Sarah followed Adam outside to try to comfort him.

The rest of us returned just as Dan's blood pressure dropped and they had to fight to save him again. Dan was finally sedated and after about an hour his life signs seemed to settle down. The staff seemed to think that maybe they had underestimated Daniel's inner strength and that he would still be here tomorrow after all. We all decided that we had experienced enough drama and emotion for one day and were literally drained, so an early night for all was planned. Obviously the hospital were instructed to call if there was even the slightest change and they promised faithfully. We all left the hospital believing that the next call we would receive would be to say that Dan was going. I made it quite clear that I wanted to be with my son if there was a likelihood of him passing on. I cannot describe the pain you feel inside believing that the person you have just walked away from was about to slip out of your life forever. My precious boy; he had struggled with dyslexia and come thorough against all odds, he had spent part of every year of his life since the age of eight in hospital with Behçets Disease, and still he had a positive attitude to life. I know that we were never promised that life would be fair but this was criminal. I know that I felt emotionally drained, weak with fear for my son, and for the first time in my life absolutely negative about the future when I had always been a positive person until now. There is only so much a body and mind can take, and looking round at the assembled group I knew that if we didn't all get out of that place for a while we would not be able to cope any longer. Adam was close to a breakdown, Joe looked like he hadn't slept for weeks, Richard was grey and the girls looked like they had all being crying for days without stopping.

Joe's estranged wife, Emma, had the children that day and was returning them at about 6.30. Richard and I decided to go and see the little boys for a little while before going home. We arrived at Joe's just minutes after Emma had dropped them off. David had gone straight up to bed, which was quite out of character for him, but we assumed that maybe Emma had been to the park or something with them and that Dave and Ricky were tired. I popped upstairs to see David in bed and he was very hot. For some reason alarm bells rang in my head. I spoke to the child and he said that his leg hurt. I turned on the light and pulled back the bedclothes. There was the tiniest of cuts on his knee but it was definitely tracking up his leg in a disturbing fashion. I just grabbed David from his bed, wrapped him in a blanket, carried him down and said that I was taking him to the Children's Hospital just in case. Joe was in such a state over Dan that he was finding it difficult to think straight. Richard took Ricky home to sleep at our house and we left Joe with Kate, saying we would ring from the hospital. The Children's

Hospital was literally one second from our house in Cotham and I took David there. As suspected, the cut was infected and the infection was tracking. He had the beginnings of septicaemia. You could tell that the little mite was unwell because he never batted an eyelid when they put cream on the back of his hand to numb it whilst they placed a tap in his hand. I explained why I had brought the lad in instead of his father and they were very understanding. I phoned Joe and he, in turn, phoned Emma. Both arrived quite quickly from different directions. It was decided to keep Dave in for a couple of days and Emma stayed the night, sleeping very uncomfortably in a chair. The next day, David looked miles better. Unfortunately, the same could not be said for Daniel. We took Ricky to school the next day and told the teachers there about all the dramas that were unfolding around us. Adam was going to take Joe down to the Children's Hospital and then on to Frenchay later, so Richard and I just picked up Sarah as usual and went out to see what was the latest. Dan's temperature was slightly lower, which was the first bit of good news for ages. Then Joe arrived and said that he could fetch David home after all as he was not happy in the hospital. He could bring him home with antibiotics and take care of him there. I took Joe to fetch David and promised the little one a visit to Toys R Us to spent a small fortune as grandmothers do.

Tuesday, 25 June – this day seemed to drag. I took Dave to Toys R Us and got off quite lightly. I was worried when he told me he deserved three things – but he only chose cheap things.

Wednesday, 26 June – another low day. Richard was looking very drawn. We decided not to go in until 9.15, and picked Sarah up on the way as usual. Going in really early hadn't proved too successful. We always seemed to arrive during ward rounds or physiotherapy so we had to hang about before we could go in and see Dan. Adam was also feeling very down today and decided not to come in until 11.30. Dan seemed unchanged, no better, but also no worse, except for the fact that he looked thinner every day. I found Dan's eyes the worst to take. His beautiful blue eyes just stared blankly – there was no spark of life and no pupil reaction whatsoever. Dan was given a couple of pints of blood. I couldn't work out why he needed blood – where had it gone? This was not the first time he had been given some! He turned out to be AB negative – he couldn't even have a common blood group.

Richard decided that it was his turn to have a talk to Dr Moncra.

He was told that, in his opinion, Dan would never get off the respirator and if he did it would only complicate things. As he saw it, nothing was going on, the lights were not on and no one was at home. Turning off the respirator was an option at the moment but if they managed to get Dan to breathe unaided and he was, as Dr Moncra suspected, a cabbage, the only way to end a vegetable state was to withhold drugs if, for example, Dan had pneumonia. The hospital is legally bound to feed patients and a court order would have to be obtained to withhold vital drugs. In Daniel's case he was not absorbing food either so just withholding fluids would end things quite quickly. It was all too depressing and distressing to think about, but Dr Moncra wanted us to think about the possibility of turning off the life support machine as he felt there was no hope of any recovery. It was the first time that Richard and I had considered the possibility of taking a cabbage home with us. We thought until now that Dan would either be dead or our old Dan. We didn't consider the possibility of a totally dependent, brain dead person sitting in a wheelchair and being fed and washed. This new thought was a frightening prospect. I cannot understand even now why this scenario didn't even cross my mind. What about Sarah? No way would we want her to experience even seeing Daniel in that condition and obviously any attachment to him would stop instantly anyway. I was actually starting to wonder if maybe it would be better if Dan just slipped peacefully away.

I needed to speak to Adam about this possible state of affairs. I still could not imagine even with the very worst scenario clearly in my mind actually giving the order to switch off the ventilator. I wanted to wait for Adam and make a couple of phone calls. Richard decided to go and tell his father the latest. I always phoned my sister every day and she informed the other elderly relatives like my Aunt Eve for me to save having to repeat everything a lot of times. There were always numerous phone calls late at night, friends and relatives wanting to know how the day had gone. It was very tiring to have spent the day with Dan and then having to repeat the same story several times when we got home. My instincts were to leave the phone off the hook, but we couldn't in case the hospital needed to get in touch. They did phone couple of times, and it makes your heart jump into your mouth, you expect the worst. I think back to when Dan was eight and first in hospital when we had a call at four o'clock in the morning telling us to get there quickly. We expected

Dan to die that day but when we got to the Children's Hospital the crisis had passed. Talk about history repeating itself.

My sister's daughter, Alex, did her work experience at Frenchay, which was quite convenient. She was considering going into nursing (and in fact has since started training) so she obviously popped in regularly. Other friends arrived from time to time, and although they didn't always go in to see Dan, they came to give moral support to Richard and me. My friend Sima, whom I have known since the seventies, popped in from time to time. Sima is an emotional wreck at the best of times so it was actually quite traumatic instead of soothing when she arrived, but she was better than would have been expected. Friends Clive and Julie Beckingham were in and out regularly. The 'friend' I had sent to fetch Richard at the start of the real drama didn't materialise ever but their son who is a gentle soul came regularly. She had obviously taken umbrage at being sent away. I couldn't worry about that at this time. I had enough to think about without added stress but it was another nail in the coffin that I could have done without. The young man,Wayne, whom Dan had rescued on the Gloucester Road even came to see him and found it all very distressing, as did ex-girlfriends who had heard the news on the grapevine and several of Dan's friends. They all found it very hard to deal with and usually left in a distressed state, something that didn't actually help the rest of us. I always tried to discourage these visitors from going in but if they really wanted or felt they needed to I went in with them for a swift visit. Richard's father and his elder brother, David, appeared from time to time in the hospital but no other relatives materialised. I was willing to excuse the elderly aunts but was considering shortening my Christmas card list considerably.

I was surprised to see a long-term friend called Helena arrive. She had lost her only son after watching him struggle on life support. I felt very touched by her arrival as it had to be quite gut-wrenching for her to walk into a place like that.

Adam finally arrived and we sat in the canteen talking over a coffee. I told him what Dr Moncra had said about Dan being a cabbage and we discussed the implications to the family if this came to pass. We both concluded that we did not want to switch off the ventilator. I didn't need to ask Joe I knew what his answer would be. My family and I are a team; we are not just a family. We are totally supportive of each other and I knew that I would have the full support of my sons if we decided to take a chance and live in hope that Dan eventually recovered. If the gamble did not pay off and Daniel turned out to be the cabbage predicted I still believed strongly that my team and I would get by.

It seemed that Dr Moncra wanted to make Wednesday, 26 June D Day. Decision Day at least as regards possibly turning off the machines. How could a parent ever make such a decision? We are supposed to be the ones who die; our children are supposed to bury us, not the other way round. Richard and I spoke at length about Dr Moncra's words and both decided that is was far too early; we would not agree for a few more weeks at least. I thank heavens for our decision, as it would have been so easy to look at the evidence and decide that enough was enough.

Adam had chest pains, obviously stress-related. He had made a doctor's appointment for the next day. Richard was shattered, as was Sarah, and it was the two semi-finals of the Euro Cup that evening so everyone decided that those interested in the football should stay home to try to unwind a little and watch the match. I, on the other hand, would rather watch paint dry than football so I stayed on at the hospital.

I was quite looking forward to a few moments alone with my precious son. I always talked away to him as if he could hear me. I didn't have a lot to tell him because I rarely stepped outside the hospital grounds. We did call into the Somerville Club most nights on the way home to drown our sorrows when necessary and to celebrate if anything positive happened, which was a rare event. Obviously everyone in the club sent their good wishes to Dan and I relayed them to him even in this coma state. I sat alone talking to Dan and the nurse told him to squeeze my hand if he could hear me and amazingly he did. It was a very weak attempt but I was taken by surprise and burst into floods of tears. I just couldn't stop crying, I sobbed and sobbed. Dan and I had been through so much together and I felt for just a moment in that feeble squeeze of the hand that he was going to make it after all against all odds and despite what everyone said to the contrary. It was as if he had heard that he was a right off and decided to show me that they were wrong. For a moment I wondered if I had imagined the pressure on my hand, it was so light. I wanted to believe it, so I chose to believe it.

I went to find Adam and he wasn't in so I went on to Joe's. I was in a right state by the time I got there. Puffy eyes, a right mess. Joe was obviously alarmed when he saw me; he thought I had come to say that Dan had gone. When I told Joe what had occurred, how Dan had squeezed my hand, he didn't look too convinced. I am sure he thought I had imagined the event but he humoured me nevertheless. I had a cup of tea, hugged the little ones and went back to the hospital. I didn't want to go home with false hopes, I needed to go back to Dan and see if I could get a second reaction before going home. The nursing staff didn't seem surprised to see me back. Saron, a favourite of mine, said she had managed to get a very weak squeeze out of Dan's right hand after I had left so if I thought I had dreamed what happened, I hadn't. It seemed that Dan was showing the slightest signs of coming out of the coma. I hurried home and my news was obviously far more thrilling than any football game. Everyone was ecstatic, though slightly apprehensive about what we would discover from here on.

When we went back the next day – Thursday, 27 June – we were almost scared to go in just in case the day before was a dream. During the night he had made slight voluntary movements as if trying to get comfortable and although there was still no movement in his eyes, he would move a finger very slightly on command. We, at last, had hope in our hearts. Joe and Adam were also taking bets as to what Dan would do first when he came round – pass wind or put his thumb up. The former won.

I bumped into Dr Chandler in the corridor and he explained to me how slow the recovery process from a coma really was. On the television, they always wake up and say, 'Hello, Mum.' But in reality it isn't like that at all. Some people can take up to five years to become fully awake and functioning again after being in a coma, especially a coma as deep as the one Dan had been in. I was quite shocked. Dr Chandler reminded me that Dan had a tracheotomy tube in his throat that would stop him speaking anyway and that if he eventually came off the ventilator he would probably have trouble talking for quite some time. On rare occasions the power of speech can be lost altogether, but not to look for the negative, think positive and watch Dan and every day we would see a little more life. I just flung my arms round him and gave him a kiss on the cheek. He didn't seem surprised so I guess this is people's usual reaction.

Friday, 28 June – Daniel remained critical but had started to show signs of coming out of his coma. It would be several days before we would know the extent of his injuries. We all left early so Dan could rest – Richard and I went to get Dan's car from the garage where it was being repaired. Joe was using the vehicle whilst Dan was in hospital having had his own stolen. He had stopped at a roundabout when someone went up the back of him, obviously at a great speed judging by the damage to the car. Adam had stayed alone with Dan and, when he tried to leave, Dan showed signs of distress. Adam phoned to tell me that he felt that maybe Dan was scared. I would imagine that he was, the last thing Dan would remember if he remembered anything would be standing outside The Showboat pub and now here he was trapped in a bed with wires everywhere, alien noises, people sticking needles in you, physio every hour, it would scare the hell out of anyone.

I returned to the hospital immediately and stayed with Dan until he fell asleep. They were intending to try to reduce the support given by the ventilator during the night which was the first stage of the plan to try to get Dan breathing for himself.

Saturday, 29 June – Dan didn't look any better though he was moving very slightly, presumably to get comfortable. He had to be put back on the full ventilator overnight as he had got very tired from their attempts on a lesser support version.

I received a letter from Ann Lloyd, chief executive at Frenchay, apologising for the treatment we received at the hands of the junior doctor at the Accident and Emergency Department and saying that he had been reprimanded, agreeing that the time lapse between our arrival and admittance was unacceptable. She also suggested that Sarah and I met with the young doctor. I wasn't very keen but Sarah was curious to hear his explanation.

The next few days were spent trying to get Dan on to a lesser support ventilator without much success. There seemed to be a problem developing with Dan's left lung. A long tube was fed down the tracheotomy hole every now and again and more and more thick creamy liquid seemed to be coming out every time. Dan's eyes were still static and it was suggested that maybe it was a simple muscle strain stopping the pupils dilating and this could take three months to settle down. We were rather hoping that this was true as the alternative was rather horrendous.

Monday, 1 July was a very sad day for Frenchay Hospital Intensive Care. Peter, the young man in the high-tech bed opposite, appeared to be in serious trouble so it was decided that all visitors should leave and an emergency double lung drain was going to be performed on Peter, a unique operation. It was his only hope. We wished his family well and left. Sarah gave Peter's girlfriend a hug as she passed. We were all worried for the lad. We had watched him struggle for so long we almost felt as though we knew him.

Tuesday, 2 July – Richard and I had just arrived, at around 8.30, when Peter lost his long fight for life. The curtains went round and the trolley was wheeled in. Everyone was silent and in a state of shock. That young man had struggled for nine weeks and had finally given up the fight for life. It was a real tragedy and the distress was etched on every one of those wonderful nurses' faces. Richard and I obviously felt very badly for Peter's fiancée and family and it made us feel a little humble that Dan was still with us, although it also brought home the possibility that the same might occur. We were always aware of Dr Moncra's words, 'The longer you spend in Intensive Care, the less likely you are to get out at all and, if you do, long-term problems were expected as a matter of course.'

Wednesday, 3 July – Dan was most unwell today – his blood pressure was low 87/58 and his heartbeat was high and erratic, his temperature was thirty-nine plus and his breathing was very laboured even on the C pack. They took blood to test and more X-rays. They actually bring the X-ray machine to the beds in Intensive Care for minimum disturbance. Daniel also seemed very unsettled, almost distressed. The X-rays showed cause for concern. The right lung was fine but the left lung was squashed almost flat. A large area of pus had formed outside the lung pushing the lung flat and stopping it operating – this accumulation of pus in a body cavity or a certain organ is called empyema. Pleural empyema occurs as a rare complication of a lung infection such as pneumonia or pleurisy. The main symptoms are chest pains, breathlessness and fever but an X-ray is needed to confirm the diagnosis and removal of a sample of the pus for laboratory examination and analysis. There are two ways of treating this condition. Aspiration (removal of the pus by suction) and antibiotics or an operation to open the infected cavity and drain the pus, as was the case for Daniel.

So they put in a chest drain. A long tube came from his chest cavity into a transparent bottle on the floor by Dan's bed. The drain seemed to work quite effectively there was quite a large amount of revolting looking fluid in the bottle quite quickly. At 4.30 we went home for a while, to let the dog out and so forth whilst they re-X-rayed. We were back at six in the evening and the new X-ray was hanging alongside the first one. There didn't appear to be much difference. The plan was to sedate Dan and leave the drain overnight and re-X-ray again in the morning. So we all went home for an early night, having been first told that if the drain did not work or the liquid was too thick to drain properly, they would remove a section of the ribcage to make the drainage quicker. It seemed that this lung problem was a real worry and they wanted it resolved as quickly as possible. We had all felt so positive when Dan seemed to be waking up but it seems that every step forward is followed by two steps back.

The next day we spoke to Dr Moncra who was not happy about the amount of fluid drained overnight. He said that pockets had formed in the cavity and that he was going to put something called Varidase in to break this up so the fluid would drain away more easily. This Varidase is like a medical drain clearer and is a haemasuruis fluid. Whatever this fluid was it obviously caused a lot of distress going in. Dan's temperature rose and his blood pressure was dangerously high. I it was obvious that even in his sedated and still semi-comatose state he could still feel the effects of this drug so it must have been very strong.

Three days of codeine to numb the pain caused by the Varidase nearly drained us all, let alone Dan. The stuff must have acted like bleach down the loo. They put the liquid in and then left it clamped for four hours, then released the drain again. The physio came to try to help the lung drain. Dan's whole body went blotchy, his face was flushed and he thrashed about continuously, obviously in a lot of pain despite the painkillers. All the nurses seemed distressed by Dan's reaction to this liquid. His eyes were full of tears for the first time.

Dan was put on to pressure support instead of pressure control, breathing wise, which was one good thing.

Sarah and I were summoned to the hospital administrator's office to discuss our complaint about Dan's treatment when trying to get him admitted. We were given a verbal apology by the powers that be. There were four of them and then the doctor concerned came in and explained how he had been tired and confused over the time span we were involved in. Sarah and I almost felt sorry for him – he looked so young and embarrassed. However, I could not shake his hand; he had caused us a lot of unnecessary stress and I was not certain in my mind that the time lapse had not caused Dan extra problems. And also it was too soon. Dan was in a serious way and it seemed a little insensitive calling us to a meeting at this time.

Dan had a lot of visitors, not that he was aware that anyone was there. His grandfather and Richard's older brother David came in and were obviously visibly moved by Dan's latest plight.

Sunday, 7 July – the chest drain was still in but no more Varidase was administered, thank goodness. We took in the walkman and headphones and tried to place them on Dan's head with a little Oasis playing, his favourite band, but he obviously wasn't ready for that yet.

Monday, 8 July – Dan was put on a T-piece (another form of respirator, which does a little less work for you and makes you do a little more for yourself), which seemed to be a good sign. Dan's blood pressure and heart rate seemed much improved. More X-rays were scheduled for today and an EMG (electromyogram) – the recording of the electrical activity in the muscles. Electromyograms take between thirty and sixty minutes to perform, depending on the number of muscles to be tested. An EMG can reveal the presence of muscle disorder or disorders in which the nerve supplies to muscle is impaired, such as neuropathy. In cases of nerve injury, the actual site of nerve damage can often be located.

Neuropathy – inflammation, or damage to the peripheral nerves which connect the central nervous system (brain and spinal cord) to the sense organs, muscles, glands and internal organs.

EMG – electrical activity is measured during muscle contractions and when the muscles are at rest. To detect the electrical impulses, small disc electrodes are attached to the skin surface over the muscle. Alternatively, needle electrodes can be inserted into the muscle. The impulses are displayed on an oscilloscope screen and a permanent record can be made on film. Changes in the electrical wave patterns can be used in the diagnosis of certain nerve or muscle disorders.

The thoracic team were to review Dan's chest problem today as well. They still seem to be getting a lot of muck off of Dan's chest through the trachea suction. Dan did not like this process and it made him cough heavily. There was always a lot of gunge round the trachea hole and I was allowed to help keep this area clean, wash him and clean his teeth (a dubious honour). Dan's lips were very dry and sore so I used to put Vaseline on them every day. Dan had a great deal of ulcers over his lips and inside his mouth, these were part of his Behçets complaint and I asked for Colchacine or a mouth spray to help him. They were reluctant to use Colchacine as it is usually used for gout; regardless of this, it works for Behçets as well. Dan's skin was so pale it almost looked transparent and he no longer had an ounce of fat on him. He looked like a reject from Belsen Concentration Camp. I was glad that Intensive Care allowed me to share a little of Dan's care even if it was the messy jobs. I had been impressed from day one over the input that was coming our way. Usually in hospitals the relatives get very little information. Certainly in Ward 2 we felt a little in the dark, but not so here.

They did an ultrasound to see how much fluid was left outside the lung cavity. Tests showed that the actual lung wall had thickened. The chest drain was removed and the site area was obviously very painful.

Tuesday, 9 July – I had decided to pursue the possibility of a complaint against the hospital for the problems with admission, something that might have seemed a little churlish in the circumstances. I did, however, need to know if these delaying actions at both Southmead and Frenchay had done any damage to my son. So I went to meet the solicitor I had chosen to represent Dan over this matter. It was one of those informal chats where I could get a free opinion and decide if I wanted a solicitor and if in fact Mr Stamboulieh was the one I would want to choose. I had obviously been looking into the possibility of criminal injuries compensation for Dan now that it appeared he might survive. I also spoke briefly about this. It seemed generally agreed that a solicitor was needed in Dan's case as the injuries were very complex. I decided that I wanted Mr Stamboulieh to act for us, I had a feeling that he was a good man and that I could happily rely on him, which proved to be exactly right. I had acquired a letter from one of the neurosurgeons at Frenchay, giving me the right to run Dan's affairs whilst he was unable to do so himself. This enabled me to sort out any bills Dan had and also close down his flat in Horfield. It was obvious that Dan was not going to return to his little flat for a hell of a long time, if indeed ever, so paying rent and it sitting there empty seemed rather foolish. We had already got Clive, a good friend who had a truck to help us empty Dan's flat. We put all the furniture in the house in Muller Road. There was nowhere else for it to go. Joe packed all Dan's china and videos and so forth, and the flat keys were handed back to Sovereign Housing who owed it. Poor Dan, there were going to be so many changes to take in when he woke up fully.

All that day Dan had been wired to an electrical impulse monitor. This released sheet after sheet of wiggly lines in rows from a machine placed at the end of Dan's bed. The mechanism was attached to Dan's head and was monitoring the activity in Dan's brain, or lack of. Dr Moncra showed us the black spots that indicated brain damage but to what degree he could not tell. There were hearing tests done and electric light impulses sent into the eyes to test if there was damage there.

The next day Dr Moncra said they were going to release Dan from Intensive Care and put him in the emergency ward down the corridor. As up front as ever, he explained that this did not mean that Dan was out of the woods, it was just stage one and many patients still do not recover even after being in Intensive Care and moving on – a cheerful thought. He also said that the results of the tests made the previous day suggested that Dan might well be deaf but his eyesight seemed unimpaired despite the still non-reactive pupils.

Richard had a word with Dr Moncra and thanked him for fighting for Dan. The doctor said he couldn't be happier to have been proved wrong about Dan and wished us all well.

It was a very emotional exit from Intensive Care. There were lots of tears shed that day and I got to hug every one in sight I think. One nurse, Saron, the one I liked the best though I do not know why as they were all wonderful, summed it up when she said it was a miracle that no one had expected. She said that it made everyone's job seem worthwhile, seeing Dan being wheeled on to stage 2 of his recovery programme. They had a secret code system in the ICU apparently, classifying who would survive and who would not and Dan was a no chance on everyone's chart. Fooled them again! I felt that every member of the ICU was a personal friend on the day we left and it was one of the most emotional days ever.

I shook Dr Moncra's hand. I had a great deal of respect for that man, not despite his total honesty but because of it. What would be the point of being positive when speaking to relatives and saying all would be well if you don't believe it yourself. Far better to spout doom and gloom and be proved wrong. I would have to say that no one in Intensive Care was more pleased than Dr Moncra to be proved wrong and at the end of the day, against all odds, that man saved my son's life. He never stopped trying despite his own belief that it was a waste of time.

The relief to go out of those doors for the last time was amazing. It had been the longest six and a half weeks of my life. I felt I had aged ten years.

Back to Ward 2

Ward 2, the emergency ward, was a different world. There didn't seem to be enough nurses and having been in such a sterile unit for so long it all seemed a bit unreal. Dan was still attached to the breathing apparatus and, although he was doing some of the breathing for himself, the ventilator pushed in added oxygen to make sure he was getting enough. Dan's weight was a worry, there was nothing to him at all, just skin and bones.

Adam and Marie arrived early in the evening so I left them alone for a while. They had both been brilliant throughout and Adam was looking very drained emotionally by the experience. I was lucky enough to have produced three wonderful boys who were obviously very fond of and supportive of each other. This had proved to be a great help to Richard and I. Adam had to return to work before he had wanted to, but if there had ever been the slightest change in Dan he reappeared like magic. He even cancelled his holiday to stay close to Dan. So this evening I decided to go and leave Adam and Marie alone with Dan for a while. Dan let Adam do things that he didn't want the nursing staff in Ward 2 to do. He had a very sore-looking arterial line in his hand but he wouldn't let the nurses touch it. He did allow Adam to clean up the area a little. That evening when Adam thought Dan had fallen asleep and he and Marie tried to creep out, Dan whispered Adam's name – it apparently hissed out through the trachea tube. Adam was both shocked and moved and stayed until Dan was really asleep because every time Adam moved slightly Dan got distressed. When he got home Adam phoned and told me of the latest happenings so the next morning I was in by 7.30 – I couldn't sleep for worrying about Dan being afraid on his own.

Dan's eyes were still not reacting so he was in permanent darkness in a strange bed surrounded by strange voices. He was lying in what must have seemed like hell, his veins breaking down, sore all over, unable to speak, not fully awake, mind muddled and then physiotherapists beating him up every now and again. The sheer terror that must have filled his mind is unthinkable, he must have wondered why we had all left him in this terrible place.

Apparently, traumatised people are inclined to attach themselves to one particular person, in Dan's case it was Adam. Sarah was a bit put out that it wasn't her Dan chose. But I felt for Adam, as this was added pressure he could really have done without, and the strain was showing. We were all looking rather washed out these days. Joe was what I can only describe as in a permanent distraught state. Dan was Joe's best friend as well as brother and he was taking the whole thing very badly. I worried for him. I felt as though we all were working on auto-pilot, walking about like zombies and trying to stay sane ourselves. I was hoping that when we could get Dan breathing for himself and talking again we would all really believe he was going to get better and the cloud would lift. We were, however, a long way from that point at this time and still did not know how much brain damage Dan had sustained.

This first full day in Ward 2 was a strange one. I didn't feel that Dan was in the right place as he didn't seem well enough to be in a ward where he was not constantly watched.

Comas are not at all like I believed them to be before Daniel experienced one. As I have said before, I always thought they really were like they are depicted on the television. I think the casual approach to them as shown in many soaps does a coma victim a disservice. They are not one moment asleep and the next saying, 'Hello, mum.' The slightest movement is identified as a possible start to coming out of a coma. Day by day the movement becomes more obvious though sometimes clumsy and meaningless. Dan was still coming round now and was not by any means awake as yet. He was sleeping eighty per cent of the day and could move very slightly during the twenty per cent he was 'awake', usually only to try to get comfortable. It is not possible to be sure what condition Dan would end up in. He could easily take the predicted five years to recover before all would be revealed. Nothing was as I thought.

I sat with Dan for the rest of that day, people came in and out but I was very reluctant to leave his bedside now that he was out of the ICU. I bathed his eyes and greased his lips and tried to clean his teeth a little. I wanted to comb his hair. Dan was always very fussy about his hair and he would have been very upset to see the state it was in now. Obviously it hadn't been washed since 31 May and there were large clumps cut out where the probes had been inserted in this head. Sarah was now only coming in at evening time as she was back at university, so I was spending a lot of time alone with Dan, talking gently to him trying to reassure him that he was safe regardless of the strangeness of the surroundings.

Wednesday, 10 July – I arrived alone to find that Dan had been sick and had diarrhoea in the night so he was on a glucose drip. I didn't think you could be sick with a tracheotomy tube in, but you can! Dan had managed to grab the feeding tube that went down his nose in the night and pulled it out. This is the first thing that all coma patients do when they start to come round apparently. I actually watched a lad in the bed opposite attempt the same procedure later that day.

Dan was moved into a side ward as it was decided that he wasn't well enough for the general ward yet and they were considering returning him to the ICU.

Thursday, 11 July – Joseph's birthday, another cancelled celebration. Dan was now established in a little side room in Ward 2. There were three such rooms and the one next door contained a long-term patient who chose the timing of our arrival to die. This brought Dr Moncra's words to mind, that getting out of Intensive Care did not mean the patient would always survive.

Dan was very sleepy today and barrier nursing was in operation. I was asked to sign a consent form for Dan to have a gastrostomy tube inserted (a feeding tube put directly into Daniel's stomach.) It was explained that if Dan did not get food directly into him in a hurry he would not have the strength to survive, so I obviously signed on the dotted line. When you consider that Dan hadn't actually eaten for over six weeks it was no great wonder that he was incredibly thin and weak. He was breathing very badly and his oxygen intake was down to 86–87. The doctor was sent for and an X-ray ordered to see if maybe the lung was in trouble again. They were now seriously considering putting Dan back into the ICU. It seemed to be that infection of the lung was everyone's main concern.

The next day the gastrostomy was the first thing planned although the doctor in charge of this procedure thought that the anaesthetic could kill Dan as he was so weak. They needed a line for drugs so the gastrostomy was necessary. I really believe it was at this stage a case of kill or cure.

The doctor tried to examine Dan and he became very distressed, banging his hands on the bed and then he inadvertently pulled his arterial line out. Blood went everywhere; it literally hit the ceiling and soaked the doctor who was not amused. The doctor shouted at the nurse and was very unpleasant to us all and left the cubicle. I applied pressure as in all good first aid manuals; the nurse and I then stopped the bleeding. Dan was given Codeine to calm him down and his blood pressure was now sky high. Dan is such a calm, good-natured person and I was a little frightened by what I has seen just in case these head injuries were going to turn him into some sort of crazy thing.

Once again Dan was starting to look like a man barely alive. He was covered in wires. His trachea, saline drip, pulse monitor, and heart monitor all gave a frightening effect. The doctor returned to try to get another arterial line in and Dan went ballistic, thrashing about. The good doctor shouted at him and Dan was actually crying. I was going out of my mind watching, I just wanted to punch this doctor. I started to cry as well and was told to go away in a very rude way. I told the doctor that I thought he had the charm and bedside manner of a dead slug and went off to literally be sick. When I returned they had Dan strapped to the bed like some sort of mental patient and it looked like a scene from medieval times. Dan had restrainers on his arms and legs and he looked petrified. I went away and once more was physically sick. I then phoned Adam as I really needed his support and thought he might be able to calm Danny down. When I returned again, Dan had worn himself out and the arterial line was in situ again. Adam arrived and sat with Dan until they took him for a sonic scan of the chest. The unpleasant doctor seemed to think that Dan might either have an ulcer on the lung or even maybe an appendicitis that was causing a problem. Also, much to the nurse's surprise, he apologised to me, saying it had been a long day and that no one had ever stood up to him as I did and spoken to him that way before and it made him go away and think. Other doctors poked and prodded Dan and it seemed generally agreed that one or the other of these complaints was possible. Adam and I went off at nine when they wheeled Dan off to have this latest scan. I phoned at 10.30 and couldn't get any information. Richard had the grandchildren that evening and he was actually quite relieved that he had missed out on today's dramas.

When we all arrived on Saturday Dan was washed and ready for the gastrostomy operation. The previous day's scan didn't show anything very definite so it was decided that a grumbling appendix was probably the best bet and that they would only deal with that if it became obviously dangerous not to. Every time anyone went near Dan he went potty, trying to punch everyone like a man possessed. It was frightening to watch. He actually had his hands firmly round the throat of one of the physiotherapists at one time. Everyone except Sarah and I decided to go back to their homes and we promised to phone all and sundry when the operation was over. Dan seemed only to like one nurse, Fiona, so when it was time to go up the corridor to the theatre she came with us. Sarah and I ran up the corridor with Fiona alongside the bed. That is the longest corridor I have ever been up and it slopes slightly uphill away from the ward. Why we had to go at a trot, I do not know, but we did. What Dan imagined was happening, I do not know. He was on his hospital bed, oxygen tank by his side attached to the trachea tube, and in perpetual motion, charging along towards who knows where. His mind must have been in turmoil. Dan looked as though he wanted Sarah and me with him so we went right up to the operating theatre door. When the doors closed behind him Sarah and I went for a drink, me for coffee and her for milk, which she drinks gallons of. Obviously, I was worried almost out of my mind knowing that this was a serious operation for someone in as bad condition as Daniel was at this time. I didn't tell anyone else of the risks involved, as I didn't see the point in everyone being frantic. I needn't have worried because two hours later Dan was back in the ward, nicely calm thanks to the anaesthetic. The idea was to keep Dan sedated for the rest of the day and evening so that his blood pressure and other signs would settle down completely. Sarah and I decided that we would, in the circumstances, go home and return the next day.

Adam, Richard, Sarah and I went to the Somerville Club that evening. We often dropped in after a particularly harrowing day or when there appeared to be a light at the end of the tunnel. Tonight we were not quite sure which we were drinking for. We were all beginning to believe that Dan was going to survive against all odds but were also worried that maybe he was going to be dangerously disturbed. None of us were sure how we would cope with that scenario.

The next day the food drip was in place and up and running.

Dan's oxygen levels were up and it was decided to stop the antibiotics before Dan became immune to their help. Dan needed to have all his hand taps out as the veins had clearly broken down and they were becoming infected. His hands were very red and swollen. Daniel wouldn't let the nurses near his hands and they were obviously very painful. He was agitated and given Codeine and he was also trying hard to remove the catheter. When you have a catheter in for as long as Dan had you get very sore.

I was still concerned about Dan's eyes. There was still no reaction to light and we had been placing dark glasses on him to help, as his pupils were so large. You could hardly see any colour in Dan's eyes, just black holes. I was particularly worried when Dan wanted his glasses removed and he didn't have them on at that time.

We took little Dave in for five minutes to see Dan. Just six years old and he knelt up on a chair next to Dan's bed and declared that he was going to look after him and nothing we could bribe him with would alter his mind. Dave just sat there staring at Dan; he seemed mesmerised by all the tubes and wires but he was careful not to touch anything. I think Dan knew he was there because he put his thumb up for Dave.

Later that evening Dan threw up all the food that had finally been put into him. Even later in the evening water was put directly into the stomach through the tube to stop dehydration.

Sarah went home that evening to Birmingham at her parents' insistence and planned to return on Thursday.

I went in alone on Monday to discover that everything moves very fast in hospitals. One moment Dan was in the ICU, the next in Ward 2 and now I was being told that Dan was being transferred to Southmead Hospital, goodness knows why. Once the wheels were set in motion everything happened at an indecent haste. I was seriously worried, I didn't think that Southmead had the facilities needed to cope with Daniel. All my protests fell on deaf ears and I was told that an ambulance was on the way to facilitate the transfer. The nurses tried to sit Dan in a chair whilst waiting for the ambulance. He didn't even have the strength to hold his head up and it was resting on his chest; he looked so pathetic. The nurses had managed to take out all the taps in his hand and they were now in his feet instead.

The doctor in charge wanted to speak to Richard and so I rang

Richard and he arrived quite quickly. The doctor came to see us and said that he felt Dan would make a good recovery although he did not know and could not guess what permanent damage had been done by the head injuries. He did warn us that we were looking at several more weeks in hospital before he would be able to think about coming home. I couldn't work it all out. Only the day before Daniel was throwing his food up. He was nothing like awake fully and yet now all of a sudden we were being told he was going to be fine, maybe. I said that Daniel seemed clearly very unwell and it was only a few days since he was in Intensive Care, only to be told that it was a matter of finance. According to the doctor, Southmead had been the original hospital to admit Dan and they were under a different hospital authority to Frenchay. As Dan was going to take a long time and a great amount of funding to get fit, Frenchay wanted to pass this expense on to Southmead. Frenchay specialises in serious head injuries and too many long-term patients would mean having to turn patients away that needed their expertise. I could follow the logic but didn't like it at all. I could not understand how Southmead could be considered the first hospital to admit Dan as all that happened there was that they kept us hanging about for six hours in A & E before transferring Dan to Frenchay. I said I thought that this hardly constituted admittance to hospital and made it clear I was not at all happy. I could see that I was wasting my time arguing.

Richard went back to work and I waited with Dan for the inevitable. I was so frustrated that I felt like crying.

When the ambulance arrived Dan wouldn't let go of nurse Fiona so she decided to come to Southmead with us and see Dan settled. Fiona was visibly distressed by the condition of the room Dan had been transferred to. They had planned to put Dan in a more appropriate ward but they weren't ready for him. I had to ask myself why we had rushed here with such indecent haste if Southmead were not prepared. I took Fiona back to Frenchay in my car.

Dan was placed in the Ear Nose and Throat Ward, in a side room. It apparently was the only room that had an oxygen supply for Dan's trachea. People kept coming in and telling us that they were not used to tracheotomy patients – not very encouraging. There seemed to be a problem at first operating the oxygen supply. When they first connected Dan up they had obviously over

Back to Southmead

Tuesday, 16 July – it seemed Dan was now in the care of Dr Ferguson, a neurologist, and they wanted to observe him in this little room for a few days before moving him to Malvern Ward. Joe and Kate came in to visit, closely followed by the policeman in charge of the criminal assault case. He seemed shocked to see how ill Dan still was. People never cease to amaze me. I lost count of the amount of people who when told that Dan was out of Intensive Care assumed he was now well, just like that. The police wanted a statement from Daniel but Dan wasn't awake enough to understand and the trachea made it impossible for him to speak. The Detective Constable was advised to report Dan's condition as still serious. We were told that the two men still facing charges of grievous bodily harm (GBH) with intent and affray were both out on bail. The original captive MB on £1,100 bail, an insulting amount that one could borrow at the post office. The one who hid for a while, M, was on £50,000 bail put up by his grandmother apparently against her bungalow. So someone loved him!

Dan appeared to have got his time clock wrong, he was sleeping all day and awake at night. Andy Broadbent, a very strange but likeable friend, went in to see Dan and the nurse seemed to think that Dan found the conversation stimulating. If you have ever had a long chat with Andy you would understand how amusing we all found this observation. Andy could wear out a fit person.

Wednesday, 17 July – Dan had his hair washed for the first time since the accident. That was quite some task. The poor lad would go spare when he saw what his hair, his pride and joy, looked like. There were obviously bald patches where probes had been and large clumps of hair missing. As he seemed to be very sleepy, Joe and I went down town to buy a radio, pyjamas, a dressing gown and other items not needed before, like a flannel and slippers. It was a very uplifting feeling to have to buy items for Dan that he might need to walk about the ward. This was something we were all beginning to think was never going to happen and now it looked as though in the near future it might.

Thursday, 18 July – the speech therapist came to see Dan and explained his role in the great scheme of things. His job was to slowly let the cuff down on the trachea and see if Dan could speak and if he could breathe through his nose. This would probably happen in a couple of days. The idea being to try to get Dan off the ventilator once and for all.

They got Dan out of bed and he shuffled across with support from two nurses to a chair. Just sitting in it wore him out. He didn't like sitting down and couldn't hold his head up at all. He just sat there with tears in his eyes looking very pathetic; I could hardly bear to watch.

Sarah came back from Birmingham on Friday and we actually got a smile out of Dan that day. He threw a bit of a paddy when it was suggested that they get him out of bed again. Sarah and I copied him, slapping our hands on the bed, and he smiled.

Dan was moved to Malvern Ward on that day. An internal ambulance arrived about 10.20 and off we went.

He was put in a very nice modern room. The Malvern Ward is sited on what was once a maternity wing and I believe I had at least one of my children in that ward – probably Danny himself, so life appeared to have gone in a big circle. The room was light and airy, with a wooden floor and French doors that looked out on to a green and trees, very pleasant. This is the only little patch of greenery at the hospital complex. The speech therapist came and fitted a cap to the end of the trachea tube so Dan could speak. It was a bit muddled but clear enough to understand. We had to hold an oxygen mask over his face every now and again when he started to struggle a bit for breath. Sarah was intending to stay until 5.30 and then Adam and Marie had promised to take over. I went into school about three o'clock for the end of term speeches and goodbyes to any staff leaving. Everyone seemed pleased to see me at work and hear first hand how Daniel was doing. I had posted weekly reports rather like royalty via the head teacher but my colleagues still wanted the details from me. I went back later and left Dan sleeping with his radio on.

Saturday was a good day but Dan was feeling unwell on Sunday, probably a touch of Behçets. His head and neck ached, his mouth was sore and his eyes looked very red. A doctor was sent for and steroids prescribed, this was the usual treatment for Behçets.

Sarah spent all day letting Dan swill his mouth round with water and spitting it out – he wasn't allowed to swallow yet. He was still being fed through the gastrostomy tube. Dan was very bad-tempered but still Sarah was patient, moisturising his hands and feet and spoon feeding him drops of water.

Lots of people visited Dan in Southmead because it was close to the majority of his friends' homes. He even had some very unlikely visitors. It was almost a pleasure to visit this little private room it was so light and the view so pleasant.

Monday, 22 July saw Dan started on a course of steroids. By now his lips were very swollen and his mouth was full of ulcers. Dan was very good-humoured with everyone that day, even the physio. Sarah went to her lodgings to pack as she was off on holiday with her parents under protest. I thought the holiday was well earned. My friend Julie dragged me off to The Beehive pub for lunch and in the afternoon I went to our house in Muller Road to do a bit of clearing up.

Tuesday was pretty uneventful but Wednesday was a good day. They took out the trachea. They untied the cord holding it in place and Dan coughed so fiercely that the tube flew out. It was a disgusting-looking hole that I could not imagine healing over. He had to wear a large plaster over it but as his chest was still a little mucky, revolting gunge kept squelching out of the plaster and it had to be changed regularly. Then at last, out came the hated catheter. This part of Dan's anatomy was extremely sore but I reckon he was very relieved to get that out of the way. We continued with the gargling and spitting out for a couple more days – by Friday Dan was getting very fed up with this routine.

Saturday, 27 July, Richard's birthday and nine weeks into the drama. Richard got for his birthday the only thing he said he wanted – his son back.

Dan had his first bath, he had to be hoisted into the water, very undignified but he enjoyed it. He, at last, actually was starting to understand what was happening. I think it was this day that he really started to come alive, not that even now he remembers anything about this time in his life. It is a wonderful thing, the human mind and what it can block out. Dan had always hated hospitals; obviously he had spent so much time in them over the years that they depressed him. I knew that if Dan was coming round, he would be trying to escape hospital prematurely.

Joe arrived and because electricians were going to work in Dan's room for a while we decided to try to take Dan out in a wheelchair for some fresh air. We managed to manoeuvre Dan into the wheelchair and Joe pushed it out of the ward. We decided to walk down to the canteen. Southmead is in the middle of a heavily built-up residential area and unlike Frenchay there is very little grass and nowhere attractive to walk or sit. Still our walk about was wonderful. It was a beautiful warm day and the first time Dan had felt the fresh air on his face for nearly ten weeks. It was a day Joe and I thought would never come. Dan looked rather sad and crumbled in the wheelchair. He couldn't sit up straight, he was as thin as could be and his head hung to one side, but he was alive and he was outside the hospital for a few moments.

True to the normal form of hospitals, one minute they were planning to rewire Dan's room so he could find the bleeper easier and the next sister decided to move Dan out of his cosy little room into a ward containing three other men. The reason being he needed the stimulation – that was a joke. The three men all had terminal illnesses and were deaf. They all had different hired televisions, on mega volume but not all on the same channel.

Dan was very unsettled and upset by this move, he cried on and off nearly all day and obviously, as a result, so did I. Surely it was obvious that Dan was happy in his own little room but as usual no amount of logical and rational argument was listened to.

Our Worst Fears

28 July – unbelievably they did move Dan out of his cosy little room into a ward holding just four beds as threatened. They had literally only just completed the rewiring of Dan's alarm button when they came to wheel him out and into his new bed. Hospitals amaze me. They are there to make people well and yet they insist on unsettling patients on a whim. I would have thought that the patient himself would have a good idea where he was happiest, surely his tears counted for that much.

It was this day that Dan actually told us that he could not see. No wonder he was so upset by the latest move. Can you imagine being blind, unwell and then shoved in a room full of noises in all directions? It must have been quite harrowing that 'stimulation' he suffered.

It was a terrible day for all the family, suddenly being confronted with our worst fears and realising that Dan was in fact blind. We should have known sooner but until then Dan had thought it was just because he was waking up. He could hear everyone saying that comas take a long time to come out of so he decided to keep this piece of information to himself. When I thought about him in Ward 2 not wanting Adam to leave and being upset by the nurses fiddling with the taps in his sore hands I could only shake my head in despair. The thought that this kind and gentle soul suffered in silence. I questioned him closely about his sight loss, hoping he meant that his sight was poor or one eye wasn't too good. Unfortunately he told us that he was in total darkness. We couldn't believe it. Hadn't he suffered enough!

We informed the hospital staff and they arranged for Dan to be taken to the eye hospital for tests. He had loads of visitors that evening and instead of being tired, he loved it and didn't want any of us to leave. I was amazed at how well he was taking the fact that he was unsighted. I could only assume that he thought it was what we all hoped, a short-term problem.

On Tuesday the speech therapist said Dan could start to swallow small sips of water and a small amount of minced food subsidised by the high protein liquid being pumped in through the gastrostomy tube. Now hospital food is dire, without mincing it to make it even worse.

The next day Dan had his first mouthful of minced food. It looked like regurgitated cat food and apparently tasted worse. He also ate a bit of ice-cream. Joe, Kate and I got Dan into a wheelchair and took him out round the grounds. You would think you had taken him to his favourite place, Alton Towers, he was so thrilled to be out.

Every day now saw Danny a little fitter. He was, however, still very weak and tired but he was beginning to come back. Generally Dan's good humour had returned with an expected few mild bouts of depression but I was no longer worried that I would be taking home a raving madman. By Saturday, 3 August Dan's food pump was only on once a day as he got used to food again.

On Sunday Richard and I had the day off. We went to the old haunts I spent my childhood in, around the Southampton and Portsmouth area. I had done this trip just after my mother died but unfortunately the film was still in my camera when we had the burglary and the camera was stolen. So I was off to repeat these shots. I wanted to go to my grandparents' grave in Hamble and Alvestoke where they used to live. It is all a lot different from when I was a child but there were still some distinguishing landmarks. Richard is very tolerant of my strange whims. We got back quite late but we popped in to say goodnight to Dan.

Monday, 5 August – I arrived just after lunch because Dan had been due to have physio between ten and twelve. The speech therapist said Dan didn't need him as he was articulate and clear which apparently is very unusual after having a trachea tube in as long as he did. At least that was one good thing to happen. A gathering of lady doctors told Dan that he was doing really well and that they wanted to send him to Bath to a Young Head Injuries Rehab Unit above the Bath National Hospital for Rheumatic Diseases. Dan was getting very agitated at the mention of yet another move to yet another hospital. All he wanted to do was go home but Richard and I knew that he wasn't fit enough to come home yet and quite frankly the thought scared us a little.

Dan spent most of Wednesday having tests in the Bristol Eye Hospital. When I went in the evening the sister said they would not have the results for about seven days. Dan was actually asking questions about his sight and seemed worried. The sister took me aside and said that the feedback she had got from the Eye Hospital was that Dan was definitely blind. She advised me not to tell him as they had experts who could break this sort of news to patients causing the minimum of distress. It amused me slightly as it was Dan who had told me that he was blind in the first place. I had obviously realised that he was having problems with his eyes but it didn't occur to me that it was a serious problem. I thought it was just muscle strain as suggested in Frenchay.

Daniel had been nagging the nursing staff to allow him to go home for a weekend. I was told that they would allow this to happen in a couple of weeks. Richard knew he would have to fit grab rails on the stairs, bathroom walls and other likely danger spots but thought he had a little time to plan this. Dan had a weakness down his left side caused by the stroke he had in Frenchay and that made it difficult for him to keep his balance even long enough to get him in a wheelchair. I decided that possibly buying a wheelchair of our own would be economical in the long run as we could not be sure how long it would take Dan to get mobile again. In the grounds of Southmead Hospital there is a unit that hires out wheelchairs and they also sell collapsible ones because they are no longer allowed on the wards for some obscure health and safety reason. Anyway, I got a good deal on a second-hand chair.

Friday came and as usual, and I should have been prepared by now, everything changed. Instead of having two weeks to prepare I was told that I could take Dan home the next day, Saturday, for the weekend. Obviously Daniel had been nagging to escape and I could hardly let him down by declining this offer. I had to cut my hospital visit short to get home and organise things for the weekend. I went to 'Nought to Ninety', a shop for the elderly and infirmed on Kelloway Avenue, to look at the grab rails I needed and bought a selection. I then went to Kelloway Building Supplies to buy a stair rail. When we moved to the School House in Cotham the stairs had a hardboard wood effect boarded-in staircase that made the hall very dark and ugly. I had knocked this out when I decorated the hall so now there was no rail on the stairs at all. Obviously I had not predicted that one of our son's would be blind when I made the stairs a safety hazard.

I was trying to explain to the men in Kelloway Builders what I needed and why when a stranger in the queue behind me asked if he could have a word with me. Intrigued, I went to speak to this man. He told me he was clearing out his grandmother's house and everything I could possibly need was there and I could have it all. Uncharacteristically I followed the stranger to a house in Bishopston and sure enough there were grab rails of all types and a couple of stair rails that, joined together, would be ample for the job I needed. This kind man wouldn't take a penny for the items. Happily there are still some good guys out there.

That evening saw Richard working flat out to get the house ready for Dan's visit home and the next day we went in to collect him. Both Richard and I were dubious as to whether Daniel was actually fit enough to cope with this weekend out of hospital but Dan was keen to be home with us. We were given a large bag of medical supplies, a huge syringe for washing out the gastrostomy tube, huge plasters and sterile cleansing equipment for Dan's trachea hole.

We managed to transport Daniel home. He was still very weak and unable to support his own weight so he couldn't stand on his own. Daniel is at least five foot ten inches and I am only four foot eleven inches so I could foresee a problem with being left alone with him. The weekend was an absolute nightmare. He wanted to sit downstairs with Richard and me but his bladder was very weak and the bathroom was upstairs. We had brought a bottle home from the hospital, the type used when a male patient cannot get out of bed and that was used a lot. Unfortunately, Dan couldn't even use the bottle without help so we all became very intimate that weekend. Daniel wasn't able to sit up straight unaided so we had to prop him up in a chair with pillows. Obviously, he wasn't able to sit on the toilet without help and had to be held in position. Everything luckily was done with a degree of good humour. Having a bath was a nightmare. Just trying to get him in and out was a mammoth task. He was so thin I half expected him to snap in half if you pulled him too severely. Although he actually weighed very little it was a dead weight and difficult to deal with.

Dan still had his stomach tap in just in case he wasn't absorbing enough food and to stop him dehydrating. We had to squirt cooled boiled water straight into his digestive system through the tube on regular intervals. Also his trachea hole needed constant attention.

Dan was very co-operative and so very pleased to be at home with his father and I. Not that he had actually ever lived in the School House having had a flat of his own prior to the incident. Dan was not at all like the person we used to know. He was strange, sleepy and forgetful but it was still early days in healing terms. It was probably Dan's saving grace that he was so sleepy. Not being able to see would have made him so bored as he just sat still propped up in an armchair big enough so that it looked as though it and the pillows were about to engulf him.

I realised that Dan would be very keen to get out of hospital as soon as possible once he had been home. I also knew the way hospitals operate having taken Dan home after hospitalisation several times in his life previously looking worse than when he was admitted. Because we always seemed as though we could cope we were always left to do just that. Looking after Dan when he was a child was a different kettle of fish than this. I knew that Dan being so much taller than me would cause problems. But also I knew that we would cope because we wanted to. That weekend was quite a good insight into just how difficult the first few weeks would be but Dan always improved much quicker at home, as do most people.

It was little Rick's Birthday today but we gave the party a miss.

The first night was a nightmare. Dan needed to use the bottle provided almost hourly so we all got very little sleep and his bed got rather wet, which was obviously unpleasant for him. Still we survived.

The next day, Sunday, we took Dan to Portishead. Portishead is a small town on the outskirts of Bristol that has a sort of beach. The water is the Bristol Channel and there is a promenade of sorts, an outdoor swimming pool and a boating lake on the front. We took Sarah with us for our stroll in the sunshine. We pushed Dan round the large boating lake; he still looked so very ill and frail. We had to contend with very strange looks from other visitors to the place. One lady asked if Dan had undergone major heart surgery. The huge plaster that covered his whole neck and part of his chest, covering the trachea hole, looked worse that it was.

There was stall for the blind by the water and I spoke at some length to the couple who were running it. They gave me a lot of tips on who to get in touch with and where to write for help that proved very helpful.

Richard's brother, David, lives in Portishead so we decided to pop over and see him for a few moments. To say that David and his wife Irene were surprised to see Daniel was an understatement.

Daniel really seemed to enjoy the visit and I felt that he was part of the family again for the short time we were there.

We had a few visitors in the late afternoon, one being Wayne, the lad who Dan had helped that fateful evening. Whilst Wayne stayed to make small talk, Sarah and I decided to drive across town and take a look at the house that Adam had just bought himself. It was quite pleasant to be doing something normal again.

Of course, come Sunday evening, Daniel didn't want to go back to hospital so I phoned and said I would bring him back in the morning. He got very emotional when I insisted that I take him back. He was not well enough to be at home really as he was weak and his head hurt all the time, just through the sheer effort it took to keep his head up off his chest.

I told Dan that he would have to stay until the hospital removed the stomach tap. I explained that he couldn't come home for good with things like that still attached. He seemed to understand this and we softened the blow of having to return to hospital by planning to bring him home again.

The general opinion before we went off for the weekend was that Dan should go to the Young Head Injuries Unit in Bath for around six weeks. They had a waiting list but Doctor Ferguson seemed to think that Dan could jump the queue. I knew Dan would be keen to leave the ward he was in; being in a room full of very deaf elderly patients was not in my mind ideal. It was definitely not the stimulating atmosphere that the nursing staff had promised. It was actually very irritating when you are unable to see; especially when strangers from different corners of the room were forever shouting him at. The patients were actually very pleasant and only trying to be friendly but they were quite wearing for someone in Daniel's condition. The man in the bed opposite Dan amused me no end. He and his wife kept saying how they had never seen anyone as ill as Daniel. The poor man was himself dying of cancer and looked like death warmed up. They were a very kindly couple and it was strange to think that they should worry about Dan when the gentleman was so ill himself.

The man in the far corner was dreadfully diabetic and had lost both his legs through this. He was also very asthmatic but he smoked heavily. His wife kept pushing him outside in his wheelchair every few minutes for a cigarette. He would come back in, wheezing and coughing, and I couldn't understand why they kept him in hospital. He was told not to smoke but ignored doctor's orders and was, as a result, making himself very poorly indeed. He wasn't going to get better because he would not help himself. Goodness knows what they fed him in there. He seemed to be a regular user of the commode and the stink engulfed the room every time.

The fourth bed in the room seemed to have a continuous change of occupant. If I took Dan for a push in the wheelchair in the morning we would invariably come back to a new patient and the same would happen again in the afternoon. I was beginning to suspect that this bed had a trapdoor that dropped each new patient down into a room below being used for spare part surgery.

Any visitors to our ward were fascinated by Dan and always wanted to know what had happened to him. I was considering taping the answers down so I could just trip the switch every time we were asked the million-dollar question.

We returned Daniel at 8.30 on Monday; as he was due to have a physiotherapy session in the main hospital at ten o'clock. He really was not pleased at all about having to return to hospital.

The nurses gathered to inspect the trachea hole and Dan's gastrostomy tube whilst Richard and I were taken into a side room for a short meeting with the sister in charge. Apparently she had been present at a meeting over the weekend, regarding Daniel's future treatment. It appeared that Bath's Young Head Injuries Unit was not keen to take Daniel on board, as they were not equipped for someone who could not see. There was a Head Injuries Unit in Southampton that specialised in newly blinded patients but they could not take Daniel because he was not mobile enough. So we were in a catch-22 situation. Sister went on to tell us that although they had still not received the results of Daniel's tests at the eye hospital, Dr Ferguson had phoned and had been told verbally what was discovered. It was thought that Daniel would not regain his sight. He was definitely totally blind in his left eye, the optic nerve almost severed at the back of his head when he struck the curb of the pavement that fateful day. Daniel's right eye only produced a perpetual shadow effect, this being caused by the optic nerve stretching when his brain swelled. The optic nerves do not mend in the way that other nerves can, so this also would be a permanent state, the condition was called optic atrophy. All in all the prognosis was very depressing and also very distressing. As there was nothing further medically that the hospital could do for Daniel it was felt that he would be discharged as soon as the gastrostomy tube could be removed and everyone was happy that Daniel was eating and absorbing food correctly. Outpatients would be arranged and Dan could go to the Head Injuries Therapy Unit as an outpatient for physiotherapy and so on once he had regained a little strength. I was scared, I felt abandoned. Richard and I came out of that room a very worried couple.

I returned to Dan's bedside and Richard went on to work. Dan was waiting to go to physio and I said I would sit with him until they came to fetch him.

When I told Dan that the plan was to discharge him in the next week or two, he was thrilled. Everyone seemed very pleased with the way we had coped with Daniel at home, I suppose we are our own worst enemy really, if we were hopeless and helpless we would possibly be offered assistance.

The physiotherapist came to fetch Daniel just after ten o'clock and she told me that it would be the last session Dan would have with her as he needed more condensed physio than she provided. Dan was wheeled away to the internal bus and I was left to think that if Dan was only going to be fed and nothing else, he might as well be at home. I could feed him and he would be happier, happiness being a state of mind needed to get completely well.

I went home for a short time and returned around lunchtime. My friend, Julie, turned up and we wheeled Dan down to the restaurant for lunch instead of staying in the ward. When we returned Dr Ferguson was waiting to speak to us. Sister had told him about the conversation we had earlier so he knew I was aware of the situation and plans for Dan's future. He had looked in on the physiotherapy unit and was rather concerned that Daniel was very immobile which would make coming home quite difficult. He had contacted the unit in Bath and persuaded the powers that be that Daniel needed their expertise and would benefit greatly from a few weeks with them. They had agreed to send an assessor on Tuesday to see if it was possible to accommodate Daniel after all. Dr Ferguson seemed to think that the hydrotherapy pool alone would work wonders. I was very pleased but Daniel was not!

I spent most of Tuesday with Daniel, waiting for the assessor, trying to keep him cheerful; he was not happy about the Bath idea.

The speech therapist came even though he had already told us that he wasn't needed. He was a very strange man, softly spoken, very slight in stature. He asked Daniel to describe how to make a cup of tea, the idea being to see how muddled Daniel was and how organised his mind was, or was not, as the case may be. Daniel was very precise in his description on tea making and we were told that Dan did not need a speech therapist as he spoke beautifully and was quite articulate. He went on to tell Daniel that he had beautiful hands and should consider learning to play the piano. As I said he was a strange man.

Sister came in to say that the Bath assessor couldn't come until Friday after all, so we were a little in limbo wondering what was going to happen next. I asked about the Frenchay Head Injuries Therapy Unit, as I knew that Daniel would much prefer to stay with me and go to a day centre from home. Their waiting list was very long and it would be January before Frenchay could take on any more patients. Sister also told us that Daniel would go down to theatre on Wednesday first thing to have his stomach peg removed.

Friends called in that evening and I went home early, leaving Dan with the youngsters and intending to return in the morning after Dan had been brought back from the operating theatre. I had promised to pick up Andy Broadbent in a morning, as he wanted to visit Dan again.

I picked Andy up as arranged on Wednesday morning and we went to the hospital expecting Dan to be back from the operating theatre. Instead of going down first thing as arranged, Dan had only been taken to theatre at eleven o'clock, so we went away and returned at 1.15. Another friend of mine of long standing, Jan Hesford, was there, waiting when we got back. We had only had a chance to say hello when Dan was wheeled back into the ward, wide-awake and very pleased to be free of the last tube. Jan had apparently been waiting some time so she couldn't stop long.

There was a social worker hovering to speak to me, so I left Dan with Andy and went to a side room to hear what she had to say. She offered me her services which I declined as I didn't feel that Dan needed a social worker; he had me to sort out any problems. She offered advice on claiming disabled living allowance and gave me the forms to register Daniel blind. Apparently, the results had still not arrived from the Bristol Eye Hospital but it was quite obvious by the forms that Dr Ferguson was not expecting anything hopeful to come out of a written statement.

A young lady doctor was sitting with Dan when I returned to his bedside. She was busy explaining to Daniel how that now he had the last obstruction to him leaving the hospital removed, he could be discharged but that she would be much happier if he decided to go to Bath Head Injuries Unit for about six weeks. She made the place sound a worthwhile idea, assuring him that he would get fit quickly there. There were other options on offer, Dan could be a day patient at Frenchay but not until January. I rather hoped I would get him fit myself by then. There was also a place in Brislington that catered for people who could not see but unfortunately took mainly older patients; we didn't like the sound of that.

As she left the doctor took me to one side and told me that someone from the blind association would be round to explain how to register Dan blind. She told me not to distress Daniel by telling him he was in fact permanently blind, they have people trained for that task.

Dan spent a restless day on Thursday, keen to come home but still unable to take his own weight. He still needed help to sit up in bed and to get in and out of the wheelchair. But Dan hates hospitals and was almost pleading with me to 'spring him'.

Friday came and the representative from Bath was due so I went into hospital early. The medicine for Daniel to take home was all prepared so it was just a matter of keeping Daniel pinned down in the ward until the Bath assessment officer arrived; luckily there was no way Dan could escape without help so he was pretty well trapped.

The lady from Bath arrived about ten o'clock. She was quite charming and spoke to Daniel at length about the wonders of the Young Head Injuries Unit that she represented. Dan showed no willingness to listen. After about half an hour of details about the hospital and all the equipment on offer there, the representative told me to bring Dan to Bath Royal National Rheumatology Hospital – to the Bath Head Injuries Unit on the top floor at eleven o'clock on Monday morning. If Dan wanted to stay, the funding was there; if he felt he couldn't cope, I could take him straight back home. There were fifteen others on the waiting list so the place would soon be filled. She seemed to think that they could get Dan reasonably mobile in a short time and could help him to cope with his blindness.

Daniel was discharged from Southmead Malvern Ward at 6 p.m., into the care of the hospital in Bath. He looked better than the previous weekend and was starting to regain his strength. Sister gave me all the relevant paperwork to take with me. The referral document called Dan a brain damaged blind patient, a charming description. I couldn't believe how fast things had happened.

Dan came home and he was a complete member of our family again, where we went he came. Dan was very sleepy most of the day but on the Saturday evening we took him to the Somerville Club for the trophy presentation evening. They run snooker, pairs and singles competitions. Dan had won the singles the previous year. They also ran crib, darts and bowls competitions throughout the year.

There were an unusual number of members in the club that evening and everyone looked thrilled to see Dan again. Adam and Joe came with us and Sarah was in Bristol for the weekend so she came as well. I think it was all a bit overwhelming for Danny and I took him home after only an hour. Everyone kept shouting hello at him and he was trying hard to work out to whom the voices belonged. Telling people that someone cannot see does not seem to register with everyone. I could see that Dan was starting to get distressed so we went home to spend the rest of the evening quietly.

Sunday we went to watch Adam play football. Richard played in Dan's usual place, as they were a man short. Dan did not enjoy this experience very much. We went on to a pub for lunch. Eating, especially when you are newly blind, is very difficult. I cut up everything as best I could but, as Dan said later, you chase food round the plate and do not know if you wanted to eat it until it is in your mouth. It was easier to use a spoon or fingers. Who would have thought that eating could be so slow and tiring. I used to try eating myself with my eyes closed and walking about in the same way just to experience what Dan was going through.

We all spent the weekend trying to assure Dan that Bath Hospital was a good idea and that we would not abandon him there; if he hated it I would bring him home. He seemed to think we wanted rid of him because he was a lot of trouble. It took quite a lot of persuasion to get him to agree that taking a look at Bath was a good idea.

Sarah went back to Kingswinford about 5 p.m. and Dan was absolutely worn out by then. Sarah being a university student was now in the middle of her long summer break and had moved back home until the next academic year began.

Bath Royal Hospital

Monday, 19 August saw the first day at Bath. Bath is a very beautiful city but parking is not so wonderful. I had been given a map of where to find the hospital so I had a fair idea where it was. It was right in the centre of Bath close to the Theatre Royal in a narrow one-way street with double yellow lines along the front entrance. This does not make bringing a new patient in a wheelchair an easy project. Richard dropped Dan and I outside and then he went off to try to park in the Victoria Park car park, which was the closest to the hospital. The Bath Royal National Rheumatology Hospital is a very old building, quite dark and oppressive-looking on the outside but very impressive once you step through the front door. There is a lift just inside the front entrance but there is also a magnificent sweeping staircase, very beautifully ornate with deep wide mahogany steps and highly polished banister rail that would not look out of place in a palace. There is a plaque just inside the front entrance listing the famous doctors that had worked at the Bath Royal over the centuries.

I pushed Dan's wheelchair into the lift and we went up to the top floor where the Young Head Injuries Unit was situated. Richard joined us there.

A very gentle male nurse spoke to us on arrival and showed us Dan's room. It was excellently equipped with its own en-suite bathroom designed especially for immobile people with plenty of poles to hold on to and space to move about in, no sharp edges anywhere. The room itself had a bed that could be reshaped with a hand control, the head end moved up and down as did the feet end, Dan was most impressed. They didn't intend to start any regime that day, it was a day just to settle in. I do not actually think that anyone was totally convinced that Dan would turn up today. There definitely seemed an air of surprise when we met anyone. As the doctor was not due to see Dan until after lunch we took him back outside and wheeled him round Bath in the sunshine. Because the hospital was dead in the centre of Bath's shopping area it was easy to spend time just wondering about, made safer by the fact that a great deal of the complex is vehicle free. It had to beat walking around the grounds of Southmead Hospital any time. Being in Bath which is fifteen miles from our home did however have its obvious drawbacks. There was no popping in for a few moments and then going back, we had to arrange to plan our days around Bath.

We returned to the hospital after lunch and the doctor, a lady called Penny North (very pretty), examined Dan and told Richard and me a bit about the unit. She also gave us his medical details; his weight was right up to nearly ten stone on admission to Bath thanks to the build-up-style fluid that had been pumped into him.

Adam and Marie arrived and they were quite impressed. We all had a tour of the Head Injuries Unit. Although the hospital itself was built in the seventeenth century, the Young Head Injuries Unit was fairly new so it was well equipped with all the latest technology. We were shown the canteen facilities, swimming pool, weights rooms, hydrotherapy room and felt that this was the right place for Daniel despite the distance from home. There were a great number of very seriously injured youngsters there, both physically and mentally. Dan looked quite well compared to some of them.

Richard and I left Dan around 7 p.m. in the evening still with Adam and Marie; we could see that he was starting to get very tired. He had tried so hard to stay awake so he could understand what was happening but was starting to struggle. He had nodded off a few times during the day, if only for a few minutes.

I didn't sleep too well. I was worried about Dan waking up in another strange place. Happily I need not have worried, as he was fine when I arrived in the morning about 10.30; in fact, he was still in bed. One of the nurses said she gave him a cup of tea about 7 a.m. and he was so tired that he went straight back to sleep. She had looked in on him from time to time but decided not to disturb him. Nothing was planned at the hospital until the Wednesday except a few tests later in the afternoon, so Dan and I spent most of the day in and out exploring Bath. We spent the day just chatting in the sunshine and he seemed quite content though he was fearful that everyone would desert him now he was so far away. I was sure that his friends would find it difficult to visit, as it wasn't easy for me expense wise, but I assured him that he had no fears that his brother's, father or I would leave him stranded.

I went home whilst they ran tests planning to return in the

evening.

On the way home I went into our house in Muller Road to see if there was any post only to find that we had been broken into. Adam used to live in the house but now he had bought a place of his own he was slowly moving everything he needed out. I had to check with Adam before I could establish what, if anything was missing. It turned out that the only thing stolen was Daniel's computer that had been stored in the back room. Dan had built this computer himself; it was a very specialised machine. Could anything else happen to Dan, I wondered! He had already had furniture from his flat that we had stored in Muller Road stolen by a lad who was renting a room there. When Adam had lived in Muller Road he advertised for a house-mate. He already had a friend of Dan's staying, the Chris that Dan used to travel with but he wasn't very keen on him because he was untidy. This fellow, in his middle to late twenties came along. Adam thought he seemed fine and he was very tidy. We trusted Adam's judgement and so long as the bills were paid we didn't mind who lived in the house within reason. The tidy fellow was all right for a while, and then he stopped paying his rent and did a bunk with Dan's furniture. We later found out that he had served seven years for armed robbery. We decide that Adam's judge of character was possibly a little flawed, as Chris, untidy as he may have been, was at least always honest.

Richard went to Muller Road to repair the windows that the thieves had broken on entry and I went out to Bath. I took Kate, Joe and my grandsons out with me. We all walked round Bath in the warmth of the summer evening taking turns to push Dan. Even little Dave pushed the wheelchair declaring he wanted to take care of Dan himself. Eventually as the little ones tired we had Dan in the wheelchair and Dave and Ricky on his lap going around. We left about 8.45 p.m. as the boys were shattered. I warned Dan that I would be a little late the next day as I had the police coming to Muller Road about the burglary. I had to tell Dan about the computer going missing. He was not thrilled but I ended up promising him a replacement as best we could.

On Wednesday morning I went to Muller Road as arranged at 10 a.m. to meet the police. Richard came in at about one o'clock and there was still no sign of any police presence. Richard phoned the police again and explained that I wanted to get out to Bath where my son was in hospital and they arrived about an hour later.

The police stayed just long enough to take a statement and tell me that the fingerprint guys would arrange to visit. I decided not to hold my breath.

I was anxious to get to Bath because I knew that Dan stressed easily at the moment and I didn't like to let him down. I like to do exactly what I say I will do; I hate to let anyone down, least of all my sons. He had his first session of physiotherapy that day. Because the room was small and well arranged Dan could manoeuvre himself out of bed and into the bathroom. It took him a little time to find his way round the bathroom but eventually he found the toilet. He wasn't able to have a shower on his own, as he couldn't stand up that well.

The next day I took my friend Julie and her son Mark out to Bath with me. Dan had his first shower with a little help. We pottered in and out of Dan's room and also out and about in Bath. I helped Dan with his dinner, cutting it up and describing the plate contents. It looked a lot more appetising that the usual hospital food.

I had to leave just after lunch as I had an appointment at Southmead Outpatients about my troublesome knees. They were stiff and painful and swelled up on occasion and the left one was inclined to actually give out on me occasionally. Usually I see someone, they bend my knee about a bit, say how crunchy they are and send me on my way with cries of arthritis. This time was different. The doctor had the X-rays that were taken in April just after my mother died. I had fallen over when the knee gave out on me and cracked my kneecap. The time before when my knee gave out I cracked my two front teeth and it cost me a fortune to get them capped. The doctor told me she thought I had rheumatoid arthritis, took a blood test and gave me a steroid injection in the left knee. The length of that needle is enough to give you pain just looking at it. If the knee was painful before I went for my appointment, it was nothing compared to after I left.

I popped in to see Richard's father and tell him all the latest news about Dan. It took Richard and me nearly two hours to get out to Bath that evening due to road works on the Bath Road. What is more it was bucketing down with rain and we had to park miles away. We were like drowned rats when we finally reached Dan's room.

Dan had apparently been taken down to the day room for

'stimulation and interaction' with other patients. No one seemed to believe that Dan was actually quite happy on his own. He used the time to try to remember events that were lodged in the back of his mind. He had apparently been introduced to and sat next to a young man of twenty-four called Paul. The nurse told me that Paul had enjoyed their chat as he and Dan had a lot in common, both having an interest in computers. She was sorry that she had to take Dan back to his room after only half an hour because he seemed agitated. Dan's version was that he thought Paul was almost brain dead and he was getting frustrated because he could not escape on his own.

People are always trying to pigeonhole Dan. Even now it is expected that he would love the company of other unsighted people by virtue of the fact that they have this common flaw. We don't get on with everyone just because we can all see so why should Dan be expected to click with everyone with sight problems. People are always asking him if he goes to this or that club for the blind and he always replies, 'Is there a reason why I should?' and they always say, 'Well, you'll all have something in common.' What? Not being able to see isn't something in common. Your interests are something in common, not you afflictions. We don't join a group just for people with big noses or sticking out ears. I am sure that Paul was a perfectly pleasant young man but just because he owned a computer didn't exactly make him an instant soul mate for Dan. Even in his still frail state he wanted to choose for himself whom he spoke to at length but this was not easy for him due to immobility and his lack of sight, which he found frustrating.

Dan was looking forward to coming home at the weekend and Sarah and I planned to fetch him after physiotherapy on Friday. I wanted to show Sarah round the hospital and bring Dan home as early as we could.

Sarah took Dan down in the lift and I took the stairs. I made a point of walking down the hospital staircase when I went home each evening. It was like something from a movie set. You could imagine Scarlet O'Hara sweeping down the steps with her gowns flowing around her. I bet that staircase could tell a few tales.

Saturday, 24 August was not a good day for Dan as he spent the whole day either asleep or holding a bowl being sick. When, on Sunday morning, there was no improvement I phoned the hospital who told me to contact our own family doctor. Dr Spence was unfortunately not on duty but a locum arrived who said that until Daniel was released from Bath Hospital he was officially in Bath's care and that we should take him back there. He did however look at Dan's tablets and suggested that we dropped one of them immediately because of the side effects. These included dry mouth, constipation, urine retention, blurred vision, palpitation, drowsiness, sleeplessness, dizziness, low blood pressure, weight changes, skin reactions, jaundice or blood changes and loss of libido. Talk about a kill or cure pill! I was never aware that one little tablet could contain so many problems. I decided not to give Dan these tablets at all.

I kept Dan on the Phenytoin, a member of the Epanutin family, used as an anticonvulsant to treat epilepsy. The side effects of this tablet sounded rather horrendous as well. They included stomach upset, sleeplessness, unsteadiness, allergies, gum swelling, blood changes, lymph gland swelling, and nystagmus (abnormal eye movement). Plenty of vitamin D should be taken when reducing the dose. All these side effects are similar to head injuries anyway so I was wondering how it was possible to tell the symptoms apart. Unfortunately, as another fit would probably have killed Dan I was obliged to keep him on the Phenytoin. Sometimes it is better not to know too much. This locum had been frightfully informative and I rather wished he hadn't.

Richard and I were intending to take Dan and Sarah, who was around for a few days, for a pub lunch but Dan still wasn't feeling well. He started to try to come down the stairs on his rear one step at a time, bumping down about eleven o'clock but he was nearly crying with pain from his stomach and just wanted to go back to bed. It seemed silly to keep him upstairs, so we decided to take him back to Bath Hospital to be on the safe side. Sarah went home to Kingswinford and Richard and I took Dan back to Bath. I gave him a Paracetamol before we left and although he was still moaning all the way there, he was feeling fine by the time we reached the hospital – sod's law strikes again!

On the Monday Richard had started a week's holiday and was planning to put a new bathroom suite into our house in Muller Road as the old bath appeared to be leaking.

Richard and I had spoken at some length about what we would have to do when Dan came home for good. We could not imagine staying long term in the School House because it was really small.

It had two bedrooms that you could get a double bed in but very little else and a third bedroom that you could not even fit a full size single bed in. There were two living rooms both of which were crammed with our furniture. I could not see that we could make Dan comfortable there. The school house went with Richard's job but our own house in Muller Road, which had been let out was far larger. I had written to Bristol City Council as the school house was technically a council house, asking what the chances were of them letting us build an extension on the side to accommodate Dan. There was plenty of room at the side of the house. I hoped that medical reasons might swing it or Richard would maybe have to seek other employment and we would move back to Muller Road.

When I went out to Bath I took my grandsons with me so Joe could help his father with the bathroom. I had to park so far away that the little ones were staggering by the time we reached Dan's room. Dan had a bout of physio and the boys and I then took him into town for a bit of fresh air. It seems that all Dan was actually doing in Bath was being given a dinner, which was just left if I was not there, and he was unable to find it, and physio, though they had promised he would be taken to the pool the next day.

I took the little ones to Bath's Victoria Park on the climbing apparatus before we headed for home again.

Tuesday and Wednesday I spent most of the day in Bath with Dan on my own. He was taken down to the pool on Wednesday and had a short splash about. They have all the equipment to lower you into the pool and scoop you out again. The short swimming experiment was very tiring for Dan and a little frightening as he still did not have full strength in his legs and arms plus the obvious disadvantage of not being able to see.

Dan told me that when he woke in the morning that day, he thought he could see and was very confused and distressed when he realised that he couldn't. It must have been a dream.

Thursday was another rather uneventful day and there didn't seem to be much happening treatment wise so I spent most of the day alone with Dan again. We were expecting Sarah to join us in the evening but she phoned to say that she wouldn't be coming until Saturday morning with her parents, as they needed the car. One small piece of good news today was the fact that Adam had forgotten to cancel the contents insurance on Muller Road when he moved out, so luckily Dan's computer was insured when stolen. I put in a claim straight away for a replacement.

Friday came and Dan was into his fourteenth week in hospital. Two outpatients appointment arrived today, one from Southmead for 12 September and one from Frenchay for 4 November and he wasn't even out of hospital yet, which amused me no end.

Daniel had a full day planned at Bath today but I was told I could take him home at about three o'clock for the weekend. Dan was very agitated today and expressed a very strong desire to come home for good. He really hates hospitals.

I watch Dan have his swim and then spent the rest of the day just wondering about Bath on my own, popping back at lunchtime to help him find his dinner. When three o'clock arrived, Dan was very keen to leave and he wanted me to take all his things home so he wouldn't have to come back. I could tell I was going to have a lot of trouble getting Dan back to Bath on Monday but I left some of his bits anyway.

Dan spent all of Friday evening trying to prove that he would not be any trouble. He dragged himself up and down to the bathroom, very slowly and painfully, refusing help. It was so sad to watch him shuffling along, so obviously unable to see and still in a degree of pain.

All of our family had been invited to a garden party on the Saturday at my friend Helena's place. She had just refurbished a sixteenth century listed farmhouse, standing in a very large garden with huge outhouses. It is a beautiful building with inglenook fireplaces, one complete with a priest hole. The building has a very well documented history, with a lot of connections with the roundheads. Bristol has a lot of local names connected with this period, Cromwell Road, Effingham Road, and so on.

Helena's farmhouse is in the middle of a built-up area but obviously would have been in open fields when built. It doesn't really look right where it is but it is a marvellous property, perfect for a garden party.

The party was a really splendid affair. Helena knows how to entertain. There were trestle tables full of wonderful food, meats of all sorts, cheeses, bread, salads, rice dishes, everything you could think of. There was also an abundance of alcohol. I have never seen so many individual bottles of wine. I didn't even know you could buy them that size. There was also an excellent band and a bouncy castle for the children. Adam, Marie, Joe, Kate, little Rick, Dave,

Sarah and her parents, Danny, Richard and I all went along. There were several people there that we hadn't seen for quite some time and we all had a thoroughly good time. Dan spent most of the time in a quiet room and started to flag about 6 p.m. so we made our way home. It was just the break we all had needed, a jovial easygoing day with friends.

Dan spent most of the Sunday asleep. Obviously the previous day had knocked the stuffing out of him.

On Monday Sarah and I took Dan back for his 11.15 physio. I had persuaded Dan to return to Bath, telling him he had to get proper discharge papers. I phoned the hospital to tell them that Dan wanted to be discharged, and was told that 'the team' was holding a meeting at 2 p.m. They planned to discuss Dan's case and see if they could advise us to take him home or try to persuade him to stay on at Bath a little longer.

Happily, the team meeting at Bath went in Dan's favour. Daniel had not been overly co-operative and seemed visibly distressed when his family was not about. Everyone seemed to think that Daniel would be a lot happier at home, and happiness is a great healer. So eventually when we got the discharge papers at five, we went home. When the doctor came to say we could go, she told us that she had just received the Bristol Eye Hospital tests we had been waiting so long for. Southmead had just faxed them on to Bath. She did, however, need time to analyse the results, so we were now leaving another hospital without knowing these important test results!

The doctor did promise to fax the details to Frenchay Hospital and hopefully, on 4 November we might actually get to hear the worst, though I thought it was a long time to wait for such important information. I was hoping that our Southmead appointment on the 12th would tell all. Bath also threatened to send us a community social worker and referred us to the RNIB (Royal National Institute for the Blind.) We also took away a detailed planned physiotherapy package for us to work on at home, designed to get Dan's legs stronger and help him regain his balance. We were also told that Bath recommended that Dan went to Frenchay's Head Injuries Unit (HITU) as an outpatient and they would write to Frenchay on our behalf.

I would have to say that Dan did seem a lot fitter when we left Bath but that could possible be put down to the natural healing process.

I went back to work the next day as it was the first day of the new term. Luckily Sarah intended to stay for a few days as she had an exam on Wednesday at the university and wanted to study and keep an eye on Daniel at the same time. No drama today and Dan slept until midday.

I was very glad to be living so close to my place of work. It could be irritating at times of course but in these new circumstances it was wonderful. Jim McKay, the head teacher, was very good to us all, I could go in and out of work as I wanted, popping home every half hour or so to check on Daniel. As I had a computer that had the same software as the school I could also bring work home to type, which I did frequently. I didn't intend to actually leave him alone for too long as getting about unaided was still a nightmare for him and steadying himself on the toilet even with the grab rail was not easy.

We started immediately our physio regime so I had to pop home to supervise that and feed Dan, of course. There was also the matter of getting in and out of the bath and manoeuvring the stairs safely. Dan could drag himself up the stairs and always came down on his bottom.

Back to the Real World

I had received a letter from Southmead Hospital Nursing Director's Office inviting me to a meeting with the senior nurse/quantity adviser, Mr Wadey, on 20 September to discuss my complaint against the hospital.

Meanwhile, on 12 September Daniel and I kept an incredible appointment at Southmead Hospital with what turned out to be an eye specialist. Bearing in mind the fact that I was told not to tell Daniel too much about his sight loss as there were experts who would do this for me, this appointment was mind-blowing.

I wheeled Dan into the waiting area and as usual there were about ten other people all with the same time on their appointment cards. After an hour Dan's name was called and in we went. Dan underwent what seemed like a very superficial examination and was then asked exactly what, if anything, he could see. Dan said, 'Very little,' and this doctor with the bedside manner of Hitler said words to the effect of 'I would be very surprised considering the damage if you can really see that much, I suggest you get yourself registered blind because the optic nerve damage is irreversible!' I couldn't believe it. Dan just looked amazed and burst into tears. Needless to say so did I. This man had been as subtle as a sledgehammer. He added that there would be no point in Dan making another appointment because he believed nothing would change. So out of the examination room we went, over to the desk with both of us in tears. The lady there appeared not to notice muttered something like, discharged and off we went. Having been told not to tell Daniel ourselves the extent of his eye injuries as special training was needed to handle such a delicate disclosure, I was flabbergasted.

We reached the car and just hugged each other for what seemed like an age. I got Dan into the car and put the wheelchair in the boot and we just sat and cried ourselves almost dry. Then we both composed ourselves with difficulty and agreed 'to hell with them' – we were going to be all right. I think these doctors see so many patients that they forget that we are people and we become just numbers.

One of our school governors, Neville Jones, kindly volunteered to come with me to the meeting with Mr W at Southmead. I had been a governor at the school before Dan's accident and knew Neville quite well. He looks rather like a solicitor, very upright, very intelligent and articulate, in his late fifties early sixties. He had taken notes on what we should ask.

It was a very strange meeting. The consultant in Accident and Emergency and senior lecturer, Mr AM, Mr W and one other were all lined up in a very official-looking way. I think I would have felt very intimidated if I had been on my own. Mr AM was at first quite aggressive but when he realised that Neville was not a solicitor, just a friend, he opened up a lot more.

We began by asking if there had been any sort of enquiry into my complaints and we were told that there had been. Neville then asked for a copy of the findings of the enquiry and we were told that, although a letter of reply and explanation had been written in June, it had never been forwarded to me as they were still waiting to hear from the ambulance records to discover why the ambulance had taken two hours to arrive after being asked for by Dr A at Southmead. They said that they felt that this was an important factor in the delay in transferring Daniel to a Serious Head Injuries Unit in Frenchay. We asked why it had taken so long to get a reply from the ambulance services and no explanation was offered. We were told that we could now have a copy of the June letter if we would like it and that the file was freely available to any solicitor we cared to employ. We never did get to see that letter. Mr. AM said that they had a letter from the doctor concerned and that she had given a reasonable account of the incident. Though her defence was totally hinging on the fact that according to her Daniel had drunk an amazing amount of alcohol. Seeing as how Sarah had been with Daniel since 6 p.m. and made it quite clear to the doctor on several occasions that Dan had hardly drunk anything, regardless of this apparently someone else had told the doctor that Dan had drunk a great deal. I think it is possible that, when asked, one of the other males at A & E that night had told the doctor what they themselves had drunk. There was no way that anyone other than Sarah would have a clue what Dan himself had drunk.

Mr. AM then told us that, at the time of the incident, it had been standard procedure to send any head injuries to Frenchay. It was an agreement between the two hospitals. We obviously asked why, in that case, it had taken the doctor so long to comply with this procedure, the reply was quite ridiculous. According to the doctor, Dan only had a broken nose, no skull fracture was seen on the head X-rays. I said that Dan never did have a broken nose and not only was his skull fractured, but the fracture stretched from ear to ear and there was also the matter of a hairline fracture of Dan's neck. Mr AM said he could not comment because he had been unable to obtain copies of the original X-rays. How very convenient. I produced, at this time, proof, supplied by Frenchay hospital, that Daniel did in fact have a compound fracture at the base of his skull as described by me on being admitted to Frenchay. Mr. AM replied that only a scan would reveal conclusively that a fracture was present and one had not been taken at Southmead. I asked if they had the facilities, apparently they have, but because they transfer head injuries to Frenchay, it was not used. He also stated that procedures had been changed since August and that they now admit head injuries to Southmead.

The doctor admitted in her statement that she had been informed that Daniel had Behçets Disease but had no knowledge of this ailment although I had in fact provided her with a detailed fact sheet on the condition. She apparently had also said that she transferred Dan to Frenchay because of his degree of consciousness and not because of any fracture. She had spoken to the houseman on duty at Frenchay, which made me wonder why he did not seem to have been expecting Daniel. There was, of course, no record of the conversation.

Mr. AM said quite clearly that he had hundreds of complaints every day and that ninety-nine per cent of them were pure rubbish but he was aware of the seriousness of my complaint and that I should follow it through and gain maximum damages for my son. He was careful not to say categorically that he felt that Southmead had added to Daniel's stress but he did say that an independent assessor might feel that there was a degree of negligence, mainly due to the time element.

Neville asked about the handling of Daniel in the form of the transport to Frenchay. Mr AM said that he felt that this would in no way have added to Daniel's condition. I asked about the possible damage done by stapling the cut on the back of Daniel's head right on the compound fracture and Mr. AM said he was not medically capable of answering that question, a worrying thought. Mr. AM then, in a roundabout way, suggested that maybe Dan had not been monitored thoroughly prior to his fit and arrest on 8 June, saying that he felt that adequate care would have allowed for the possibility of this happening and checked it on the onset. He said I should get a second opinion as to whether signs of brain disturbance before the fit could or should have been detected and therefore the effects' lessons. He said he was not qualified to give this answer but that a solicitor would arrange for someone who was. I had not thought along these lines at all before.

Mr. AM was quite open at the end and I felt he was a good man with a lot of integrity. He said that the file on his desk was open to inspection and we could go and see him at any time for further discussions. He added that it was not his job to cover up incidents but to look into them.

I asked just one more question before leaving and that was why had they taken so long to arrange a meeting with me. Mr. W said he had tried several times to telephone me but I was never in. I had to laugh and told him that of course I wasn't in because I was at my son's bedside, some of the time just a few feet from his office, when Dan was in Southmead.

It was an interesting meeting that I was promised an account of. When we started we were told not to bother taking notes as minutes were being taken and we would receive a copy of the meeting in full. (Oh yeh!)

On 15 October I still had not received the promised typed minutes of the meeting of 20 September, so I wrote requesting them. I had a reply by return telling me that it was 'in hand'. Meanwhile, also on 15 October, Daniel received a summons to appear as a witness on 4, 5 and 6 November in the case of MB and H. This amazed us all as everyone knew that Dan had no memory of events of 31 May.

A couple of days later I received the said copy of the minutes of the meeting with Mr. AM and Mr. W. The letter was dated 17 October 1996. It was absolute twaddle and had no similarity to the meeting whatsoever. I was very pleased that I had taken notes and typed them up immediately whilst they were still fresh in my mind and also that I had an independent witness.

I am going to repeat the whole letter in full and hope it does not bore anyone reading this book too greatly, but it is so unbelievable.

The letter started by thanking me for meeting with Mr. AM and Mr. W on 20 September and apologised for keeping me waiting so long for it to be arranged and hoped I had found the meeting helpful.

The letter went on by saying that Mr AM had started the meeting by reading a report that he had written summarising Daniel's care from the time of his arrival by ambulance at 23.58 hours on 31 May and his departure to Frenchay Hospital at 05.45 hours.

Mr. AM had stated that his report was based on information from my letter of 15 June 1996, the Accident and Emergency notes made at Southmead Hospital by Dr A, the nursing observation chart, an X-ray record made at 1.30 hours on 1 June, and finally the ambulance record describing events between 23.35 hours and 23.58 hours on 31 May.

The report contents were summarised as follows:

Daniel arrived at the Southmead Accident & Emergency Department at 23.58 hours on 31 May. Daniel would not open his eyes to speech or pain. The ambulance staff had noted that Daniel had a wound at the back of his head but stated that he had not been knocked out. The ambulance staff had been told that Daniel had fallen backwards on to the road. Apparently, Dan's blood pressure, pulse and breathing were normal.

So this was the first contradiction in terms. Dan had arrived according to the report unable to open his eyes to speech or pain and yet the ambulance reported that Dan had not been knocked out!

Apparently, nursing observations had begun at 0015 hours on 1st June and been repeated every fifteen minutes. Also the report stated that Daniel had been seen by the duty casualty officer at midnight who noted that Daniel was under the influence of alcohol, was responsive but incoherent.

Dan was not even slightly drunk and now it seems the good doctor has changed her story and decided that Dan was not unconscious but responsive and incoherent!

Nursing observations began at 0015 hours on 1st June. I have no disagreement with the nurses on duty that day but I do strenuously disagree that the duty casualty officer that night saw Dan at Midnight – it was more like one o'clock, an hour after we arrived. Apparently, examinations to the nervous system had revealed no abnormality. The doctor also had noted that Daniel had been assaulted and punched in the face, had fallen backwards and had not lost consciousness. She went on to say that Dan had drunk three pints of beer and five measures of spirits that night.

Where did this woman get this ridiculous information – I have witnesses who spoke to Dan when he left the Somerville club at 10.20 p.m. and who will state that he was perfectly sober. He would had to have swallowed a huge quantity of alcohol in less that half an hour to catch up with the amount Dr Al says he drank. And please tell me where she could have got the information seeing as how Sarah made it quite plain that she had been with Dan since 6 p.m. and that Dan had drunk less than two pints all night. Also, everyone that night said that Dan had gone down like a skittle, making no attempt to stop his fall and that he was unconscious from that moment on – he certainly was when I got to the scene!

The report continued by saying that Dr A had given instructions that neurological observations should continue and had placed Dan in a hard collar and had requested X-rays of Dan's skull and cervical spine. The X-rays had been taken at 1.30. Dr A then examined the X-rays and noted a fracture of the nasal bone and had discussed Daniel with the orthopaedic registrar. She decided to transfer Daniel to Frenchay Hospital's Accident and Emergency Department and this took place at 05.45 hours.

This amazed me as Dr A had assured Sarah and I at the time that this was all that was wrong with him. Also, why did it take so long to decide to transfer Daniel to Frenchay?

The letter went on to tell me that after reading the report Mr AM had subsequently examined Daniel's X-rays, including those taken on 1st June, except that no X-rays of the nasal bone and no lateral view of the skull were available to him. The letter went on to say that the X-rays showed no evidence of a skull fracture.

What a load of twaddle. The man had examined X-rays that were not available to him and could not see a skull fracture that was there and life threatening.

The letter went on to explain that Southmead's procedure was always to transfer suspected serious head injuries to Frenchay, which is what Dr A had done. (Six hours later!) Also it was stated that it was never appropriate to ascribe a reduced level of consciousness to be the effects of alcohol alone.

The letter ended by saying how sorry everyone was about

Daniel's injuries and hoped that our meeting had proved helpful. It added where and to whom I should write if I decided to pursue a legal angle and it was signed by Mr. W – senior nurse/quality adviser.

I was very annoyed about this letter as it was pure fantasy. I wrote immediately to Mr. AM expressing my disgust at the letter I had received from Mr W and line by line dissected it. I send a copy of my four-page reply to Mr. W and received, by return almost, a very grovelling letter apologising profusely and saying that the letter was entirely his responsibility and not the fault of Mr.AM. Apparently he had passed the file to Mr Rixon, administrator, Trust Headquarters, to take over responsibility of communicating with my solicitor.

I had another letter from Mr Rixon saying he now expected a letter from my solicitor.

Yet another letter arrived, this time from P Chubb, chief executive, it was long and detailed. The letter began by agreeing that my compliant had been handled badly, lethargically, and Mr Chubb apologised unreservedly for this. He said he noted that I had attended a meeting with Mr. AM and that he had been open and frank, which he would have expected of Mr. AM. Apparently Mr W had taken notes during our meeting and had subsequently lost them, which is why the letter written later did not completely reflect what was said during the course of the meeting. He added that he was not surprised that my response to the letter I received was one of anger. The letter went on to say that Dr A said she had been told that Daniel had drunk a large amount of alcohol by another young person although she could not say if this information was correct. The next matter that was covered was the time discrepancy between when I say Dr A saw Dan and when she says she saw him on the 31 May 1996. Mr Chubb said that the truth of the matter was that Dr A could not remember what time she had first seen Daniel. Apparently the doctor was now working in Scotland but when contacted she could only say that she had seen Daniel as soon as possible after his arrival at casualty. Apparently the ambulance records showed that Dan arrived at the hospital at 23.58. I had booked him in at 12.06 at reception. The doctor then apparently picks up the patient's card when going to make an examination and inserts the card into a clock stamping machine – the card was stamped with the time of 00.00 – six minutes before I had booked him in and six minutes before the card would even have been available to the doctor, which proves that the clocking machine was faulty, which apparently explains the mistake in the times! It was never Mr. W's intention to deceive me in this respect. Dr A never noted any times on the records that night, though she did say that the A & E department had been very busy. I knew that, I was there, and everyone there that night was involved in the same incident.

There was a whole paragraph about the X-rays and how Mr. AM had requested them and they were not available and how no one was trying to deceive me. There seemed to be a breakdown of communications over this point.

The next paragraph was about Dan's state of unconsciousness that night. Apparently the ambulance records stated that Dan was 'not K'od', but went on to report that Daniel's condition was monitored by using the Glasgow Coma Scale which quite clearly showed that Daniel was unconscious.

Amazingly enough, it was this information that influenced Dr A's decision to send Daniel on to Frenchay. Talk about a turn around. I know now that Daniel arrived at Southmead with a Glasgow Coma Scale of six, which is very serious, and that he should have been transferred immediately to Frenchay.

The last paragraph apologised again and said how sorry everyone was about Daniel's injuries. The letter was signed by Mr Chubb, Chief Executive.

I could not believe how contradictory each letter I received from Southmead had been and was starting to think seriously about what I should do about them. I wanted to follow up the complaint, I felt sure I had a good case. Part of me was worried about the cost to take up any complaint and another part of me thought that maybe it was petty to pursue these people after my son's life had been saved, all be it at the cost of his sight. I did feel, however, that these people added a tremendous strain to my already heavy burden.

I decided to get in touch with Hector Stamboulieh, our new solicitor, and see what he thought about this issue. Obviously he would be dealing with a claim for criminal injuries compensation, which I felt must be our main prerogative. Our decision to pursue a complaint against the A & E Departments of both Frenchay and Southmead is covered in the last chapter of this book.

Magistrates' Court

4 November 1996 – the day we had all been both waiting for and dreading, the day of the court hearing. I didn't know quite what to expect. Joe had taken the kids to school and I picked him, Kate, Sarah and Kate's parents up from Bishop Road and dropped them down town. I got back home only to discover that Dan's wheelchair had a flat tyre and I had to run down to the nursing home down the road to borrow a chair from them. Once organised Roger, the caretaker at Charnwood, the annex of the school my husband and I worked in at the time, took Dan, Richard and me down to the Magistrates' Court. We were in Court number seven. There are steps up to the court, not very handy when you have someone in a wheelchair. Luckily, a member of staff had the decency to take Dan up in the inner lift that was really only for employees. It runs from the parking area under the building and we were allowed to return by that route after lunch.

It is a really primitive place. You come in through the front door. No one actually searches you. They just ask you if you have anything offensive on you, as if you are likely to say, 'Yes, I have a submachine gun in my handbag' if you had. They open handbags and look in without disturbing anything and then when you get upstairs and find the court you are looking for, everyone waits in the same waiting area, witnesses for both defence and prosecution. Luckily there were none of MB or H's relatives there.

We were assigned Court seven and a few feet away was Court eight and another group of individuals, I believe the first ones were waiting to answer a summons about a motoring offence. You have to go through the Magistrates' Courts for a decision as to whether the case in question is serious enough to be forwarded to Crown Court. I couldn't believe there would be any doubt about our case.

First all the witnesses had to go into court and read the statements they had given to the police, to refresh their memories. (I often wondered how people remember such complicated details after a long time.) Then they all had to gather outside without discussing the case at all not knowing what order they would be called in. Dan, Richard, the parents of the prosecution witnesses, were also there. We all went in to listen. Dan had and still has no memory whatsoever of the incident so was allowed to listen to all witnesses. His wheelchair was placed at the end of one of the rows. The DC in charge came over and shook Dan's hand. It was the first time I had seen a member of the police force since we arrived at the court building. There were about six rows dedicated to the general public, all facing the judge's bench. The witness stand was on the left and the defendants were in a box to the right. There were another half a dozen shorter rows in front of the public rows. These contained the barristers, solicitors and so on.

First they read out the charges to decide if they were all going to be used. There was a long discussion about Section 18 as opposed to section 20, the difference between GBH with intent and ordinary GBH. The main difference is, of course, the sentencing. The lesser charge carries a five-year sentence, the other up to life. They decided that it seemed inevitable that it would go to Crown Court. They were just testing the water to see if the witnesses would stand up and be counted at the end of the day. MB and H were sitting in the dock – they were not asked to plead. They were just asked their names and addresses. MB couldn't even remember his so-called address. He was supposed to be staying with relatives in Gloucester as part of his bail restriction, but we all knew that he was never anywhere near Gloucester except to sign in at the local police station once a week. The rest of the time he was spotted round and about Bristol as usual.

These morons sat the whole time with fixed grins on their faces. They showed no shame and no remorse. MB is quite tall, six foot plus, I would say, with short dark hair and a goatee beard. H is stocky, about five foot eight inches, with a square face and cleft chin. They were both dressed casually, almost scruffy. There was no similarity between these two men whatsoever and they were both very distinctive to look at. The shorter of the two looked quite strong, whereas the taller looked almost weedy. Strangely, before I actually saw these men in court I had pictured them and they were not at all as I had expected.

MB actually has quite a pleasant face and the other I didn't like the look of at all. I had always wanted to give H the benefit of the doubt. He had kept well out of sight since running away, hiding and being found. I actually thought he might be sorry for what had happened. As soon as I saw these two men I could see they were not sorry at all. The sight of Daniel, blind and in a wheel chair did not send a flicker of emotion across their faces even for a second. I couldn't take my eyes off them throughout the time we were in court.

MB and H had separate solicitors. Both looked rather smarmy. The charges were dropped over the minor assaults on Babe, Rachel and Jason, so already we appeared to be losing ground.

The proceedings seemed ready to begin at last and the first witness for the prosecution was called. It was Wayne. Wayne was eighteen at the time, about five foot six inches maximum with very dark hair, pale skin and a flattish nose. He is of slight build. As he stood in the witness box which faces the defendants I thought how very unnerving and intimidating that must be.

Wayne was sworn in and had to give his full name and address, strange because if he hadn't known MB anyway, now they would know his address! He was told to speak clearly and loudly, quite understandably he was looking very nervous.

As the kids gave their evidence the scribe repeated every sentence into a tape recorder, a lengthy and off-putting process. You lose your thread when you can only say a couple of words at a time. Wayne told how he had arrived at the Somerville Club at about 6.30, left there and arrived at The Showboat at about 9.15 and how, as he walked across Dongola Avenue, by the Lloyds Bank and was immediately grabbed by MB. Wayne said he had been pushed into the wall, cutting the back of his head. MB had allegedly asked Wayne if he had been in a taxi with his girlfriend and Wayne had denied that he had. Wayne went on to tell how MB had slapped him again and repeated the question with the same reply. MB had allegedly said, 'Tell the truth and it will all be over,' to which Wayne had replied that he wouldn't have done what MB suggested because he wasn't stupid and he knew that MB could 'knock the shit out of him'. Eventually Wayne decided to say it was true to save himself a further beating and MB had shaken his hand and as he did so had slapped Wayne again. He shook his hand again and did the same thing. Wayne estimated that MB had punched him three times and head butted him twice. Wayne had then, on being released, gone into the pub. This, the original assault, had left Wayne with a cut head and a swelling round his left eye.

Apparently Gary, a friend of Wayne's, had dropped Wayne off at The Showboat and had then gone to park his van. As he passed the incident Gary had asked Wayne if he was okay and rather foolishly Wayne replied, 'Yes.' Wayne had told Gary to 'go away', he didn't want him to get involved.

Wayne then began to describe the second assault on his person by the accused. He told of how on or about 11.10–11.15 p.m. he and a group of friends left The Showboat and started to walk towards the Southern Chicken place a few doors down. Wayne was walking in the front of the group. When he got to Tile Flare he said that MB, H and G were walking up towards him. When asked if he knew the accused before the incident Wayne said he knew MB because his mother had babysat MB's younger brother. He also knew MB through school though MB was a lot older than Wayne. He knew H from both school and football. Wayne went on to say that he had been slightly in front of the others coming out the pub. Apparently MB and H said to Wayne that he had got off lightly, and MB hit him again. H stepped forwards to hit Wayne and MB said words to the effect of 'Leave it, this is my fight,' and laid into Wayne again. He had punched, head butted and slapped until Wayne went down. At this point Wayne vaguely remember Dan Gallimore walking over. Wayne said H told Dan to 'F— off' and Dan said, 'No, I think you've had your fun and he's had enough,' or words to that effect.

Wayne continued by saying how he had struggled up on to his feet and then was either head butted or punched from the side. Wayne said that he thought it was H who hit him and this time he stayed down. Wayne added that MB hit often but not as hard as H.

I thought to myself that H sounded like a real charmer – he waits until the victims are almost on their knees and then he joins in.

Wayne continued his evidence by saying that after the last blow everything was hazy. Wayne had heard Kate scream and saw her head move and knew that MB had hit or kicked her whilst standing over her.

Cross-examined, Wayne was asked what he had drunk that night in the three hours before he reached The Showboat and Wayne said three pints and three or four rum and blackcurrants. He said he had stayed at The Showboat a further two hours but only had one more pint. The defence were very keen to make something out of the amount of alcohol drunk.

When asked for more details about the alleged attack, Wayne said that, as Dan approached, he had seen H strike Dan as well. He knew it was H because it was a far more powerful punch. Wayne was asked if Babe had helped him to his feet and he said he knew she was there but felt it was a male. The defence went on to ask Wayne if he had seen other witnesses, whom they named, close by. Wayne explained that while being punched repeatedly by the likes of MB you do not notice other people. He was asked if it was dark and explained that Tileflare was lit up and made the area very light. Asked if he was capable of making a mistake, Wayne said everyone was but he hadn't in this instance. Wayne was asked about G, the third man. Where was he? What was he doing and so forth? Wayne said he could hear G's voice egging MB and H on but was too busy concentrating on MB and H to notice G too much. G appeared to be behind him.

Wayne was asked to describe the three men and it seems they all had skinheads and possibly goatees as well. This point seemed irrelevant to me; if you know someone, you know them, it is as simple as that. But I could see where this line of enquiry was going, the defence was trying to say that maybe H wasn't the second thug, G was, there was a mix-up. Wayne had gone to school with G so he knew the fellow even though G had been in a couple of years above him.

Wayne was asked what everyone was wearing and he could not be sure. Wayne mentioned that MB had been downtown later bragging to Wayne's brother that he had 'hit the shit out of Wayne'. Wayne was asked if he had ever spoken to H before the incident. He said he had because they played football and you are inclined to speak when doing so. They tried to confuse Wayne but he was excellent and stuck to his story. Asked finally who had hit him, Wayne said he knew it was MB and H.

Wayne was excused, and the bench decided that we would take a short recess for lunch before the second witness was called. We all disappeared to the canteen for a cup of tea only to discover that the accused were in the same place, so we all went outside for fresh air instead.

I was amused by the fact that no one bothers to search you at all in the afternoons, so you could bring in a sawn-off shotgun after lunch if you wanted to and don't think I wasn't tempted!

We got back to Court seven waiting area to find MB and H already there. Richard couldn't resist following MB when he headed towards the toilets. MB turned and decided that he didn't fancy being caught in an enclosed area with Daniel's father and he decided to keep his legs crossed instead.

The second witness was another Jason who so as not to confuse the two; we will refer to as JP. JP was eighteen at the time, about five foot ten or eleven inches, with short fair hair and of stocky build. He was sworn in and gave his full address.

JP began his evidence by saying that he had gone to The Showboat at about 8.45 with a friend of his called Aaron. He had met a small group of friends that he knew and had stayed at The Showboat until about 11.15 p.m. JP, who incidentally was Wayne's best friend at the time, played the drums in the same band that Wayne was in. The group of friends were at The Showboat together when MB arrived and called JP outside. JP knew MB, G and H and usually spoke to them. MB had spoken to JP about Wayne, asking him if he knew anything about Wayne and Louise, MB's girlfriend. MB was obviously furious about something and told JP not to tell anyone about the conversation they had just had. MB repeatedly threatened JP but eventually let him go back to The Showboat where he immediately told his friends what MB had said. JP explained how he had wanted to warn Wayne but did not know where he was at that time. Later Wayne came to the pub and JP could see that Wayne had already encountered MB as he had marks on his face. JP said he had left with the group at closing time. They were heading for Southern Fried Chicken when they saw a commotion at Lloyds Bank en route.

JP was asked several questions relating to where he was standing and who else he could remember in the vicinity. JP's main piece of information was that he had allegedly seen MB strike Dan. He did not know if Dan was hit again as he had gone immediately to The Showboat for help. The defence solicitors asked JP how much he had drunk that night and he said four pints. He was then asked what sort of mood MB had been in when he called him outside the pub on the evening of 31 May. JP said that when MB had approached him at first he had been like a mad man, but had calmed down by the time he walked away from him. He went on to say that he had been eager to get word to Wayne that MB was after him because he was afraid for his friends safety. Asked if he was sure that MB had floored Dan, he said he was. JP was told he could stand down and should wait to hear his evidence read back to him.

They then recalled Wayne, read out his evidence word for word and asked him to sign it. Then Wayne was told he could now go if he wished as he would not be recalled.

The third witness was then called and sworn in. Brian was another eighteen- or nineteen-year-old, about five foot eight inches, of slight build, rather a nice-looking young man with a very pronounced stutter. It was Brian who had phoned me on the night of May 31st.

Brian gave his account of what had happened on the evening of 31st May 1996. As it did not correspond totally with JP's I knew that the defence would score points. For example, Brian said he allegedly saw MB push Dan over the rail and Dan then got up. He said he was two foot away from Dan when H hit him on the chin and that knocked him out. The defence made a big thing out of the fact that Brian did not notice JP near the scene but he did add, 'Who looks around at a time like that?' Several of the things that Brian said did not correspond with other witnesses but I think they were all young and were entitled to get a little muddled during such a horrendous experience. I think that Brian may have actually seen H strike Dan the final blow as he said he did but did not witness the alleged blow administered by MB earlier. Brian was the last witness of the day.

It is quite frustrating listening to a court case and not being able to discuss the witness statements afterwards. I wasn't, however, going to give the defence any excuse to get away with what they had done to my son.

JP was recalled to the dock to listen to his evidence but we had to wait nearly an hour for Brian's statement to be read out and signed and then the bail restrictions were explained. MB on £1,100 bail bond put up by his mother – not to come to Bristol – not to contact witnesses.

H on £50,000 bail bond, put up by his grandmother and to report to Southmead police station between seven and eight on Saturdays. It all seemed very strange to me. Considering what these men had done to my son, why would they allow my husband and I to know where they would be and at what times! People with different ideas about justice might have taken advantage of this information.

Throughout the proceedings I found it difficult to take my eyes off the defendants. I was looking for a sign of emotion or conscience. There weren't any. In fact they seemed to be treating the whole thing as a bit of light-hearted entertainment, with silly grins almost permanently on their faces. They looked particularly amused when Wayne was on the stand, almost as if they were trying to goad him into getting annoyed or upset. I admired Wayne's guts that day, I must admit. As I did all the other witnesses throughout the whole ordeal. It couldn't have been easy for them standing face to face with the people they were accusing, especially as it was obvious that they were violent men without scruples.

Whilst I was watching the accused Richard was watching Daniel to make sure he did not get upset by the proceedings. Not remembering anything that was being talked about must have been quite frustrating. It must have seemed as though they were talking about a different person, not him. Hearing about himself and not remembering the events must have been a difficult concept to perceive.

All the witnesses left together that day. Richard took Dan down in the lift and I went down the stairs with Joe. I was amazed when we reached the outer door to discover that the defendants were heading in the same direction. Most of the other youngsters were already outside, waiting for us to join them, looking very emotional. MB and H pushed through the group, muttering death threats and laughing. There was no police presence and I was only grateful that Daniel had gone out by a different exit. The girls were hysterical and the young men were genuinely scared witless. It was disgusting that a decent bunch of youngsters should have had to face such an additional ordeal. We vowed at that moment to always arrive in groups and leave the same way. No one was to be left vulnerable, as it was obvious that we could not rely on the police to protect us. I couldn't believe how lackadaisical everything was.

5 November 1996

We were here again. Most of our witnesses turned up to support each other, careful not to talk about the case, just to give moral support. There was still no sign of MB or H's hangers-on, though they themselves were waiting outside of court when we arrived.

The first witness of the day was Babe. She is a tall, slim girl of eighteen with a very slight brownish complexion, of mixed race with very dark shoulder-length hair. Her parents were in the waiting area and they seemed very pleasant. They had spoken to a Detective Constable before Babe went in about the fact that MB and his mother had been to Babe's place of work and threatened her – it was on record as the police had been called. MB had also harassed Wayne outside his own home. Wayne's mother who is a widow and vulnerable was understandably very nervous about events. The Detective Constable said it would be taken into account. Needless to say, it never was.

Babe was sworn in and began her testimony by saying at what time she had arrived at The Showboat, adding that she knew most of the people there that night. She went on to say how she had seen G, H and MB come to the pub at about nine o'clock. She explained that she was sitting outside with a group of friends when MB came up to the table and asked to speak to JP. Babe said she had known MB for about a year. She described MB as having a skinhead and goatee beard as did the other two. Babe also knew G and she had spoken to him before but she did not, however, know H. She said that she did not know who H was until later that day, apparently she had got his name from a friend.

Babe went back to the events of the fateful evening, explaining that someone had fetched JP and he had gone round the corner with MB, out of her sight, towards Lloyds Bank. Five to ten minutes later she saw JP return and he sat with the group. She said he appeared to be quite shaken.

A bit later Babe said she saw Wayne start to walk towards the group then turned back towards Lloyds Bank. Jason and Rachel, who were a couple at this time, joined Babe and her friends, and when they asked where Wayne was were told not to look. Babe continued by saying that a little later Wayne appeared round the corner with a marked and swollen face, especially round the eye.

Apparently Wayne and JP then went off and had a discussion then returned to the group. She thought that was the end of the dramas for the night.

Babe said that the next thing she remembered was Joe, Kate, Sarah and Dan arriving to join them at about 10.45. They all went into the pub for a drink but Dan only stayed inside for a few moments, leaving closely behind Jason who had gone outside to wait for Rachel. About 11.15 the group started to leave The Showboat and head for the Southern Fried Chicken for a takeaway – they didn't reach the place. When they got to the tile shop they heard shouting. Babe said she turned round and saw Wayne on the floor but she didn't see how Wayne got to the floor although Babe said she saw that MB was standing over Wayne. Babe told how she went to help Wayne and when she turned round she saw Jason being held up against the wall of Tile Flare by his throat by MB. She was only a few feet away. Jason was trying to push MB off and asking him to get off. Babe said she went over to push MB away from Jason but after she turned her back, MB had grabbed him again. She remembered seeing Joe on the floor with Kate kneeling by his side. She did not see what had happened. Babe said that she also saw Dan fall but she didn't see who hit him. She went over to Dan and knelt by him, intending to see how badly he was injured but Joe said, 'Don't touch him!' so she moved away. When she got up she saw Rachel and Sarah running after MB and H who were walking past The Showboat towards the top of Ashley Down Road. Rachel hit MB on the back and MB swung round and hit Rachel in the face. Rachel stumbled but she still followed MB and she hit him again. MB pushed Rachel into a car and she fell into the gutter. Babe continued by relating how she rushed to help Rachel and was also pushed by MB and fell on to Rachel. She then helped Rachel up and they went into The Showboat. Babe spoke to the bouncers and the manager – they went up the road looking for MB and the rest. Babe described the scene as bordering on pandemonium. People were running around saying, 'Call an ambulance.' Babe said she started walking back towards Dan but Brian and someone else were walking towards her carrying Wayne who was covered in blood and when they sat him down he asked for her.

Babe was then asked details about the group she had left the pub with and where they were going, trying to establish where each of the witnesses were at this time. When asked who had been nearest to Dan when he fell, she was unable to say with confidence.

The next person to be called was my eldest son, Joseph. At twenty-four, Joe was a bit older than the majority of witnesses. He is about five foot ten inches and has a mop of light brown hair. He is slim but muscular and has quite broad shoulders.

Joey was sworn in and refused to give his address out loud only to be told that all witnesses had the right to write down their

142

personal details. Shame no one thought to mention this to the previous witnesses!

Joe explained how he had started at the Somerville Club at 6.30 with Kate, Dan, and Sarah. They all stayed at the club until 10.20, then Dan drove them up the Gloucester Road to The Showboat. Reaching The Showboat Joe spoke to several people he knew then got a pint. When last orders were being called they left to join Dan. Dan was already outside because he didn't like the heavily smoky atmosphere. Joe said that he had left the pub with Kate and that they were behind the main group. There was a group ahead and they were all heading for the takeaway. Joe went on to say how when they reached Lloyds Bank corner they encountered a disturbance. Joe said that at first he didn't know what was going on. He saw a crowd of about fifteen but didn't know what was occurring at that time. Joe said he started towards the group and saw Wayne fall out from the crowd but his view was obstructed as to how he fell or why. Joe said he speeded up, telling Kate to 'stay put' and when he reached the other side of the road he saw Jason being pinned against the wall of Tile Flare by MB. Joe said he did not know MB as such, he had spoken to him before but really only knew of him by reputation. Amazingly, he was not asked to explain that remark. He was asked what MB had been wearing that night and replied that he didn't make a point of noticing what men were wearing.

When asked about the assault on Jason, Joe said that MB was shouting into Jason's face and that G was shouting what sounded like encouragement at MB. Joe was asked to describe G and gave the usual description, shaved head, goatee beard. Joe went on to say that when he saw Jason against the wall he stepped forwards to help him but as he got close MB turned and walked towards him causing Joe to step backwards, tripping over the curb as he went and to fall to the ground. Joe recalled MB standing over him and the expectation of feeling a boot in his face but Kate had joined the fracas and had got in between him and MB. He did not actually see MB kick Kate in the face, though he heard MB and G shouting. Joe said his attention was caught by other events. He had looked to his right and seen Dan on the floor. Joe went on to explain how he got up and hurried over to where Dan was lying. He could see it was serious. He remembered sitting in the gutter with Dan's head in his lap. There was a lot of shouting for an ambulance. He did not know what else happened that night as he was too busy concentrating on Dan and thought he was probably in shock.

Cross-examined, Joe said he did see Wayne in The Showboat for a couple of seconds and noticed that he had a marked face. He also said he had seen JP for a moment. He was asked how much he had drunk that night and then asked why he had only drunk such a small quantity of alcohol during such a long evening, 'Was he a slow drinker' were the actual words (the defendants' solicitors were so sarcastic all the time). Joe explained that he and Dan had been playing snooker in the Somerville Club and that you need to be sober to play well. Obviously all the interrogations were a lot more repetitive than I have written in this book but I don't want to bore the reader too much with detail. Every witness was questioned closely about the clothes and appearance of the three suspects. Everyone's alcohol intake seemed to be of particular interest to the defence as was where the witnesses were standing and whom they had seen at the time. Everyone seemed to have viewed the event from a slightly different angle and there were a few glaring discrepancies, but everyone seemed to agree on the basics points on issue. Who struck the blows and who egged on the assaults. I was starting to get a clear picture of the evening's events and wondered how Dan was feeling about the whole thing.

We broke for lunch. The lunch hour was peppered with the usual problem of where to go that wouldn't mean we had to sit in the company of the alleged assailants. So we headed out of the court and down into the town centre to a pub with outside seating and a cheap and cheerful bar menu. Staying all together at all times gave the witnesses confidence and it certainly made me feel more comfortable. We made a point of not discussing the happenings at court, which wasn't easy to do. It must have been frustrating for the witnesses yet to testify not to be able to ask what it was like at least. It was very strange sitting outside a pub downtown at midday whilst in the middle of a court case. Everything seemed a little surreal.

The afternoon came and the next in the hot seat was Rachel who is short and slim, about five foot four or five inches, with very dark hair and heavy-looking eyes. She was probably about eighteen or nineteen. I remembered seeing her at the hospital on 31st May with a very swollen eye.

At the time Rachel, who comes from the Midlands, was at

Bristol University. She speaks with a very heavy Birmingham accent, which I found hard to follow. She is, however, a very straightforward young lady, honest and upfront. She said she had arrived at The Showboat with Gary and Wayne, in Gary's van. Gary parked round the corner from The Showboat, although she didn't know the name of the road. Wayne went on ahead and she waited for Gary to lock his van. As they approached Lloyds Bank, she saw Wayne with 'some chap'. The 'chap' was a lot taller than Wayne. Rachel couldn't, however, remember much about him, neither did she hear what they were saying. As they passed, Gary asked Wayne if he was okay and Wayne said 'Yes.' She supposed because they kept walking although she didn't actually hear the reply, probably because she had already drunk, by her own admission, six or seven Southern Comforts with lemonade. Rachel said that she then went into The Showboat and met up with her then boyfriend Jason. She had three or four pints of cider. When she left The Showboat she was heading for the Southern Fried Chicken. The rest was, not surprisingly, a blur. She remembered Sarah saying Dan had been hit and saw Sarah start to run after 'three chaps', thought better of the pursuit and returned to Dan. Rachel did not recognise the three men. She said she remembered f—ing and blinding at the taller of the group and that he struck her. She said that Jason had sat her on the curb for her own safety and that she had stayed there until Dan was taken away in an ambulance.

Rachel was cross-examined and the defence kept harping on about the amount of alcohol she had drunk, accusing her of being a heavy drinker. Rachel was asked if she was drunk that night and she said no. MB's solicitor gave a slimy grin and said, 'Are you telling me that you consumed that much alcohol and do not consider yourself drunk. What would you call your condition?' Rachel replied, honestly, that she was paralytic. Which caused a bit of hilarity. She also said that she couldn't remember much because of her condition. Her honesty shone through.

Dan's then girlfriend, Sarah, was next to take the stand, after Rachel had her testimony read back to her and she had signed it.

Sarah is about five foot six inches tall, slim with long, straight, light blonde hair. She has a very pale complexion, a tiny nose and large blue eyes. Sarah was also eighteen and from the Midlands but has a softer version of Rachel's accent. Rachel and Sarah were at this time at university together in Bristol doing the same course.

145

Sarah said she was in The Showboat on Gloucester Road and listed who was with her. She wasn't familiar with everyone there that night as she was fairly new to Bristol. Sarah said she had arrived about 10.30 with Joe, Dan and Kate and had previously been in the Somerville club from 6.30ish. She said that she and Dan, who was her boyfriend, had intended to go for a curry after they left The Showboat. Sarah said she was a bit slow leaving the pub because she was talking just inside the door. So when she reached the fracas Wayne was already on his knees with his head in his hands and Babe was walking towards him. She watched as Dan also walked towards Wayne from a different angle. She saw Dan step over the chain link fence round the side of the tile shop and walked over to where Wayne was kneeling. Then a man who she did not know said, 'It's got nothing to do with you,' and the man's fist hit Dan on the right cheek. When challenged by the defence solicitor she said she saw the punch connect. Asked to describe who punched Dan she could only give a rough description, she said about five foot seven inches so it couldn't have been MB, the height wasn't right. Sarah continued by saying that when Dan fell he was pole axed and she assumed he was unconscious when he hit the floor. There appeared to be several people closer than she was but Sarah said her view was not obstructed. Asked who these people were she said she did not notice who they were as she was too concerned about Dan. She said she thought John, the security man from The Showboat, carried Wayne towards the pub.

When cross-examining Sarah, the defence was very keen to get her to change her mind about the height of the assailant she had seen strike Dan, but she would not budge. There was a lot of to and fro about this man's height. Sarah said he was shorter than Dan. So this led to a discussion about Dan's height and I piped up that Dan is five foot ten inches. The solicitors for H were trying to make it look like Sarah had mistaken H for MB. Because they were from out of town neither Sarah nor Rachel had ever seen any of the alleged assailants before that day which is why a police identity parade had been a necessity. Sarah said she thought there were people closer to the heart of the incident than her but she could only remember Babe who was concerned with Wayne. Sarah said Wayne was about ten feet away.

If the prosecution had been able to ask Sarah if she saw the man who hit Dan in that room that day I bet she would have picked out

H because I watched her face when she first caught sight of him. Unfortunately, I could not ask Sarah if H was the man at this time! The lack of a police line-up was really starting to worry me.

Wednesday, 6 November

The third day. The group was all assembled as usual. There were a couple of extras today, One being Isabelle's then boyfriend, now husband, yet another Jason. Daniel and Richard had both decided not to attend today's proceedings, Dan had heard enough and was finding it all a bit distressing, which was understandable but I was there of course. Isabelle was first for the torture today. She knew everyone because she used to work in The Showboat public house.

Isabelle was maybe nineteen or twenty and is about five foot eight inches, well built but not fat with fair hair to just below her ears. She has a pretty round face with rosy cheeks, clear eyes, and an easy smile.

Isabelle explained how she had been with friends in The Showboat and then had gone to The John Cabot, returning to The Showboat about 10.30 where she saw Wayne and observed that he had a black eye. She said that she had seen Wayne earlier and he did not have a black eye at that time. She had apparently left The Showboat at about 11.15, heading for the Southern Fried Chicken takeaway, walking with a friend called Alice. Isabelle said that she did not reach the takeaway. She saw at some point MB pass her going in the other direction; she turned to see where he was going and saw him strike Wayne near the tile shop. Isabelle said she was about thirty feet away when MB hit Wayne and that there was no one in front of her to obscure her view. She said that she had definitely seen MB thump Wayne in the face and watched as Wayne subsequently fell to the floor. There was a lot of shouting, mainly by MB and Babe. Isabelle said she heard Babe shout, 'Leave him alone!' When asked she said that although she knew MB and G, she did not know H before that evening, although she knew of him. Isabelle said she used to live and work in The Showboat and had been warned about H. He was a friend of MB's and MB was banned, as he was from most local pubs. Isabelle said that later she saw H hit Dan. He punched him in the face; she saw it connect and Dan fall. She went to The Showboat to call an ambulance and stayed there until it came. She explained that she used to work in The Showboat and was good with faces and names and she knew she could not mix these people up at all. Isabelle was adamant that she knew who G and MB were even if she did not know H and added that MB was over six foot tall and slim where as G and H were both stocky and a lot shorter. She was sure that it was not G or MB she saw hit Dan that night, she knew who those two were. She said yes when asked if MB was the tallest. She said he was one of the tallest of everyone there that night. Asked if she saw H prior to the assault and she said yes and explained that all three had been in The Showboat at about nine o'clock for a couple of minutes, before they were asked to leave.

The defence was very keen to confuse Isabelle as she had made some quite damaging remarks about the defendants. They did, in fact, manage to make the poor girl cry before she left the stand much to the assailants' amusement. Isabelle had been the most nervous of all the witnesses, as she felt vulnerable because she knew so much about the defendants. I was beginning to wonder who was on trial here. The witnesses were upset and the defendants were having a great time. Our barrister was not very forthright.

It appears that the tape had broken towards the end of the cross-examination of Isabelle so we had to have a break and the next day the solicitors and barrister planned to get together and reconstruct the missing part. So Isabelle was told that she would have to come back the next day and have her statement clarified. She left the court in tears and I was glad that her boyfriend was waiting outside. She was not looking forward to having to return the next day though I felt she had been a very good witness. The two defendants seemed to take a great deal of pleasure out of watching the female witnesses squirm under the pressure. They both spent the whole time smiling at each other, looking totally unruffled by the whole experience. I felt as though they were privy to some information that the rest of us did not have. As time went on I understood their confidence. The defence, realising that the witnesses were honest and unshakeable, were building on the possibility that G was the second man and not H, thus throwing the whole case into confusion. I assumed at this time that MB's cocky exterior was based on the 'one out, all out' theory, thinking they could not condemn one if they cleared the other. I very much hoped I was wrong but I had a very bad feeling about the whole thing.

The next witness was Kate who was eighteen and about five

foot six inches, with a shock of red curly hair that really hits you. Kate had the kind of hair that was everyone's dream; it is splendid. She has pale skin and brown eyes. She is a slim, striking-looking young woman who speaks very clearly and is very articulate.

Kate explained how she had gone to the Somerville Club at about 7.30 and left about 10.30 p.m. with Dan, Sarah and Joe. Then they had gone to The Showboat to join Babe and Wayne, who, she noticed, had a swollen face.

Kate said she left The Showboat at about 11.15, coming out with a crowd of people. Kate said she had walked with Joe and was aware of Wayne being behind them. They reached the tile shop and heard something going on behind them. Kate said she heard Wayne shouting and another voice. She did not hear exactly what was being said, but knew that MB was shouting at Wayne. Kate said she was standing with several people on the corner of the pavement but had not taken notice of who they were, except Wayne and MB. When asked how she knew MB's name she said she had known who MB was for about eight months to a year through The Showboat but was definitely not a friend of his.

Kate continued by saying that she had seen and heard MB shouting at Wayne for a short time, then she saw MB hit Wayne with his fist several times. She walked towards them and saw MB punch Wayne twice again. She saw both punches connect and Wayne went down. She said she was by the tile shop with friends around her at the time. Then next she remembered seeing MB standing by Rachel. She saw him pull back his fist to punch Rachel but did not see the punch connect. Then she just saw Rachel's head jerk back. Kate told how she had seen Babe try to separate MB from Rachel but he pushed Babe and she fell on Rachel.

Next she said she saw MB holding Jason against the window of the tile shop by the neck. Kate went on to say how she turned and saw someone else on the floor with MB standing over him but that she was not aware it was Joe until she ran over. Realising it was her friend Joe she screamed, 'No,' and hit MB in the face to prevent him kicking Joe. Kate went on to say that she then knelt by Joe, looked up at MB and he called her a bitch, kicking her in the face as he spoke. Needless to say Kate said it hurt a lot and was swollen and bruised for several days but fortunately an X-ray showed that no bones were broken.

Kate, on being questioned, said that she knew prior to the events of that evening who H, MB and G were. G, because he was at the time going out with a friend's sister. She also made a point of making it clear that she did not, however, socialise with any of them. They were the sort of people who were known and whom you were polite to because of their reputation.

Kate continued her detailed account of 31 May 1996. She said she had seen Dan start towards MB and that MB had gone across and pushed Dan over the rails round Tile Flare. Dan broke his fall and got up. She explained how well the area was lit with lighting above the cash points on the side of Lloyds Bank and high lamp style lighting round Tile Flare, as well as street lighting, so it was very easy to get a clear picture of events that night even though it was late in the evening.

Kate went on to say how after she had been kicked she had turned round to see if Wayne was okay and when she turned back she saw Dan fall and hit his head on the edge of the curb but she had not seen who knocked Dan down.

Kate described a large pool of blood that was appearing where Dan had fallen. Joe was hysterical and insisted on nursing his brother's head in his lap, getting himself covered in blood. It took quite a lot of persuasion to get Joe to move so that Kate and Sarah could put Dan in the recovery position.

Cross-examination was very brief. Kate had been so precise and clear in her evidence that the defence commented on this fact. Clutching at straws, they asked Kate what she had drunk and she said she had only had a couple of halves so they dropped that line. (They could have picked up on the fact that most of Kate's evidence was out of sequence – the part with Babe and Rachel. I believe this was a little later than Kate described, actually when the men were walking away from the scene.)

The next witness for the day, but not until after lunch, was going to be a young man I had seen briefly talking to the police after the incident. He had not been in the hospital on the evening of the drama and did not know many of the other witnesses prior to the court hearing. His name was Michael. Michael looks about twenty-four and very like a bank a manager. He is about five foot eight inches, quite well built, wearing a double breasted suit that fitted him as if it was his usual apparel; it looked right on him. He had a good head of dark hair and wore glasses. He looked like he spoke; intelligent, articulate and mature. You could tell by looking at him that if he had actually seen anything he would give a good and clear account. He should have looked tired that day because he had driven all night up and back to Leeds but he looked fine. Apparently Jason, who was at Leeds University, had not been contacted and he was needed as a witness. So Joe and Michael had decided to drive up to Leeds and do what the police didn't seem able to do, tell Jason he was needed in court and bring him to Bristol. This is exactly what they had done that day.

There was a break for lunch, the youngsters went off together and I decided to wonder about alone for a while to clear my head and read over the notes that I had made that day in court. I got back before the crowd, and H and MB were sitting on one of the benches. I purposely sat next to them and was joined quite quickly by the victim support lady, Wendy, who wanted me to change seats. I said out loud that I wouldn't as I was fascinated watching MB read the *Sun*. I said loudly that I didn't think he would be able to read anything that intellectual. MB just sneered at me. I didn't want these people to think I was afraid of them and, strangely enough, I wasn't.

MB and H got up and went into the court. The victim support lady went to get us both a cup of tea. I sat alone for a short time and then the two defence solicitors came out, talking to the lady prosecutor. They were laughing and joking. Another solicitor or barrister walked by. He clearly knew the group and asked how things were going. MB's solicitor joked that MB was sure to walk as he was obviously innocent and everyone laughed. I stood up and asked the solicitor if he would find it so amusing if his own son was blinded by a yob like MB and he said he had not meant to offend me. I replied that it was too late, he had. The lady prosecutor later told me that the solicitors were nice men really. I said that I rather doubted that. I could not then, and I still cannot, understand how anyone could fight tooth and nail to get obviously guilty people off any charge. I firmly believe that every unpunished crime is an insult to the law-abiding people in the world.

Everyone started to gather again for the afternoon session and Michael was sworn in. This afternoon I appeared to be the only person in the public gallery; this didn't bother me, I just continued to take notes throughout, breaking off occasionally to stare at H to try to unnerve him a little.

Michael began by saying that he had been at The Showboat that evening with his fiancée, Serena, two other young women and Brian, who had already given evidence. He had not been drinking. He said he left at about 10.30 with Serena to take a friend of hers home. He had gone back to The Showboat to give a phone number to the doorman who was also called Mike. He had returned about eleven o'clock and had gone into The Showboat, leaving Serena and her friend Linda in the car. Michael said he gave the phone number to Mike, returned to his car and started the engine when he saw a disturbance in his rear-view mirror. Michael said he could see that someone had Jason by the throat against a wall outside the tile shop. Michael recalled that the man holding Jason was taller than Jason and wore a checked shirt and black trousers. Michael then got out of the car and walked towards the group to join Babe, Brian and JP. He said there had been about ten people in all. Wayne was laying on the floor. Michael only knew him as Wayne at that time. Michael observed that Wayne was rather battered. Then he saw a man waving his arms about – he was around five foot nine inches with short hair and a goatee beard – he was also wearing black trousers and a brown checked shirt. He was shouting about people messing with someone's girlfriend. This man then walked up to Dan and punched him. Michael said he had seen Dan fall and hit his head on the road, his arms staying at his side. There were other people whom he did not recognise but he saw that Brian was quite near. Michael said he heard Dan's head crack as it hit the floor (a little bit more information than I needed to hear). Dan's assailant had then stepped over Dan, and Michael saw two girls run after him and the assailant shoved one of them. Michael was then asked if the same person who held Jason hit Dan, and Michael said no. Michael went on to say that the two violent men later walked up Gloucester Road with a third person he did not know.

Michael said that the police had shown him a checked shirt at the station when he made his original statement; it was a brown checked one with red in it. Michael said he identified it as being very like the one that Dan's assailant was wearing that evening.

The defence nearly buried themselves. First they asked Michael if he had been drinking and he had not, so they moved on to insinuate that Michael's eyesight was bad because he wore glasses. Asked why he wore glasses, Michael said he had a lazy left eye. The solicitor for the accused then suggested that in that case he was only seeing clearly from one eye. Michael was quite definite in replying to that ridiculous suggestion and explained that because he wore the glasses it did in fact correct his problem and he saw perfectly. The prosecution then made a big thing out of how late at night it was and Michael explained that the lighting in that spot made it like daylight. He explained the lighting much in the same way that Kate had. Then they picked on the point about the shirt being shown to Michael at the police station and Michael explained that he had already given his statement to the police and described the shirt before it had been shown to him. The solicitor jumped on this, exclaiming how come there was a mention of the fact that Michael was shown the shirt in his original police statement. Michael then said that if the solicitor read the statement clearly he would see that actually halfway through his statement he had described the shirt. He was then shown it and asked if this was the one and had he seen it that evening. Michael said he had told the police that it was very similar if not the actual shirt. It was like some strange point scoring game that happily at this moment Michael seemed to be winning hands down. Then the defence wanted to know why it had taken Michael a week to make his statement. Michael explained that he had given his phone number to police on the scene and they had said they would be in touch. In fact, they did not get in touch with him for nearly a week and Michael adding that he would have been more than willing to have made his statement sooner had he been contacted. It was then suggested that he would have discussed the matter with others in the week prior to making his statement but Michael said that he did not really know the rest of the witnesses at the time, only Brian. He did, however, add that he had only discussed it briefly with his fiancée who was, unfortunately, a witness, so I knew they would make something out of that.

Michael was told to step down. He had been an excellent witness and I liked him a lot. He had held up very well considering how tired he must have been having just got back from Leeds with Jason in tow. Jason was someone that the defence seemed worried about and the prosecution badly wanted though I found it amazing that despite this fact, the police had made no effort at all to fetch him themselves. Jason was very tired and, unfortunately, was the next in line for the third degree.

Jason is a coloured lad of eighteen, about five foot six inches tall and very slim with very short black hair. He had been at The

Showboat with several people that he knew on the night of 31 May. He had arrived at about 6 p.m. and left just after 11 p.m. He had only drunk three pints of Budweiser all evening due to the financial restrains of being a university student. Jason said that he and Daniel had gone outside the pub just after eleven to wait outside for their respective girlfriends and then head for the takeaway. Jason continued to explain his movements by saying that he and Dan had sat in front of the tile shop display window on the metal uprights that the chains hung on forming a sort of small courtyard round the large picture window. The tile shop is past the Lloyds Bank and next to The Showboat and over a road called Dongola Avenue on the same side of the Gloucester Road. He explained that you cannot actually see the pub from this point as The Showboat is set back off the road hidden from view by the bank. He remembered Brian sitting behind them balancing on the wooden trim at the bottom of the window. They sat there for a short time. The pub started to turn out and some people he knew had passed them and were on their way to the take away and there were others following behind. Jason went on to say that as Wayne came walking along, MB, G and H appeared and approached Wayne. It seemed that MB and his pals had come from the direction of the takeaway, walking up the Gloucester Road towards The Showboat. Wayne was about three or four yards away at this time. Jason said he knew MB. He had known of him longer but only started speaking to him about six months prior to the incident. Jason said he had heard of H but had not spoken to him. He said that G made up the trio that night and that he had known him for about six months as well and had spoken to him before.

Jason went on to say that MB had grabbed Wayne with both hands by the collar pushing him backwards. Wayne had said something like, 'What's going on?' MB and H were both shouting for Wayne to stay away from someone called Louise, and said that they hadn't taught him a good enough lesson earlier. Jason said he saw H try to head butt Wayne but MB pushed Wayne back and H struck fresh air instead. Jason then heard MB say, 'Stay out of this, it isn't your fight!' Several punches were rained on Wayne, and Dan was fidgeting uncomfortably and at that point stood up. Jason said that he warned Dan against getting involved because H and MB were not people to mess with. Jason said that Dan told him he did not know any of the three men who were hassling Wayne. Dan sat back down for a few moments but when he saw that no one else appeared to be going to Wayne's defence he stood up and went over and asked what was going on. Jason said he saw Dan bend down to help Wayne to his feet, saying something like 'enough is enough' and that was when H hit him. Jason said that H came from behind Wayne slightly and just leapt forwards and struck Dan an uppercut to the jaw and Dan went down. Jason said it was a right-hand uppercut. He could not have been mistaken because it happened right in front of him. Jason said that he did not see Dan get up. The prosecutor should have asked if Jason thought it possible that Dan might have got up from such a punch and more importantly where Dan had landed to establish whether we are talking about the first punch that took place or the near fatal one, but they didn't. Obviously it had to be the first punch and Dan did foolishly get up. There was a lot of palaver about where everyone was standing, I understood exactly what Jason was saying but the bench seemed to have a problem with it. I think that they understood perfectly well and that they just wanted to wind Jason up a little which unfortunately they managed to do.

Jason continued by saying that he saw MB hit Wayne again several times and that he clearly saw the punches connect. Jason said he watched as Wayne got to his feet but stumbled and fell again. At this point Jason decided that he should help Dan but was himself held by his throat against the wall of the tile shop by MB. MB told Jason to stay away from his girlfriend. Jason said he did not reply because he realised that the assailants had completely lost the plot by now. MB let him go and turned round, he pushed someone over the chains of the tile shop, he did not know who. Then he saw Joe on the ground and MB looked like he had him pinned. Jason said he then went over to Wayne who was lying on the floor trying to get up. He saw Wayne get to his feet, take a couple of steps and fall. All the time G appeared to be standing against the window of the tile shop, shouting encouragement but not actually participating in the violence. Jason said he had been very shocked by the violence he had encountered that evening and had gone to the hospital with the injured out of concern.

Cross-examining, the defence wanted to know if three pints could have affected his memory and Jason said, 'Hardly.' The defence expressed a doubt that Jason had only had three pints over such a long period but Jason went on to explain that he only had

£10 that night and he bought a packet of cigarettes as well so he could only afford three pints. Asked if anyone had bought him any other drinks that evening, he said they had not because in his financial position he could not afford to return the compliment so he always refused if offered. Once again the defence suggested that maybe Jason had confused G and H but Jason said he knew H from school and would not mistake him for anyone else. They tried generally to discredit Jason's statement by picking up on the fact that he was held against the wall after Dan had been struck. No suggestion was made by the prosecution that maybe there were at least two punches laid on Dan. The solicitor for H described Jason as hostile and with an attitude. I think he was tired, scared and had taken a dislike to the solicitor, which I could quite understand.

I think that Jason's statement was pretty close to what happened that night. I think he was sitting with Dan where he said, with a good view. He saw what happened to Wayne and saw Dan step forwards and be struck by H. No one asked him if Daniel was pole axed or if he put his arms out to break his fall. If Dan did the latter then the statement makes sense completely. Obviously there was a second punch that knocked Dan out. Joe himself had said that he looked to the right and saw Dan on the floor. I do not think even MB could be in two places at once so I think H placed a second punch to Dan's head causing him to fall unconscious and crack his head on the pavement. I remembered how shocked Sarah looked when she first saw H. I believe she recognised him, she too had only seen one man and one punch. I believe that, as the two men, regardless of the same haircuts, same clothes and same beards, actually look nothing like each other, in height, build or physically, Sarah would have picked H out at a line-up. I watched her face, she looked at MB but didn't flicker; she looked at H and gasped. At the time I could not ask her without compromising the case but obviously I did speak about it afterwards and she confirmed my thoughts.

Also Jason's account puts Brian in the exact spot he said he was in so he could very easily have seen two punches? Medical evidence said there had been two prime punches to the face as there were only two obvious bruises, one on Dan's chin and the other on his temple.

Everyone went home that afternoon, looking thoroughly drained. At least we did not have to run the gauntlet of the accused any more. A complaint had made the police arrange for MB and H to use a different exit point. This didn't stop anyone encountering these dreadful people on their way to court of course or in the lunchtime.

Thursday, 7 November

Today was Serena's turn for the Spanish Inquisition. Serena was, and I believe still is, engaged to Michael. She is about five foot seven or eight inches – slim, with long, very dark, curly hair tied back. Pale skin and smartly dressed, she spoke very nicely.

Serena's evidence was much a mirror of Michael's only she had watched from inside the car so her view was obscured. This point alone made her an easy target for the prosecution council. I do not really know why Serena was picked as a witness. The police said there were over thirty witnesses that night and that they had narrowed the field down to thirteen to give evidence. I think I would have dropped Serena as well. All she really did was confirm that Michael had returned to The Showboat, when and why. Also that Rachel and Babe had been struck and bounced off Michael's car. Serena did, however, offer a good insight into how frightened everyone had appeared to be on that night, and how reluctant the majority of those gathered appeared to be to approach the three 'wild' men.

The last witness for the prosecution was Linda. Linda is a hysterical type who lives on her nerves. She was in shock at the scene and had seen very little. I would have expected the girls with heavy involvement to be shocked. Linda's evidence did not lend any weight to the prosecution. I can't imagine why she was brought in to give evidence for the prosecution. I thought that it was very cruel to put someone as highly strung through such an ordeal especially as she had seen very little. We had to wait for the rereading of the statement by Linda then we all left to go to lunch, having been told to return at about 2.15 for the verdict. Would this go to Crown Court or not? I wasn't keen to rush back for this part of the proceedings as I had a horrible feeling that H might have got off and MB landed with the whole thing. If that happened I doubted there would have been a conviction at Crown Court.

I didn't hurry back and actually arrived just as everyone was coming out of the courtroom. Thank heavens, the case was referred to Crown Court.

Although the police had brought up the fact that MB had hung about outside Wayne's house to intimidate him and had gone to Babe's place of work with his charming mother to shout abuse at her and try to frighten her, both men got bail. MB, who was on an insulting £1,100 bail, was not to come to Bristol. And H, whose grandmother has put up her house as £50,000 bail was to report to Southmead Police Station every Saturday. H actually had the cheek to say he was in fear of his life from witnesses and wanted protection from me. I am four foot eleven inches tall for goodness sake!

So now we had to wait again for the real court date – we were told that it would probably be in March or April 1997.

Unbelievably, we all left court by the same exit again. Most of the witnesses were crying, there was no police presence at all. MB and H pushed through the group, muttering threats of violence and laughing once again. They seemed very confident that they would walk free. I was not at all impressed with the prosecutor we had been given. She was a very pretty, young-looking blonde who appeared to make no attempt whatsoever to cross-examine in a positive way. The only time I thought she was any good was when she mentioned casually that the defendants had been up before her on a previous occasion, so the judge would know that they were not innocent young men snatched off the street at random. It had been a harrowing experience for these young people and I was very proud of each and everyone of them. They had experienced an ordeal that I hope they would never face again. Being in a courtroom certainly was an eye-opener for me. Everyone who was a witness now appeared to be firm friends, fused together by the night of May 31.

I think we all went home quite relieved that day, believing that justice might actually be done. I phoned home to tell Dan what had happened, went for a drink with the crowd and then went home, tired but happy with the day's events.

Goodbye to Sarah

My family and I needed to get back to some semblance of normality if we were going to get Dan well again. It was hard not to dwell on the thirty witnesses mentioned by the police and not to speculate why so many people would have allowed such a thing to happen as that which happened to my son. Fear, too much alcohol, who knows why some people will put themselves on the line and others only watch. At court I had taken notes throughout and had spent hours sorting them out in my mind. There had been so many muddled points but it seems that everyone had seen one moment clearly and I was trying to fit these moments together like a jigsaw. The whole sequence of events kept going round and round in all of our minds and we needed to put our energies into something different.

So as a result 30 November was party night. With the Magistrates' Court ordeal behind us all we decided to throw a big party in the Somerville Club. Joe and Adam decided to try to raise some money towards the talking software that Dan would need for the computer he had just received in place of the machine that was stolen. So we decided to make this party a fund raising event. We knew that Dan needed £1,800 and that Dan could not get a grant because he was living with his father and I. Grants are means tested.

Joseph is a musician and said he could get quite a good band together. Kate's parents, Sue and Tim, are both semi-professional musicians. Sue has the most beautiful voice I have ever heard. They sing and play mostly Irish folk and sixties' style protest songs but they can perform any style of music brilliantly, having the talent to be able to play several instruments. So with this talented couple playing guitar and flute, Joe on electric piano, Wayne on another guitar plus a cousin of Tim's, we had a winning combination. They didn't have much time to rehearse so it was more like a large jam session than an actual band.

The Somerville Club was more than keen to provide the venue

to celebrate getting Dan back alive. I organised raffles, writing to everyone I could think of and received some really uplifting replies. I wrote to a couple of top Bristol restaurants. Michael's Restaurant sent me a beautifully worded reply and tickets for a free meal for two. Sealey's reply amazed me. The sons of the proprietor had only just taken over the running of the hotel and restaurant due to the sudden death of their father, followed almost immediately by their mother, and yet they still took the time to be kind to us and help our cause. Hearing from people like that certainly lifted my spirits a little. I was beginning to think that the world had gone quite mad.

I bullied long time regular members of the club to let me borrow baby photographs and I made booklets to sell on the evening. The idea was obviously for people to guess who the photographs were of. I also printed out quiz sheets to be bought and filled in during the evening.

It was a brilliant evening. I have never seen so many people in the club before. Everyone wanted to contribute to the evening so there was no shortage of volunteers to sell quiz sheets or raffle tickets. Clive Beckingham, the friend who had helped clear Dan's flat, volunteered to have his thick, almost shoulder-length hair cut off, donations per snip. He ended up almost a skinhead but you had to admire his nerve. Isabelle, who used to be a hairdresser, tidied up the end product and we videoed the whole event.

We raised a very large amount of money but at the end of the day Daniel decided that he wanted to donate the money to Bristol Royal Institute for the Blind as he felt they would make good use of it. Adam managed to get the then TSB to double the amount we raised and we arranged a presentation evening for a couple of weeks later.

We have organised several other musical fundraising events since, usually in the Somerville Club, but none as successful as that one. We also do occasional charity quiz nights and Adam ran the Bath half marathon for the BRIB. Things we would probably not even have considered doing before the assault.

Christmas was a strange one that year. It was wonderful to all be together but difficult. It was Dan's first Christmas since losing his sight and the little ones' first Christmas as a split family. We were all determined to try to make the event a good one. After all we had been blessed with the return of Dan so we had something to celebrate. Sarah had wanted to have Dan go home with her at

Christmas but he was too scared and insecure to be away from home so soon. I told her it was too soon. I did make a compromise and took him up halfway to Kings-Winford and handed him over to Sarah for the New Year. Unfortunately, Dan was feeling sick and was apparently sick several times before they reached Sarah's house. I think it was pure nerves. I ended up fetching him back the next day and I think that was the beginning of the end of Sarah and Dan as a couple. She had been very supportive when Dan needed her most but I could tell that she was finding the new Dan difficult to cope with. She was, after all, very young. Dan had no real short-term memory, or a memory at all, of the months prior to the incident, including, unfortunately, actually going out with Sarah. I suppose on reflection he didn't even really know who she was or what she looked like. Dan was at this time a sleepy, clumsy, forgetful young man. He had a long way to go before he would be really fit and even I didn't realise how long it would take although I had been warned.

My birthday was on 13 January, a date I share with Kate. A large group of us, including Sarah, Kate and her parents went to what was my favourite pub, The Station House at Hallatrow for a meal to celebrate this joint event. The Station House is like a huge junk shop inside. There are weird and wonderful articles hanging from every part of the ceiling and from the walls. You could spend hours just looking about and taking it all in. It has great food and a really good atmosphere. It has changed hands recently and unfortunately been tidied up a bit, nothing stays the same.

Sarah was behaving very strangely and refused to sit next to Daniel. Dan was obviously not very accomplished in the art of eating as yet; eating in the dark is not easy! At home I was placing his food in the form of a clock, meat at three o'clock, potatoes at six, and so on. However when you eat out a great effort is made out of making the food look pretty and the plates are cluttered. So Dan could not be sure if he wanted to eat what was on his plate until it was in his mouth, and finding his mouth wasn't his greatest skill at that time either. Dan had lost his sense of taste and smell as well as his sight, so the texture of food played a big part in his enjoyment or dislike of certain foods. Apparently everything tasted like chicken according to Dan. I spent ages sorting out Dan's dinner and taking off the plates anything I knew he wouldn't eat through choice. I do not think Sarah was too enamoured by this palaver and

The Warning

It was 28 January 1997 and Joseph was walking home from The Showboat with Kate and was suddenly aware that two men were following them. Joe was literally a few yards from his home but decided to keep walking as he felt there might be a problem and did not want these people to know where he lived, fearing for his small sons. These men were arguing as to whether Joe was the person they wanted and when they were parallel with the young couple, they decided Joe was in fact who they wanted and without warning, head butted him, breaking his nose.

The men walked away still asking each other if they had hit the right person and making sure that Kate and Joe knew where they were from. We took this to mean that it was a warning of some sort connected to the pending court case.

Kate screamed after the men, asking them if maybe everyone in their neck of the woods shared just one brain cell and that enough was enough. She couldn't really remember exactly what she shouted, she was so angry and a little scared that violence was going to be a way of life from now on.

I received a phone call at 11.30 that evening from Joe asking me to take him to Southmead Accident Department as someone had broken his nose. I hurried to Joe's house to be told that a friend with a car had called and taken him to the hospital, so I drove up there to join them. The staff at Southmead Hospital saw Joe quite quickly, after about an hour's wait and said it was too swollen to mend. They gave him painkillers and said they would make an appointment for him in a couple of days' time to come to the Hospital for reassessment and resetting. Joe is not an easy patient and he was pacing about all the time, obviously very annoyed and in a lot of pain.

The following Tuesday, 4 February, Joe went with his father to the outpatients. It needed a proper operation to correct the damage to Joe's nose as it was a nasty break, so they rescheduled for the following Tuesday for Joe to have the operation.

163

At 8.30 on 11 February, I took Joe to register that he had arrived, and then on to Ward U at Southmead Hospital. Kate came with me and stayed with Joe all day, leaving only for a short time whilst he actually had the operation. He had the operation at 3.30 p.m. and I collected him and brought him back home at nine o'clock the next day, taking little Rick in with me. Rick was most concerned that if his Dad was in hospital like Uncle Dan had been, he might not be able to see when he got back home! I felt that showing him that his dad was perfectly fine and that blindness was not the outcome of every hospital visit was the best plan and little Rick was obviously relieved. After I collected Joe from the hospital, I took the little ones home again with me to give Joe a chance to recover from the operation. His face looked very sore.

I was beginning to wonder if life was ever going to get back to any semblance of normality again. I felt as if we were all in the middle of a 'B' movie; it was a little scary to realise how much your life could change from an average family to living through an episode of *The Godfather*, all in a matter of months.

I had thought that 1996 had been the very worst year of my life and that it would be impossible to ever experience a year like that again and stay sane. When I think back on 1996 the words 'stop the world I want to get off' spring to mind. Now we were into 1997 and life didn't seem to be improving a lot.

Dan was now being taken up and back to the Head Injuries Unit at Frenchay three times a week. We were all trying to fit in work and our normal lifestyles, it wasn't easy. Dan was getting stronger, which was something.

We had all been affected by Dan's plight, not just because we took care of him but emotionally as well. I could cry all the time and found it very difficult not to. I couldn't even be polite to people who I felt were irrelevant to my life now. Work was starting to become a chore when I had always loved working at Cotham. Richard had shaved his thick head of dark hair off. I felt it was a sort of protest. The only good thing about that action was that all the people who could not understand why he still had very little grey in his hair and thought he dyed it could see it was natural. I hated the look of Richard with such short hair. I associated hair that short with the people who injured Dan and I didn't like the constant reminder. Richard said it was just one less thing to think about which is why he did it.

Adam was suffering from mild depression and it was putting a strain on his relationship with Marie. It is strange that a group of people can go through such a harrowing and binding experience together and, as the light at the end of the tunnel starts to show, drift apart. I think the destruction of relationships through temporary personality changes is quite common after major trauma. Coping with your own emotions and having to worry about someone else's as well is not an easy task. It seemed that Adam and Marie were casualties of this syndrome.

Joe was very low all the time and short-tempered. He had put his great love, music, on hold for a while to concentrate on Dan and his young sons. It isn't easy to fulfil your ambitions when you have responsibilities and Joe has a great deal of talent which must be very frustrating. Kate was a real friend to everyone throughout, babysitting or just talking things through. There was a lot of maturity in that young woman.

When you read about incidences you never think beyond the person directly concerned. You never stop to wonder how the family of the victim are coping. Well, I can now tell you from personal experience that they do not cope very well. We were very lucky to be such a close family. Whenever I felt I was drowning my boys were always there to throw the lifeline. In turn when the events of the past year started to get them down their father and I would try to prop them up. But it wasn't easy. We all were able to make allowances for each other's off periods although it was difficult at times. I think we all lost our sense of humour for a while and that is a terrible thing to happen. You need humour in your life to survive. In some ways in those early months Dan got off lightly emotionally because he had no memory of life before the incident. His frustrations started as his memory returned, not that he has even to this day regained all his memories. He certainly still has no knowledge first hand of the events that caused his sight loss, several months previous to that event or several months after.

The Crown Court

It was 28 July 1997, a year to the day that we discovered that Daniel had lost his sight and it was the first day of the intended trial by jury of his assailants. Richard dropped Dan and me outside the court building in Small Street at ten o'clock. It was important that Daniel attended the first day's hearing so the judge and jury could see for themselves what these people had done to him.

The Crown Court is a vast improvement on the Magistrates' Court building. At least you felt that you were safer here. There were proper security guards at the entrance and a scanning device for handbags and so forth.

Once inside the building, having passed through the security system, Dan and I made our way up to the second floor in the lift, to the witness support area. Wayne, JP, Michael (who had brought Wayne down), Brian, Brian's girlfriend and father were all there already, being informed of procedures. Soon after this, Joe and Kate arrived. Babe had been due to give evidence that day as well but was in Tenerife. She was, however, flying back early the next day so she could attend court on Wednesday at a cost of course. This was the first of many cock-ups. Everyone had been given forms to fill in saying when they would be unavailable due to holiday commitments. Babe had said she would be away with her family at this time, so naturally they booked her into appear in court two days before she was due back from her holiday!

My sister, Judy, and my niece, Alex, were in the waiting area much to my surprise. Everyone was very nervous but Wayne was petrified, physically shaking like a leaf. His mum was there and she turned out to be a dinner lady at the school where my sister used to be deputy head. Irrelevant, but it just shows what a small world it is. A detective constable tried to help Wayne get over his nerves but I think he was beyond talking to at that time, he just wanted to be sick. The victim support ladies were all very helpful and pleasant. An ex-teacher of ours at school, Mike Jefferies, was and still is one of their colleagues but was not there that day. He did, however, phone and speak to Dan to wish him luck. It was as it turned out more than luck that we needed.

We were due to be in Court number ten but the case from the previous week had over run and they were summing that up and sentencing that morning so this meant we had to wait. At midday something started to happen. I had been told that it would be best to take Dan in after the jury had been sworn in. Time was needed to explain to them that Dan was an observer and not a witness as he could not remember the incident or even some time prior to it happening. My sister and niece did, however, go in before us and reported what had happened. There was still no jury present but MB and H were in court and the charges were read out – GBH against Wayne, GBH against Daniel, GBH against Kate, affray and two cases of intimidating witnesses. Apparently, the defendants were asked to plead; MB pleaded guilty to one account of GBH against Wayne, and affray. H pleaded not guilty to everything.

Then the defendants' legal people started their appeal. They started quoting all sorts of previous cases of mistaken identity and cases where police line-ups were not carried out going back to the year dot. My sister did not understand where all this was leading but I was pretty sure that I did when she related the events to me later. The case was adjourned until after lunch. We were told to return at two o'clock when they would decide whether to swear in the jury or wait until Wednesday. Nothing could happen until Tuesday, even though Sarah was due down from Birmingham because one of the barristers for the defence had a previous appointment – cock-up number two, though I did wonder if maybe he knew something we did not.

So we all traipsed down the road to a pub that had seating outside (the very pub we used in the breaks during the Magistrates' hearing), had a pint and a sandwich and returned for two o'clock. Dan and I decided to go in this time. We were there for an hour and a half whilst H's barrister waffled on about one case after another where mistaken identity had made conviction unsafe. He read out passages from each of the witnesses' statements. Every witness referred to H by name and a big thing was made out of the fact that only a few witnesses knew this person prior to the case and yet everyone knew the name H. The defence suggested that the remaining witnesses had been told who the person was, thus putting his identity in their minds. If anyone was at such an incident as this and men were behaving in the way that these three were behaving, a natural question at the time would be 'does anyone know who they are?' Obviously Wayne did as he went to school with all three, so did Isabelle because she was a barmaid in a pub they had been banned from. H admitted to being at the scene with MB and G (the third man who was mentioned continuously by the defence) but said he had tried to prevent MB from hitting anyone – absolute rubbish. The judge could not understand why a police line-up had not been arranged to identify who had in fact done what on the evening in question, something I had always asked.

The barrister went on and on about the fact that all three men had goatee beards, shaven heads and were dressed the same so how could anyone in the evening light, be sure who did what? The area was in fact very well lit. Other cases were quoted and the police were asked to produce photographs taken at the time of the three people charged. Originally the third man had been charged with affray but the charge had been withdrawn for some unknown reason. The judge wanted to see the photographs to either prove how much they looked alike or how much they did not – which we will never know because apparently they were lost in the computer system even though they had been asked for on numerous occasions by both defence and prosecution. The judge went off to think things over and returned about fifteen minutes later. By this time it was only Dan and me in the courtroom along with H's aunt or some such woman relative of his. MB's mother was not allowed in due to the harassment charges against her. There were also several press people. Joe and the rest had all gone home having had their days to appear rescheduled. Joe now had to come on Thursday, which was wonderful as he had arranged for Emma to have the day off, Tuesday, his original date to testify, to look after the children whilst he went to court – another cock-up.

I was surprised that Dan wanted to hang about but I think he felt, as I did, that something was in the wind and we would not like it at all! Judge Darwell-Smith returned to the courtroom and began by saying that he felt that the seriousness of the crime was such that a long custodial sentence would be called for but in view of the fact that there had been no line-up and the witnesses had obviously spoken to each other prior to the case, convicting H could only occur if the jury were allowed to hear the evidence without any of the witnesses being able to say his name or indicate who he was. I was most confused. I couldn't see why the witnesses could not simply be asked, 'Can you see this man here in court today?' MB and H do not look alike, MB is six foot two inches and slim, and H is about five foot eight inches and stocky.

There was further discussion by the defence and prosecution about the rights and wrongs of the proceedings. Our barrister, who was the same one we had been given for the Magistrates' Court, was totally useless and made no objections to anything said by the defence and the obvious happened. The judge, in his infinite wisdom, decided that in view of the confusion, H could go home an innocent man. He didn't free him under an unproven cloak but as not guilty. The prosecution barrister didn't even protest that the affray charge should at least stay. She said nothing and H walked. Guilty as hell but as free as a bird. Needless to say Dan and I were furious. MB was taken down to return on Wednesday so the judge could decide his fate. We followed H out of the court and into the corridor. He was outside with an older female relative and as I passed I stopped, looked at him and said, 'I hope you sleep well tonight you little shit,' and walked on. As we banged on through the double doors towards the lift we could hear feet running behind us, it was a detective constable and one of the victim support ladies. The policeman grovelled and apologised, said he knew how I felt and I assured him in no uncertain terms that he did not and left him in no doubt about what I thought about him and the whole police force at that moment. Which in a way I felt sorry about because the detective involved was a decent man and, try as I might not to, I liked him. I was as mad as hell; in fact, I cannot recall ever feeling as furious as I felt that day. I am normally a very even-tempered person, not given to uncontrolled rages. My vocabulary even at this point did not include any heavy swear words. I think my words to H were as ugly as I could be speech wise. The support lady came down in the lift with us obviously very concerned over our distress. It wasn't distress I felt, I felt insulted. I just wanted to get as far away from that place as possible and scream very loud. We knew that we had to reappear on the Wednesday and that MB was going to court accused of everything but Daniel's attack. This, the major reason for going to court in the first place, apparently was not to be mentioned by any of the witnesses as it is now *'irrelevant to the case'*. My son, blind and in a wheelchair, was classed as irrelevant. That made my blood boil. I felt that MB was obviously going to stand up and say that everything he was accused of was not down to him but it was H who has already been let off so he didn't have to defend himself. So there we have it, one continuous cock-up by the police leading to an obviously guilty person going free. Dan is now blind and no one will be made to pay for this. So obviously Dan threw himself down on the pavement fracturing his own head and so forth. It wasn't MB or H after all! I do not think to say I was anger would cover my feelings at that time. I clenched my fist so hard that my nails went into my right palm. Dan was so calm, it amazed me. I thought that maybe as he was still not totally 'with it', it was probably a blessing.

I could understand exactly how Doreen Lawrence must have felt when the five men accused of murdering her boy continued walking about as if nothing has happened. Maybe, and just maybe, they were actually innocent. But these men involved in the incident with Daniel definitely were not.

It seemed amazing to me that anyone ever gets convicted of anything the way the law works in this country. All it seems you have to do is simply go out in a gang dressed the same with the same haircuts and you can commit havoc and mayhem until the cows come home. You can even go down town bragging about your crimes, have thirty witnesses who saw you do them but don't worry no one will convict because you look alike, even if in truth one of your gang includes a two-headed midget. It all seemed very suspect to me that the defence barrister had booked Tuesday off in advance obviously that confident that H would walk. I wondered if everyone but us already knew what the outcome would be. My faith in British justice took one hell of a knock that day.

I phoned Richard to ask him to pick us up, thanking God that he had not been in court. If he had been, I feel sure he would have thrown H out of the nearest window closely followed by the nearest policeman. We drove round to tell Joe. I knew a lot of the witnesses would be there propping each other up and it seemed only fair not to phone them but to tell them in person. We had just arrived and finished relating what had happened prior to the police calling to tell them the same news. Kate was in floods of tears. Wayne was as mad as hell. I knew that no one would have pressed charges if Dan had not been so seriously hurt. All the witnesses were unused to tangling with the law and the thought of doing so appalled and frightened them.

We went home and very soon had a phone call from the Detective Constable in charge begging to be allowed to come round and apologise to Dan personally. I was not very polite, I'm afraid, and he said he would phone again the next day. He also said that the prosecution barrister wanted to come and see us. It seemed pretty clear to me that someone was worried about us looking into police negligence. I intended to phone my solicitor the next day.

Richard's brother, David, and his wife turned up in the early evening. They had been to the cemetery as it was the anniversary of my mother-in-law Marion's, death. It actually seemed quite appropriate timing as we couldn't be feeling any more depressed than we all were.

My Jewish American friend, Sima, had promised to call in for the past few days and was now on her way home to America without saying goodbye, which added to the day's gloom. It probably wouldn't have bothered me under any other circumstances.

Dan, Joe, Kate, Wayne and I all went to the Somerville Club in the evening for a short while. Wayne had calmed down a little by then and was determined to stand up and be counted on Wednesday. Maybe at least we could see MB put inside for a while, though I rather doubted it.

I phoned Dan's solicitor first thing in the morning and he said that the judge could rule on practically anything he wished to as he had that much power. He added that if the judge felt that there should have been a line-up, as clearly there should have, and there wasn't, it was within his power to dismiss the case.

There was a phone call from a press freelance journalist called Howard Wheeler who wanted to come round at three in the afternoon and we agreed to this.

Dan had a MIR scan in the morning at Frenchay. We went into the local pub there for a swift drink before getting back for the press conference.

Howard turned out to be a very nice young man who works for *South West News Services* and sells his stories to whoever wants them. He had a very pleasant young camerawoman with him who took several shots and then left us to get a story together.

During the day the police had contacted most of the witnesses and informed them that they had now been whittled down to nine from thirteen – no explanation was given. They were told that it was intended that the case would start and finish on Wednesday. None of us could quite understand how we were going to swear in a jury and get through nine people's evidence in one day. To me it smelt of a deal. I quite imagined that MB was going to walk away as well the judge maybe ruling that if it was right for H it must be the same for MB.

That Wednesday was a very strange day. Richard drove Dan and me to the court, picking up Joe and Kate and the little ones en route. He planned to look after the boys for Joe whilst he was in court. There was a large gathering of press and cameras outside the court waiting for us. We got Dan out of the car and into the wheelchair. It was very strange indeed having to run the gauntlet of the press. Happily, they managed to get a shot of MB arriving as well.

Everyone gathered as before in the witness support area. Babe had returned from her holiday very brown. Dan wasn't keen to come at first but then had decided to come after all. He wanted to see things through to the bitter end, which I felt was quite brave of him. We also decided that we would sit in on everything that day.

It wasn't long before a representative of the CPS came to see us all and explained that MB had now decided to change his plea slightly. He now wanted to plead guilty to everything except GBH on Dan and witness intimidation. Babe and her mother were taken into a room by the police to discuss what they wanted done about the intimidation charge and were talked into leaving this on file and not pressing it at this time. Babe was told that if she went on with the intimidation charge she would have to give evidence, but if she dropped the charges she would not have to give evidence at all. Obviously, as she was only eighteen at the time the thought of giving evidence scared her, so she went for the easy option.

Dan, Joseph and I were taken into another room to talk with the detective constable in charge who was visibly upset by the whole thing and wanted to put his case to us. The female barrister who had attempted quite pathetically to prosecute also came in a little later to apologise and explain where everything had gone wrong. I already knew where and when things had gone wrong: it was the moment the police allowed G to walk away without charge. I think everyone but us had known for quite some time that this was going to be a bit of a farce.

The CPS went on to explain to everyone what would happen

next. Because MB had pleaded guilty there would now be no formal trial and no witnesses called. So by 11.30 on Wednesday it was all over bar the shouting. Dan, my sister Judy, Alex, Kate's mum, Sue, and I went into Court ten to hear the charges read out again to MB. There was quite a heavy press presence. Then the rest of our group was allowed in later to hear MB plead guilty. MB's mother was allowed in court for the first time now that harassment charges against her had been withdrawn. Also, unbelievably the third thug who was not formally charged but in our opinion should have been was also in court. I placed Dan's wheelchair in front of the visitors' rows and sat next to G, which made him look uncomfortable. Our witnesses all quashed into the row in front of me. MB's mother was behind me.

Financial bail restrictions were lifted and it was agreed that MB could reside with a relative in Nailsea, not as if any of us believed that he would ever go anywhere near Nailsea. The judge ruled that MB should appear in Gloucester Crown Court on 22 August for sentencing. Why Gloucester, I do not know. And that was that, out of the court he walked, still with that smug face.

We all left the court and had to walk past MB who laughed and gave obscene gestures. That fellow had to be seen to be believed. We had to restrain Wayne as he was furious and was ready to take a swing at MB. The girls were all crying but at least I felt we might get some sort of justice if it was only for Wayne and Kate.

We all went back to the witness support area to calm down. All the ladies who give their services for free were very sympathetic towards everyone concerned. A newspaper reporter from the *Evening Post* came over and asked for my comments. I was just about to give them when Howard appeared and asked if we could keep things exclusive to him, which was a bit difficult as the *Evening Post* had actually interviewed Dan and me a week earlier. It was not as if we were being paid for any exclusive interviews.

We all left the court and went across to the Bar Oz almost opposite the court building to talk things over. There was a lot of bad feeling over the way Dan had been treated and we had already decided to put in an official complaint against the police. I tried several times to phone Richard on the mobile.

Howard found us in the pub and we spoke for a while. I eventually got hold of Richard at about 1.15. He had taken the little boys to the park. Richard then took us home.

Dan went to Joe's for the evening, Adam joined them there and they stayed the night.

The phone rang continuously all evening. One of the calls was from the police who were still trying to talk Richard into meeting them, but Richard was still far too angry.

The next day, Thursday, 31 July, was to be like no other. The day started about 7.30 in the morning with a phone call from Radio Bristol asking for an interview that they would use later in the day. About an hour after that Detective Inspector Tunks called from Southmead asking if there was any chance of him coming and talking to Dan – there wasn't. He was, however, very polite and offered any assistance we might need in the future. My sister called later to tell me that we were on the front page of the *Western Daily Press*. It was a very fair and accurate account of the story and I was quite pleased. We were also on page nine of the *Sun* and later the front page of the *Evening Post*, with a postscript relating to my father, and the incident that he got involved in many years ago. When my father was seventy-six he had gone to help a woman being assaulted by a man with a stick and for his pains got a compound fracture and brain haemorrhage. Although he survived the initial incident, the man was never caught and my father was never quite the same again. It was a lightning strikes twice type scenario.

We had visits from HTV and the BBC news teams and appeared on the local news later in the day. It was all very odd. But the oddest of all must have been the arrival of a very smart car sent by Deputy Chief Constable David R Kenworthy QPM LLB (Hons) AKC and a gentleman carrying a letter for Daniel that he had wanted delivered by hand. It said how sorry the deputy chief constable was to hear that the case had gone so badly and that he would be looking into the details to see if the police were at fault. We learned later that the *Western Daily Press* had received a similar one which they intended to print the next day. The lady from the *Western Daily Press* who phoned said it was an unprecedented move by the police. I feel that maybe heads might roll. The silly thing is that at the end of the day the wrong people get the hassle. So some poor policeman gets hauled over the coals for messing up, but it doesn't alter the fact that the bad guys win again. Nothing could change that and nothing at that time could give Daniel back his sight.

Later in the afternoon yet another press photo call was set up, this time to picture Dan with Wayne. I assumed that that would be that and all would be forgotten the next day, though we did also get a call from Kilroy who wanted Dan and I either on a 'have a go heroes – is it worth it?' or a 'So the police have messed it up again' programme. Not to be organised until September so I felt that we might well have been forgotten by then.

My sister Judy rang to say that our elderly Aunt Freda in Swansea was to begin radiotherapy as a biopsy the hospital had undertaken on cells removed from the small intestine during a colostomy operation she had undergone a few days previously showed that there was a problem. My Aunt Phylis from Southampton was coming to stay with Judy and Judy was hoping that I would help her transport Phylis and my late mother's other sister, Eve, to Swansea to see Freda. I am afraid I was not feeling very charitable. I felt that I wanted to do almost anything for Judy but at that time but I had just had enough of hospital visits. Also I felt rather bitter that none of my cousins or elderly aunts for that matter, though their age could excuse them, had managed to visit either my poor old mum last year even though it was obvious she was dying of liver cancer, or my son Daniel. It is not as if they weren't in hospital long enough. My mother was in Frenchay for six weeks and Dan was in different hospitals for fifteen weeks. It seemed that Judy and I are were always the ones that did the running around. I suppose I was feeling a little sorry for myself maybe and a bit like the poor relation whose only use was for transport and deliveries.

Anyway, whatever the reason, I said I wouldn't go, knowing I would feel bad about it for months if only because I had let Judy down.

Once again we made the news on the Friday. The *Evening Post* and the *Western Daily Press* both ran the picture of Dan and his 'best friend' Wayne with a caption 'Friends for life!' It was starting to become an episode of a rather bad soap opera. I also knew that Wayne and Dan would never be friends regardless of the dramas they had been through, they had nothing in common.

Life went on and we tried to behave normally whilst waiting for August 22nd and the sentencing of MB. Richard and I intended to do a bit of work on our house in Muller Road and move back there. The head at Cotham had decided to change Richard's job description so we could move out of the little school house. Muller Road would not have been my first choice but it was all we owned at the time so it had to do. I had already organised a bank loan so we could do the work needed to make the house more suitable for Daniel. On the plus side, the house in Muller Road was a good size and only round the corner from Joseph and he could really do with our support with those little boys. Also Joe would be close at hand if Dan needed anything during the day, so we could help each other. So life went on, not quite the same as before. We had all lost something, Dan his sight, Richard his role of protector of the family, Joe and Adam the friend and brother they knew and me, as I have already stated, my sense of humour. Hopefully not for ever but I couldn't see much to laugh about at that moment.

My whole family including the grandchildren were invited to join Kate's family camping in Cornwall as a relaxation project before the next court date. We all went. The weather was scorching but we decided that camping with Daniel was almost an impossibility; it was just too difficult for him. All those guy ropes to trip over and the long walks through fields to the toilet bock were a nightmare for him.

The sentencing of MB was changed from Gloucester to Bristol and brought forward a day. So on 21 August 1997 the witnesses and I all decided we would go to this event together. I rather felt that MB would only get a slapped wrist but I wanted to see this thing through to the bitter end.

We all gathered at the front of the court and went in as a group. Dan had decided that he did not want to be at this event just in case it turned out to be another travesty of justice. MB was waiting outside Court ten with his mother, father and another adult. I glanced down the corridor at him and could see that he looked very confident and relaxed, laughing and joking with his relatives. Just looking at this little group made me feel so weary and utterly drained. I didn't realise before what a real 'them and us' situation there is out there and how naive I was. I always thought the bad guys got caught, punished and the good guys won. I used to think that what goes around comes around but it is not true. There are people out there without conscience, brought up by a similar-minded people. They get away with crimes and produce offspring that go on and make other people's lives a misery. It is an endless destructive circle.

I waited with everyone else until the case was called and we could all go in. I sat in the row behind the rest of our group. Everyone looked very tense and worried. Wayne was particularly worried that MB would walk out of court that day and be looking for him.

We all stood when Judge Darwell-Smith came in. Everyone then sat down and the barristers began telling the judge what a wonderful person MB was, how he had a good job that he would lose if he went to prison. The judge was handed a pile of references but as the majority of them looked like they were written on the same violet-coloured paper, he seemed to glance at these and dismiss them quite quickly. The judge did have a letter from Wayne's doctor saying how Wayne had been suffering badly from nervous exhaustion since the incident, which he commented on. The defence then went on to say that MB had no violent record – the whole row in front of me sniggered at that comment. MB only had convictions for handling stolen goods and other such offences, no violence, and apparently he would willingly pay compensation to Kate and Wayne for any damage done which he would not be able to do if he lost his job. I glance round at MB and could see that he was still looking cocky. Also apparently because MB had been incarcerated for a couple of weeks whilst on remand, his barristers felt MB had suffered enough – poor soul! Also the poor boy had been forced to live away from the family home for several months – like hell he had! I felt sure that these slick talking barristers were going to get this animal off and he looked like he felt the same way.

The to and fro talk seemed to go on for ages and then suddenly the judge brought everything to an end by saying that the evening of 31 May had been a terrible night full of unnecessary violence instigated by the defendant. He also said he was not swayed by the fact that MB had decided at the eleventh hour to plead guilty. He mentioned each incident involving MB in detail, except Daniel's attack, saying how appalling he felt the attacks on the young women, especially Kate, were.

I suddenly felt for a moment that we were actually going to get a result that day. I had fingers, toes, legs, all crossed. I had written to Judge Darwell-Smith after we had returned from our 'holiday' in Cornwall. Dan had looked so pitiful, unable to move, getting burnt to a crisp on the beach whilst his brothers and nephews charged in and out of the surf. I just had to write and say that I hoped that H never repeated his treatment of Dan on another innocent young man and ruined their life in the same way. I had received a very formal but polite reply from the judge's officers saying how sorry he was that he had been forced to rule as he had but blamed the police.

After a short silence the judge said he was ready to pass sentence. He continued by repeating that the seriousness of MB's behaviour and outcome left him with only one course open, a custodial sentence. Fifteen months for the assault on Wayne and a further fifteen months for the assault on Kate, to run concurrently. There was a huge gasp from the front row then the girls all burst into tears. MB's mother was also in tears, not with happiness, I suppose. I didn't look at MB but apparently his bottom lip quivered. At last, that knocked the grin off his face.

MB was taken down to start his sentence and we all trailed out of the court. Obviously there were press people outside waiting to record what I thought of the sentence. I moved the press away from the court door, after all MB's mother was there and she was a mother and must have felt terrible without me rubbing salt in the wound.

I said I was obviously happy for Kate and Wayne. At least they had seen some semblance of retribution for what they had been through, though obviously I would have been a lot happier if the men concerned had been punished for what they had done to my son. I also didn't understand the concurrent running of sentences and no one seemed able to explain the logic of these. Kate and I both gave our Detective Constable a hug, he was obviously elated by the verdict. We all went to say goodbye to the victim support people and made our way out of the court. In the foyer MB's parents were waiting to say goodbye to him. The father, who is estranged from Mrs B, actually stood in front of his wife in a protective way. This amused me no end. What sort of people did they think we were? Obviously not the type they usually mix with. As if any of us would even want to speak to these people, let alone touch them.

We all gathered outside. The detective constable came out soon after and he told us how MB would have been taken straight down to the cells to wait for the prison van to take him probably initially to Horfield Prison. Kate was delighted to hear the details of the indignities MB would suffer, strip searches and so forth. I found it difficult to actually relish in this unpleasant young man's misery regardless of what he had done to Dan. It just seemed a waste of two young lives to me and it had all been so unnecessary. I still wanted someone to come up to Dan and say how sorry they were about the whole episode and how they would make it up to him by helping him get over his disability as best they could. But I guess that only happens in the Waltons and fairy tales.

The Detective Constable in charge of the case was and in fact still is an honest hardworking policeman. He was in the firing range at that time and took the flack on the chin for all the decisions made regarding the case surrounding my son's assault, whether he concurred with them or not. He was visibly shaken by the events and I knew that he felt for Dan and the family as a family man himself and as an upholder of the law. Unfortunately although I liked the man immensely he was the symbol of a rather ridiculous law as I saw it at the time, that had let my son down. I did feel for him though as he knew that justice had not been done and also that it was simply the wrong decision at some level that had allowed this to happen. I myself felt that we were not important enough to have had all the i's dotted and t's crossed that would have convicted my son's assailants. That is a feeling that has never really left me to this day.

We all decide to go for a drink in the Bar Oz opposite the court before going home. I had to go down the road and phone Dan at home first; needless to say he was thrilled. I just had one drink. My instinct was to get totally drunk out of my mind but I wanted to get home to Daniel and celebrate with him.

I felt at that moment that we all were bound together for ever. We little group of witnesses, bound by an invisible force but unfortunately for ever isn't very long nowadays. I knew that Kate and I would remain friends though. After all I felt she had prevented Joe from coming to harm as well that terrible night and that would bind me to her.

Gold Star, Liverpool and Robbie Williams

Richard finally allowed the hierarchy from the Avon and Somerset Police Force to come to the house and try to explain why our son's assailants walked away scot-free. Richard was still very angry and wasn't really that receptive to these officials. We were amazed when they suggested that we take out a private prosecution, offering us all the paperwork they had relating to the case and assuring us that they would guarantee that we would get a conviction. We were aghast and wanted to know how come if conviction was assured for us it had failed them. We never did get a satisfactory explanation to that question and I suppose never will. If it wasn't such a pointless exercise, as private convictions do not carry a custodial sentence, I would have been tempted to take out a private prosecution if only so I could name and shame without retribution. Still the Stephen Lawrence case didn't get a conviction and everyone still continues to name the suspects. I often wondered why, having been cleared in a private prosecution, the five men accused never brought out libel suites against papers that name them. Nervous that a second hearing might not find in their favour, I guess. I felt it would be a little hard on the young witnesses to put them through that ordeal once again, especially as there would be no meaningful outcome. When I was told that a lad who worked on a building site with H heard him bragging about his notoriety I was tempted to rethink the private prosecution issue.

Our solicitor was at this time working on getting Daniel a decent criminal injuries compensation payment and that was more important.

For Dan, 1997 was a series of outpatient appointments mainly at Frenchay Head Injuries Unit, physiotherapy and mobility training being the main aspects of the visits.

August, we went to Cornwall camping for a short time with a group of friends as mentioned in the previous chapter. Dan went a couple of days ahead of Richard and I with Adam. When we reached the camp site at Treyarnon we were quite shocked. Adam had a face that looked like he had been beaten up. Apparently he had fallen on some rocks and caught the side of his head not long after he arrived. Daniel looked like a boiled lobster. It had been really hot and because he couldn't move about much, he just cooked. His feet were purple and swollen and he was in a lot of pain. Because Dan didn't get any more comfortable, we took him home. We decided that we would give camping a miss until Dan could get about more easily.

On 12 September Daniel went to a presentation dinner at the Marriott Hotel in Bristol. It was the Bristol *Evening Post* Gold Star Awards Luncheon. Throughout 1997, every month, a different person was chosen as a Gold Star winner and featured in the *Evening Post*. July was Daniel's turn when he was nominated for his bravery. The award is funded by the Birmingham Midshires Building Society.

It was a star-studded event in minor terms. There were several local celebrities present, but Daniel was only really impressed at meeting Ian Holloway, Bristol Rovers' football team manager at that time. He was very kind to Daniel and invited him to be his guest at any home match he wanted, an offer Dan took up just once because he didn't want to take advantage of the situation. It was the first event that Dan attended without a wheelchair and he soon looked tired.

Richard, Adam and I had accompanied Dan to the luncheon and I have to admit to shedding a few tears when Adam helped Dan up to the podium to accept his award to the sound of Bette Midler singing 'The Wind Beneath My Wings'.

We had some really nice people at our table and Dan thoroughly enjoyed himself. One of our companions was the then Miss Bristol who turned out to be a girl who Dan was at school with, Leah Mason. Adam got on really well with her fiancé and they got into conversation about the limousine hire firm that he ran with his father. It was Dan's birthday the next day and they hatched a plan to take him by limo to a nightclub accompanied by Leah. Leah was involved in promotion work for Oddessy's nightclub and she arranged free passes for Dan, Adam and a group of friends. Oddessy's got their publicity and Dan had a good night with free champagne.

In October the whole family went to Paris for a few days and I think Dan had a good time despite the obvious disadvantages of not being very mobile. We took the wheelchair as we knew Dan would not be up for endless walking. He loved Euro Disney and we jumped every queue. Disabled people are allowed in the front of the line. I think Dan enjoyed himself more than our grandchildren. Obviously we didn't tell the people in charge that Dan couldn't see or they might not have let him on the rides.

In November we were invited on the Kilroy show, all expenses paid, it was quite an enjoyable experience. At least it made us realise that there are a lot of people out there who have suffered as badly if not actually more so than us. Kilroy isn't half as smarmy as I thought; he actually has quite a charming and soothing way about him. The programme was about 'Does the punishment fit the crime?' There were people who felt a terrible sense of injustice about how people who had violated them in some way had 'got off lightly'. I could relate to that.

We were driven to and from the station to the studio in very smart cars that had tinted windows. Going back we had the largest man I have ever seen behind the wheel. I do not mean fat; I mean a mountain of muscle. He seemed to take up the whole of the two front seats. His neck was as thick as the headrest. He was really a lovely man who was a minder really but was driving that day and the car had been especially adapted for him. I decided then and there that I wanted a minder. No one would mess with anyone that had a man the size of that guy step from the car.

Christmas was brilliant; it went on for days. We spent a great deal of time singing round the table with Tim, and Sue, and other members of Kate's family including her grandfather who were all great company.

We were now into 1998 and Dan had mixed feelings about his retirement from Cotham Grammar School on the grounds of incapacity, but it is a large site school and would have been difficult for him to work in. Obviously his original job there would have been nearly impossible anyway. He used to strip computers to update or mend them and keep the network running. To be fair to Cotham, the bursar was more than willing to adapt the switchboard for Daniel to use but that would have been rather a dead end job and I had to agree with Dan that concentrating on getting fit at that time had to be top priority. Dan's short-term memory was still a little dodgy and I would not have wanted him to have anything to worry about unnecessarily.

Daniel has been working very hard from day one to get fit and was getting more mobile by the minute, despite a little extra weight.

Whilst Dan was still in hospital, Sarah and I had written up to Liverpool football team to express a desire to get Dan there and meet them when he was fit enough. On 1st May we went to fulfil this dream. Daniel, Adam, Richard and I went up to Liverpool at the team's invitation to meet them all and visit the training ground and Anfield, of course. We met John Barnes, Michael Owen, Dominic Matteo, Robbie Fowler, Steve McManaman, Paul Ince, Jason McAteer, and the rest of the team, and had a cup of tea with them. This was followed by a private look round Anfield.

The next day Dan and Adam had front row seats just by the players' tunnel, and watched Liverpool beat West Ham five–nil. Everyone was really nice to us all and we had a thoroughly good few days away. It was all a bit lost on me as I do not like football even remotely but Dan had been a Liverpool fan since he was a young lad, I just wish he could have seen his heroes properly.

As a result of the *Evening Post* Gold Star Awards Dan and I received an invitation to a reception at Buckingham Palace on Monday, 1st June 1998, signed by Michael Jephson, Master of the Household's Department. A vehicle pass came through the post along with a gold-edged invitation. Along with the majority of people, I had never met the Queen and I was unashamedly honoured on behalf of my son.

31st May – Dan, Joe, Kate, Kate's sister Hannah, my niece Alex and a friend, all had tickets in the stalls to see Robbie Williams at the Colston Hall in Bristol. Julie and I had seats in the balcony. Dan's interest in music has increased since his sight loss; a concert is one thing that he really enjoys. The support act was dreadful. I thought for a moment that I was too old for live music, but was reassured when I discovered that the group below didn't think much of the support act either, so much so that Kate and Hannah had gone up to the bar whilst they were on.

In the interval our surname was called over the loudspeaker asking us to go to the mixing desk in the centre of the stalls. I thought that maybe Dan was feeling unwell and hurried down. Joe spotted Julie and me at the desk and brought Dan across to find out what was occurring. Apparently Robbie had asked if he could meet Dan in the interval, having heard about him.

Before we knew what was happening we were ushered round

the back of the stage, manoeuvring numerous obstacles such as lighting and sound cables. We waited for a second or two and Robbie appeared. He was so nice, absolutely charming and the thing that struck me was the fact that there was no publicity angle, just a genuinely decent young man wanting to meet another. His show was brilliant as well. Kate and Hannah were really sick that they had missed meeting Robbie but unfortunately we didn't have time to find them; it all happened so fast. The annoying thing for the young women was that Julie had a hug and kiss from Robbie Williams and she didn't really know who he was. I had dragged her along literally to keep me company.

Dan and I got home on a high as we were dying to tell Richard what had happened but he already knew. Amazingly enough Robbie had phoned our home. The conversation had gone like this.

'Hello, this is Robbie.'

Richard – 'Robbie who?'

There was an exasperated sound then Robbie asked,

'Is Dan in?'

Richard – 'No, he's gone to a concert.'

Robbie – 'Whose concert?'

Richard – 'Robbie Williams, at the Colston Hall.'

Robbie – 'That's me, I am Robbie Williams.'

Richard – 'Oh yeh!'

Robbie – 'Never mind, I will catch him at the show,' but he left his mobile number in case he missed us.

Richard just didn't believe it was actually Robbie Williams, who would?

Apparently, Robbie had intended to send a taxi for Dan if he had not been at the concert. Dan told him that we were going up to meet the Queen the next day but he reckoned that meeting him was better. It was a strange experience. We all just wondered back to our seats as if nothing had happened and he made some firm fans that evening. When I read outrageous stories about Robbie Williams I just remember that conversation he had with Richard and smile. Never believe all you read about people. Sometimes their whole public lives are a performance when the real person is quite a different kettle of fish.

The Palace

1st June 1998 was a day and a half. Daniel had received a formal invitation to a reception in the State Rooms at Buckingham Palace in the presence of the Queen and Prince Phillip. It was a Young Achievers' Award Ceremony. If you had a handicap you could bring a companion with you either to push your wheelchair or to guide you if necessary. You could choose to bring a guide dog if wanted. Guide dogs, wonderful as they are, are not psychic. They only follow trained routes and would have no more got Dan around London than fly, not as if he had a dog anyway. Luckily for me, Dan asked me to accompany him on this auspicious occasion and I was more than pleased to do so. Dan was determined to actually attend this event on his feet, and this he did.

The *Bristol Evening Post* had nominated Daniel to attend this event. There were a couple of young people there who had also received the Gold Star awards on the same day as Dan going up to London with us.

We went up by train. I had intended to drive and had been sent a pass for the Buckingham Palace car park but decided that negotiating the London traffic was not an attractive idea. My decision to take the train was confirmed when the *Evening Post* offered to pay our fare. We travelled up in the train with the reporter, a young lady called Jessica who had looked after her invalid mother since she was young, and Peter Calder. Peter was a remarkable young man who had battled cancer since soon after taking his A levels in 1996. Eventually having his leg amputated to stop the spread of this disgusting and indiscriminate disease. He had not been well enough to attend the Gold Star Awards so this was the first time we had met him. Peter had gone on to Nottingham University to study biochemistry despite his illness but had unfortunately had to drop out when the cancer returned in his second term. He was an inspiration, determined at this time to get his degree. This was unfortunately not to be because he died a short time after the Palace visit from a tumour on his lungs and spine. If anyone deserved to survive it was that young man. He was so matter of fact about his illness and so easy to talk to. He was a lovely young man and his parents must have been immensely proud of him.

We stood outside the Palace and waited for the rest of our group who had chosen to find their own way there. One of the young people was Scott Calder, whom Dan particularly liked. Scott had received the Gold Star Award for rescuing his then girlfriend from drowning and Dan and him seemed to get on like a house on fire. There was also a very pretty girl called Miriam who sings to raise money for charity. These young people were the representatives from the West Country.

The whole of the area around the Palace was cordoned off and the area was buzzing with tourists all wondering what the obvious event was all about. There was such a crowd around the gates that the police formed a sort of tunnel for guests to walk along.

At 5.15 we started to go into the Palace. We were ushered through the main gate into the first courtyard once we showed our invitations. Then we walked on though the central arch into the inner courtyard. We approached the entrance and a sweeping staircase into the Palace.

The interior of the Palace is indescribable. It is really beautiful and ornate. I have been to Versailles a couple of times and although it is amazing it is also really rather vulgar whereas Buckingham Palace is more subtle but still magnificent. There is an amazing central corridor bigger than our house (the Picture Gallery), with the walls covered with magnificent paintings. Off the gallery is a series of doors leading to the State Dining Room, the Blue Drawing Room, the Throne Room, the White Drawing Room, the Music Room, the Green Drawing Room, the West and East Galleries and Ballrooms. All the connecting doors were opened and everyone could walk around where they wished. We were issued with a map of the state rooms, detailing where the toilets were. The toilets were actually hidden behind secret panels. The men's toilets had tapestries draped over the entrances, so no wonder we needed a map.

There were 650 young achievers at this event and some of these people were amazing. There was a great many disabled young adults there, several of them in wheelchairs or unsighted. We were given a booklet each with a list of everyone invited, in alphabetical order. Daniel's write up read – Daniel Gallimore, Good Samaritan, blinded trying to stop a fight. There was the usual splattering of famous faces, quite a few of them were lost on me but Dan seemed fairly pleased to be in their company. Eternal, All Saints, Zoë Ball (whom Dan spent a considerable amount of time with), a couple of young soap stars and Denise Van Outen, to name but a few.

The front page listed the royals present – the Queen, the Duke of Edinburgh, Prince Charles, Prince Edward, the Duke and Duchess of Gloucester, the Duke and Duchess of Kent, Viscount and Viscountess Linley.

The royals just wandered about speaking to people here and there. I think we spoke to most of them briefly. The Duchess of Kent seemed the most genuinely interested in replies she was given. Dan amused me when Prince Edward stopped to speak to him. Edward, to his credit, had the sense to touch Dan on the shoulder so Dan would be clear that he was being spoken to and Dan, thinking Edward was just a guest, asked him why he had been invited. To which he replied, 'It's Edward,' and he continued chatting to Dan in a casual way. Dan didn't have the vaguest idea who Edward was. A rather well-spoken young ex-army captain spoke to Dan straight after Edward and Dan thought he was still speaking to the same person.

The only person that you did not approach was the Queen. She was very short and appeared to be surrounded by personnel wherever she went. Her ladies-in-waiting or whatever (they seemed more regal than the actual royal family) wandered about and spoke to people, some of which were then taken to be introduced to Her Majesty. Daniel was amongst those chosen to actual shake the Queen's hand. Dan had stood with Zoë Ball, who is very tall, watching the Queen as she approached. They were giggling very loud and I was surprised that Dan was actually picked to meet the Queen, considering. He seemed so confident that day, talking to all sorts of people that under normal circumstances he would never have come into contact with. One time Dan wandered off with a beautiful tiny ballerina from the Royal Ballet. Because most of these young people were on their own they seemed more inclined to talk to anyone close enough to hear them. Beverley Hammett, a young lady who had acid thrown in her face whilst babysitting in a case of a mistaken identity hit, was there alone and I felt rather sorry for her. I did try to speak to her but she was very shy and reserved. Having been recently in close contact with total morons thanks to Dan's heroism, it was a real pleasure to actual spend time with such a large group of people who looked and sounded as if they would and could make a difference to the world. I felt proud to be in such exalted company.

There was endless champagne and miniature size hors d'oeuvres. Every time you took a sip a footman seemed to appear from nowhere and fill the glass back up. Very quickly I was glad I had chosen not to drive. A rather fine-looking footman was telling a group of guests about a very ornate, gold-leafed spinet in the corner of the room that had belonged to Henry VIII. It was worth enough to wipe out the national debt. So I had to ask the obvious question: why didn't they photograph it, hang the picture on the wall, sell it and wipe out the nation debt? This rather grand-looking gentleman was not amused.

Dan spent most of his time wondering about with Scott and I spent quite a large portion of my time with a charming unsighted young woman who had brought her guide dog and needed a human guide to describe the decor. She was a private secretary at the House of Lords.

The royal family withdrew at about 8.30 and the invited guests started to file out closely behind them, although Dan and I stayed until we were nearly thrown out at nine o'clock. Dan and I were having such a good time that we planned to get a much later train home than the rest of our group who had hurried off to catch the 8.30 train.

Dan and I were both hungry because we had not eaten anything but hors d'oeuvres since breakfast, so we decided to find our way to the Chinese quarter and indulge in a meal there. We took advice on which restaurant to use from the taxi driver and eventually caught the 10.30 p.m. train home. It was the best day either of us had ever had. Dan slept all the next day; the occasion had worn him out.

HTV, Walley Cowen and Manor House

Dan appeared on a programme called *Sherry's People* on HTV at the beginning of August. Sherry Eugene, a local newsreader, fronted this. She interviewed Dan at home and then they went walk about. She was very pleasant. We told Sherry how we had received strange phone calls from people who remembered me from the days when I worked in Horfield Prison. I think they meant well but they were actually a little unnerving. People were phoning offering to 'do something about the people who had hurt Dan'. This is the drawback of having an unusual surname; you can be easily traced. I had been ex-directory whilst I worked in the prison and returned to this state fairly quickly after Dan's assault mainly to try to stop the silent calls that we were still getting. The phone rings, you pick it up and hear breathing but no one speaks. As for the potential hit men I am only glad they did not phone me after the assailants walked free from court or I might have been tempted. At the time of the calls I still believed in the British justice system.

Just when we thought we had been everywhere and done everything, Dan received a letter from Mrs Anita Smith, personal assistant to the chief constable, Avon and Somerset Constabulary, informing him that he had been awarded the Walley Cowen Award for his actions when attempting to prevent a man from being attacked by three others. Apparently the award is similar to one called the 'Binney Award' which is presented to people in the London area for services in support of law and order. It was a monetary award originally but after the fund ran out it became just a certificate and a commemorative piece of glass. This presentation was to take place on 24th September at 10.30 a.m. at the police headquarters in Portishead, near Bristol. There was a stamped address envelope enclosed, a map and details about the award. It seemed a long time after the event, a bit of an afterthought maybe generated by all the recent publicity, or were the police a bit edgy and wanted to make amends? Whatever, we decided to attend this event. Why not, after all, we are all on the same side.

I wrote to the chief constable and suggested that Kate should receive a similar award as I felt her actions on the night of 31st May were heroic as well. As a consequence Kate received an invitation to be presented with a Walley Cowen Award at the same time as Dan in recognition of her re-enactment of the Pocahontas and John Smith incident, which I believe had saved my eldest boy from injuries on the night. Her parents were absolutely as proud as could be although they, like us, had lost a lot of faith in our legal system for other reasons apart from the incident involving Dan and Kate.

Kate's grandfather came, my sister Judy, Alex, Joe, Adam, Richard and myself.

There were several people collecting similar awards as well as a couple of awards to policemen who had acted with bravery, beyond their normal expectations.

Daniel was presented with his award, a large inscribed cut glass vase, by the High Sheriff of Gloucester. He was dressed in his formal attire, complete with sword, and, because he appeared to be at least six foot six, dwarfing everyone including Richard who is six foot two, he looked most imposing. He actually was a very pleasant man who spent quite some time talking to Richard explaining how he came to be appointed high sheriff and what the post entailed.

There was a short press call. The police hierarchy tried to be friendly, several of whom I had met before when they were trying to explain what went wrong in 1996 and 1997. I was still a little touchy about these events but all in all it was a good day.

Dan had by now finished attending the Head Injuries Unit and was on his own two feet so to speak, still a little unsteady but getting there. I still could not imagine him breaking into a trot but he could now walk a reasonable distance if not rushed.

There has been very little improvement sight wise but he seemed to be getting used to the little sight he did have. Eye contact is the thing he misses most. You do not know when someone is actually speaking to you if they do not make it clear. It is also almost impossible to detect if a member of the opposite sex is interested without eye contact.

Daniel was waiting to go to Manor House at Torquay, a rather splendid building near the harbour especially designed to train newly blinded young people in the art of life skills. Ironing, cooking, organising their own lives, getting on and off trains and buses, shopping, things that everyone else takes for granted and things that are needed if a full and independent life is be reclaimed. They also intended to show him how to make the best use of his usable sight, that obviously was the main attraction.

Every day I saw a little bit more of the 'Old Dan' returning. He was now back to telling terrible jokes, something he was quite famous for. His sense of humour had always stayed intact and he put everyone at their ease when they did not know what to say to him by saying something frivolous.

Dan appeared to have regained all his social graces and I hoped that Torquay would give him the boost he needed to become independent again. After all, as much as I love my son being around all the time, he was now twenty-four and I wouldn't be here for the rest of his life, so independence was essential.

Dan was always a very laid back young man, which I believe has proved to be his saving grace during this trying time for him. You lose spontaneity when you lose your sight; everything has to be planned. Everything has to be kept tidy and returned to the same place; this is something Dan was never very good at when fit but I hoped Manor House in Torquay would help with this.

Dan had a week-long assessment at Torquay, which he thoroughly enjoyed, mainly because there was a good bunch of youngsters there at the time. The organisers thought that a nine-week course would get Dan firmly on the right road and I believed at the time that Torquay would help him to plan the rest of his life.

Dan was already making long-term plans. He hoped to have a place of his own again one day and was planning to start producing a tape magazine for the blind and disabled that gave details of forthcoming events that would be suitable. He also wanted to include restaurants and pubs that have easy disabled access and toilet facilities. On the lines of the *Talking Newspapers* but more focused towards teens to thirties, whereas the *Talking Newspapers* cater more for the older age group. He sent out loads of flyers locally and had some very encouraging replies, so it was just the funding he needed to work out. It was a project that had his mind working again which was the main point of the exercise.

The rest of 1998 was pretty uneventful apart from a trip we took in the October half-term to Paris yet again. I love Paris and it always seems quite easy to get a coach party up for a few days' visit. We did, however, decide that this was the last Paris trip for a while; we would try pastures new in the next October half-term.

Just before we set off for the Paris trip we were burgled again and it made me uneasy about leaving the house. We had all been at Richard's niece's wedding, his sister's daughter. It was a really good day but Dan had started to flag about seven o'clock so I decided to drive him home and then return to the evening do. I arrived home, opened the front door and was immediately aware of a draft so I knew someone had been in the house. They had shut the dog in the living room and she was barking like mad. I think they were actually still in the garden when we entered the house having heard us approach and left in a hurry because there were two bags packed and yet left behind. I couldn't leave Dan alone in case they came back so I phoned Clive and Julie, and Clive came over to be with Dan whilst I went back to fetch Richard. He couldn't believe it. We were beginning to think that we were not allowed to enjoy ourselves any more. Despite Dan's room obviously being set up for a blind person and press cuttings on his wall, it was his room that had been mainly targeted. All his electrical gadgets and CDs were taken. I was as mad as hell. The police wondered if maybe because of all the publicity about Dan the perpetrators thought he had money. They were quite wrong; he hadn't even received his criminal injuries compensation yet.

All my jewellery except the ring I was wearing, Christmas presents I had already bought, cameras, CDs were now in the hands of others. There were a few CDs in the bags that had been left behind and some video films. They had cleared most of Dan's shelves of items, half of which I am sure will be of no use to them. When you have to replace things that are particularly designed for the blind it is a very time-consuming business, it is not as if you can just walk into Woolworth's and pick the things up. It is maximum disruption.

These light-fingered animals had destroyed the French doors leading to the garden so Richard had to nail them up until he could get someone to fit new ones on Monday. Saturday evening is the worst time to be burgled, if, in fact, there could ever be a good time.

I was particularly upset because the only thing I had of my mother's was her engagement ring. It wasn't her original ring as she had lost that, it was a replacement my father bought her about ten years before she died and she loved it. It had been given to me and now it would be sold for pennies to strangers.

Eventually we got a date for Torquay, January 1999. As it was a few months since he was last there and obviously the same people would not be there, Dan's enthusiasm has dulled. Actually arriving there was a great disappointment. They had shelved the life skills temporarily (the main reason that Dan wanted to go) due to building work and the fact that the society was selling America House, a large property close by that housed the life skills section. With the money gained from the sale of America House they were building extensions to Manor House so this part of the work could be placed there. Meanwhile, it was just keyboard skills and other hands on workshops set up to put newly blinded people back into the work market. This was not what Dan needed at this time. Having Behçets gives Dan a definite disadvantage work wise without the added disadvantage of having very little sight.

Manor House ran like a college, breakfast at 8 a.m., start lessons at 9 a.m., lunch at midday and then work through until 5 p.m. Seeing as how Dan could only manage a fifteen-hour day before he received serious head injuries, it was all too much for him and he became quite distressed and thoroughly worn out after just a week. Then he got the flu and I brought him home. Needless to say Dan did not want to return but I persuaded him to give it a little longer, so reluctantly he went back. His head injuries had made him a little insecure and he got it in his head that we were trying to get rid of him, which is why we wanted him to go to Manor House. Whilst at home he always wanted to go wherever I went. He used to come to the supermarket almost as if he was afraid I would desert him. He was rather like a small child again. He was starting to get over this phase and then Manor House seemed to have made him regress instead of moving forwards.

After another week, Manor House themselves accepted that Daniel was not fit enough for the devised programme and I took him home. He looked as though I had sprung him from Wormwood Scrubs; he was so pleased to be going home. It was a bit of a pointless trek forward and back twice a week if he wasn't enjoying the stay. I think we had actually gone too soon. Dan was only just starting to return to his old self, not as if I expected to see him fully recovered after such injuries. Another year and he might have wanted to be at Manor House. Back home he started to get his confidence back again and I decided that places like Manor House were not for him, we could get him fitter at home.

We still went to the annual ex-Manor House reunion weekend in Torquay at Easter, regardless of the fact that we felt as though we were not worthy to be there. It was a thoroughly enjoyable weekend although I doubt if we will ever go again. The organisers were too keen to push him into joining groups of other youngish men because 'he would enjoy their company'. Daniel wanted to choose his own company and was inclined to withdraw into his shell if pushed to socialise without actually volunteering.

Just When We Thought It Was All Over

I came home from work on 14th May 1999 to find a rather pretty young lady taking photographs of Daniel in the front room. To our amazement we were informed that Dan was a finalist in the Pride of Britain Awards, run by the *Mirror Group* and sponsored by Richard Branson. There had been a list of categories printed in the *Mirror* for a few weeks earlier in the year and readers had been invited to vote for who they thought should get each award. The young lady photographer filled us in as best she could about the forthcoming event. As she had said that Dan had been nominated I naturally assumed that the photographs were just in case; I could not imagine how Daniel could possibly end up as an award winner as I felt that he had probably not been heard of sufficiently nationwide.

The categories were Courageous Children, Teacher and Nurse of the Year, Lifesaver of the Year, Charity Fundraiser and Good Neighbour of the Year, Outstanding Bravery, Pioneer, Inventor, and Entrepreneur of the Year. As well as an award for Animal Welfare, Outstanding Contribution to Public Life, there was a special award to Helen Rollason who was a sports presenter, which is an achievement itself in a male dominated TV area, who was also battling with cancer. Most Inspiring Young Sportsperson and a special award to Lennox Lewis after the travesty of justice that robbed him of the title Undisputed World Heavyweight Boxing Champion. There had been international outrage when the ringside judges declared Lewis's fight against Evander Holyfield a draw. There was another Special Award for Doreen and Neville Lawrence to mark their tenacity and drive for justice and unflinching quest for the truth in connection with the racial murder of their son Stephen in south-east London in 1993. Finally there was an International Award given to His Late Majesty King Hussein of Jordan and Her Majesty Queen Noor. The late king had worked tirelessly behind the scenes for charity, much of it in Britain, and his generosity knew no bounds. He had acted as a behind the scenes mediator during the Gulf War and it was his personal pressure on Saddam

Hussein which helped bring about the release of British hostages. King Hussein could be considered one of the greatest forces for peace we have seen and the world was saddened when he lost his fight against cancer whilst still a relatively young sixty-three-year-old. Queen Noor, as well as advancing women's rights in Jordan, travelled the world building invaluable links between the West and the Arab world. She also took on the job of patron of the Landmine Survivors' Network after the death of Princess Diana.

None of the recipients were known at this time and although we were told the awards were imminent we rather assumed that it might be best to put this to the back of our minds. Then amazingly, at the weekend we had a phone call from Fran Plews of the *Mirror* telling us that Daniel had actually won an award. Thank goodness Dan had bought a suit to wear to the Palace I, however, searched through my wardrobe but happily was dragged downtown by Richard to buy something a little special to wear. A letter followed the phone call on the Monday setting out the itinerary and enclosing the train tickets for three of us. I had requested at the weekend that my middle son, Adam, came as well because I knew Dan would like having him around.

When we received the letter we realised that the event would be at the Dorchester and that we would go up the day before and stay at a hotel nearby. We still did not realise the enormity of the event. We knew it was lunch in the ballroom of the Dorchester and that we would meet Tony Blair but I was still thinking low-key event. How wrong I was.

Wednesday, 19th May arrived and we got ourselves organised for the 14.06 train from Bristol Parkway to London Paddington. Richard took Dan, Adam and I to the station and away we went, still not really grasping what it was all about. When we arrived at Paddington a large gentleman greeted us by holding up a card with my name on. We were whisked away in a beautiful limo to the Chequers of Kensington where we were to stay with others involved in the next day's events. This hotel was absolutely wonderful. I had a single room that was like a studio apartment, decorated in art deco, shades of the sixties fashion. It was silver chrome thin tube legs, Habitat/Ikea style fittings, upwards shining wall lights, polished wood floors, rugs, vases and ornaments, a computer, huge telly, and what looked like a wall-to-wall wardrobe hid a stylish kitchen with sink, utensils for two, a microwave and so on. There was no restaurant in the Chequers, you rang out to get food delivered and presumably popped it into the microwave. There was a beautifully fitted en-suite bathroom with both shower and bath. I felt for a moment that I had been transported into a different world. Adam and Dan had a twin room that was a small flat, not a hotel room. It was the sort of hotel where very wealthy businessmen would stay for a while and conduct business from their rooms.

We had been asked to be in the bar for eight o'clock so we obviously did as requested. There dignitaries from the Mirror and Paul Burrell, Princess Diana's former butler greeted us. Other people who were to participate in the award ceremony were also staying in the Chequers; there was a light but elaborate buffet laid on and endless wine. There was quite a large Irish contingent from Omagh. I was thrilled to be able to meet twenty-three-year-old Donna Marie McGillion and her new husband who had taken the force of the Omagh bombing whilst out with their baby niece Breda, buying items for their impending wedding. Breda tragically did not survive that fatal day. Donna Marie had suffered sixty-five per cent burns mainly to her face and upper body, a cut across her head that needed fifty-six staples as well as lung damage. It was a miracle that she had survived at all. She didn't let the perpetrators of this heinous crime against humanity beat her, she went on to walk down the aisle as previously planned with Gary, he himself having sustained thirty-five per cent burns. I could quite understand why Donna Marie was receiving a bravery award.

There was a father and son, Nick and James Leeds, who had been rescued by the Port Isaac lifeboat crew in appalling conditions. Nick had dived in to rescue his stepson when he fell from rocks; both were trapped and swept into a deep cave that was rapidly filling with water. By the time the little lifeboat reached the pair they were in a sorry state. Nick had a dislocated shoulder, was semi-conscious and badly bruised. James had hypothermia. There were three men on the lifeboat, Kevin Pringle, just twenty-two, Mike Edkins and Paul Pollington, and it was the most treacherous mission they had ever faced. As they headed into the bay, massive waves slammed the boat against the roof of the cave, knocking out the radio and killing the engine. Kevin and Mike were thrown out into the cave. Paul managed to get the boat back into open water and tried in vain to restart the engine. All four, trapped in the cave

197

clinging to the rock face, cajoled and coaxed each other to keep conscious. Happily, five hours later a helicopter rescue team winched everyone to safety. I felt humbled to meet such men as these who risk their lives regularly for no pay in those tiny lifeboats. I do not think that there are awards big enough for such people. It was definitely an honour to be in the same room as them.

I didn't really get to know who anyone else was that evening except for Diane whose daughter Sarah was to receive a Courageous Children Award, and rightly so. I liked Diane a lot, she was my type of person and easy to talk to. Her car had plunged down a steep bank and flipped upside down in a fast-flowing freezing river. Both mother and daughter were trapped as the water flooded in. Diane was upside down, unable to free her seatbelt, and with her head and shoulders submerged in the icy water. Sarah, who was only fourteen, stayed calm, managed to free herself, dragged her mother from under the water, kick the jammed driver's door open and pull her mother out of the car. Diana had passed out so Sarah revived her mother and trekked across fields for help. No mean feat for one so young. Her mother was so proud of her it oozed from ever pore, though she, like me, wondered why her child had been chosen. Funnily enough Diana thought my son more than worthy and I felt likewise about her daughter.

Paul Burrell, who I have to admit I didn't have the vaguest idea who he was until I asked someone, was charming and spent a lot of time with Adam, Dan and I. He told us that there would be quite a few celebrities at the Dorchester the next day. This did not, however, prepare us even slightly for what was to come. He went on to say that they were hoping Sir Paul McCartney would appear but it would be touch and go as he had not been out since the loss of his wife and soul mate and it was the anniversary of Linda's death. We were told not to approach Sir Paul as he was very emotional still. It must have been something really special that those two had in their relationship, it must have been devastating to lose someone that you are so totally in tune with. The next day when I actually saw the great man I could see the pain etched in his face.

After this rather amazing evening we were expected to go to bed and sleep, a coach was coming to pick us all up at eleven the next morning to go to the Dorchester.

The Dorchester

On 20 May the coach arrived at the Chequers as arranged and off we all set on this great adventure. We had to sit on the coach for twenty minutes when we reached the venue as the police were running late and had not arrived to sweep the rooms with dogs, something always done when the Prime Minister was expected. Eventually though, we disembarked and ran the gauntlet of photographers into the building (rather reminiscent of the Crown Court in Bristol back in 1997).

The entrance of the Dorchester is impressive enough without going any further. We walked through a round room with ornate ceilings and mirrored walls, were handed name badges and taken on into a further much larger reception area that was full to bursting with celebrities. It was at this moment that I realised how big an event this was going to be though I wondered how we would figure in it exactly.

Glancing round the room, we seemed to be surrounded by most of the cast of *Coronation Street*, *Emmerdale*, *EastEnders* (probably left behind after the soap awards at the Dorchester the previous day). We chatted to Barbara Windsor for a while and I asked her if she would play me if I ever finished the book I was writing about Daniel and a film followed it. Barbara and I are much the same height and although she is a few years older than I am it would be hard to tell, she looks so trim and fit. I looked about me and it was all a bit too much to take in. The youngsters with our party were busily gathering autographs until we were ushered into a side room to meet Mr Blair and Queen Noor, who, incidentally, is stunning.

There were several other awards recipients in this other room that we had not previously met. The charismatic Northern Ireland Secretary Mo Mowlam who received an award for her Outstanding Contribution to Public Life, a wonderful woman fighting her own battle against a brain tumour with the same fearlessness that she uses in her political life.

I was particularly honoured to be in the same room as Helen

Smith, a young woman I had read about with horror. She must be the vision of everyone's nightmare. Her beautiful face and smile make you feel really humble. The young woman was twenty-four and studying for her doctorate at London's Imperial College after graduating from university in Bath when she was cruelly struck down with virulent meningococcal septicaemia. Whilst she lay in a coma surgeons amputated both her legs, most of her left arm and her right hand. I cannot begin to imagine the horror of waking up to find yourself in such a situation or, in fact, the pain her parents must have felt seeing her in such a terrible state and having to make the sort of life or death decisions they had to make. An amazing girl, fighting back and determined to have a full life despite everything and having this plan hampered by her local health authority who insist that she must wear primitive false legs and a hook instead of modern false limbs. Undeterred Helen is raising money herself for the limbs she deserves and also counsels other amputees and their families. Who would ever complain about toothache after having met that young lady.

The award winners were all herded on to a stage for a group photograph. Whilst this was happening Zoë Ball came into the room, spotted Dan and made a beeline for him, remembering him from the Young Achievers at the Palace the previous year. The beam on Daniel's face was a picture.

The photographs were finally completed and then we were all asked to take our places at the tables in the ballroom. There were place plans around the room and we were on table twenty-one, which I thought would be at the back but once again I was wrong.

We walked into the Dorchester ballroom; it was a stunning room. The large round tables were set out in rows of five about ten rows deep. It was exactly how the Bafta Awards look on the television. Our table was left of the centre table in the front row just in front of the stage. The tables had place names in situ and I had Carol Vorderman who was hosting the event on my left, Adam on my right and Dan was sitting next to Cilla Black who was pure delight and never stopped chatting. Next to Carol was a really delightful man, I am afraid I do not have a clue what his name was but he was definitely one of the *Mirror* hierarchy and very kind to me throughout the afternoon. I was too overwhelmed to look about too much but I imagine that every table had one of the awards recipients and several celebrities. On the next table to us, the central front table, clearly the head table, sat Queen Noor, Tony and Cherie Blair, Richard Branson who sponsored the event, Piers Morgan, then editor of the *Mirror* and now one of my favourite people as he made my son so happy that day. There was a place set for Sir Paul McCartney who arrived a little later almost unnoticed.

We ate the cordon bleu meal after the loyal toast. I ordered vegetarian and even though it was very attractive and tasted fine, I still do not have a clue what it was that I ate. Dan and Cilla discussed the possibility of slipping out for a burger and then finally as the last plate was cleared Carol took her place on the host's rostrum to start the proceedings and that is where she remained throughout.

Carol's rostrum was in the centre of a raised area. To the left of her was a very large screen placed high enough for those at the back to see. To the right of Carol was another podium, it was bright red with *Mirror* blazoned in white across the front. There was a bright red path leading up to this podium, it went in front of the tables and turned up a slope to where the speakers would stand. In fact the whole effect was very red.

Everyone listened in silence as Carol Vorderman explained why we were all there and how the proceedings were intending to go.

Piers Morgan took the long walk up to the podium and introduced himself and the awards, followed by a speech from Richard Branson who explained why he wanted to sponsor such an auspicious event. He apparently had his first suit on, bought at the insistence of his parents. He looked very good in it.

Tony Blair took the long walk next and spoke of the Kosovo crisis and his hopes for Northern Ireland and why he wanted to support this Pride of Britain Awards. As the Prime Minister had to go shortly and he was giving one of the awards, he remained on the podium whilst Carol explained how the judges, Richard Branson, Paul Burrell, Mel G, Dr Miriam Stoppard and Piers Morgan had sifted through the thousands of nominees sent in by *Mirror* readers and how difficult the task of picking winners from such a wonderful selection of entrants had been.

The first award was for the Teacher of the Year and it was given to Helen Ridding who, at only twenty-five, became the head teacher of a tough London school and turned it from an inner-city nightmare into an exemplary school praised by Ofsted, the government's education standards watchdog.

Firstly, the screen showed pictures of Helen and newspaper cuttings and then she was asked to go up and collect her award. The screen continued to show whoever was standing on the podium so the whole room could follow the proceedings totally.

Secondly, Queen Noor was asked to receive a posthumous award for her late husband King Hussein. She gave a long and passionate speech about her ties with Britain, and one of the many youngsters that the king had helped came up and handed her a bouquet of flowers. She was Emily Casey, two years old, and King Hussein had paid for her to have a life-saving heart operation in the US after life-or-death NHS surgery was cancelled five times. She was just one of the many people of all nationalities that this great man had helped.

Next, Sir Bobbie Charlton presented Liverpool footballer Michael Owen with the Young Sportsperson of the year award. Followed by Mo Mowlam with the Outstanding Contribution to Public Life.

Lifesavers of the Year were the wonderful crew of the Port Isaac lifeboat rescue unit. The father and son that they rescued on the horrendous day went up to the podium to praise their rescuers.

There was the Good Neighbour of the Year given to Irene James who had helped take care of her neighbour since he was born twenty-five years ago, giving his parents a much needed break from time to time.

Nurse of the Year was Yvonne John who worked at the Royal London Hospital in Whitechapel, East London, and spent her spare time working voluntarily for a disabled children's charity.

Charity Fundraiser was Sandra Howard whose severely epileptic son inspired her to start a charity called For a Better Life with Epilepsy – FABLE – after she discovered a revolutionary new treatment that was not available on the NHS and decided to raise money herself. Over the past three years Sandra's charity has raised nearly £100,000.

Then we moved on to Courageous Children, the awards presented by a couple of the Spice Girls and Josie Russell, that dear little girl who lost her mother and sister in a murderous hammer attack.

The first child up was Lucy-Rae Tamulevicius. When she was just ten months old she was diagnosed with a rare form of childhood cancer, neurolastoma, which affects the nervous system.

Doctors found a tumour in her chest, which was treated with chemotherapy. She is now eleven and in long-term remission but has developed a condition similar to arthritis and she has a curvature of the spine. Despite all this Lucy-Rae has continued dancing and won more than one hundred awards.

Sarah Dinsdale was next. We had met her and her mother, Diane, at the Chequers of Kensington the day before. A wonderful family.

Then there was a posthumous award for two dear little souls Rhys and Charly Daniels who had lost their long fight against the crippling illness, Batten's Disease. Their parents told how the children's courage and cheerfulness throughout had given them strength to cope. The Daniels have just seen the opening of their first two homes in Bristol, where Rhys was treated. They have set up the Rhys Daniels Trust which has raised nearly a million pounds to provide homes to be used by families of seriously ill youngsters whilst the child is having long-term treatment.

It struck me that Mr and Mrs Daniels deserved all the awards wrapped into one, having lived through such a nightmare.

Then we moved on to the Outstanding Bravery Awards. Adam and Dan looked calm but I was starting to get nervous for them. The first two were involved in the horrendous Omagh bombing. Twenty-nine people lost their lives that day and 250 were injured. The screen showed slides of the devastation, it looked like a war zone. How a human being could inflict such misery is beyond my comprehension.

Michael McNally was sitting in the bus depot when he heard the device explode. He drove his bus into the heart of the carnage and ferried dozens of the badly injured to hospital, literally picking people off the street despite the possibility of a second device which was still being sought at the time.

Next came the amazing Donna Marie McGillion. She gave a marvellous speech about her hopes for peace in Northern Ireland and got a standing ovation. There is one brave and determined young woman.

Then Carol started to tell the audience about my son, Dan. It was a strange experience having him spoken about so highly and seeing the newspaper cuttings flash across the screen along with photographs of him in hospital. Adam led Dan up the slope to the foot of the podium where Lisa Potts, herself having received the

George Medal for bravery, was waiting to present him with his award. The award was a large engraved piece of glass on a stand. Adam mounted the steps to read a short speech partially prepared by Dan, saying how thrilled he was for receiving such an award. Adam spoke about how every now and again you have to make a split second decision and that Dan's was whether to try to stop a fight or live with the consequences of doing nothing. Dan had obviously decided to intervene so his conscience was clear but as a result, unfortunately, the same could not be said of his eyesight any more. Adam went on to say how thankful Dan was to his family who have helped him to come to terms with his new lifestyle. Adam added his own ending by telling everyone about Dan's previous illness and how Dan was already registered disabled when he went to the aid of the young man he saved, making his actions even more amazing. Adam ended his speech by telling Dan than he loved him, coming down from the podium to give him a hug. Needless to say, everyone rose to their feet. It was amazing to see all those famous faces crying over my son. That moment, if I could have it frozen in time, would be the moment I would want to keep forever. I smiled at Cilla and we hugged, both having three sons I feel gave us something in common that day.

The last Bravery Award was to the wonderful Helen Smith, wheeled up the ramp, still with that illuminating smile.

There were just seven more awards to go. Richard Emanuel of DX Communications, Entrepreneur of the Year. Viagra scientists represented by Dr Nick Terrett took the Inventor of the Year. Pioneers of the Year were Richard Noble and Squadron Leader Andy Green who at 763 mph broke the land speed record. Special Awards to sports presenter Helen Rollason whom Dan had a long chat with before the ceremony and who has very sadly since died of cancer, Lennox Lewis (to compensate for the most outrageous sporting decision ever) and Doreen and Neville Lawrence, the parents of Stephen murdered because of his colour. The very last award was given by Paul McCartney in his late wife Linda's memory for work in connection with animal welfare.

A different celebrity gave each award. How the organisers actually chose which of the many famous faces there that day were actually going to present each award I do not know. Irish Ronan Keating, once lead singer of Boyzone, was the obvious choice for Donna Marie as he had visited the Omagh victims; he has a very gentle way about him as well.

I do not think there was a dry eye in the place at the end of the awards and to my amazement people swarmed over to our table to speak to my sons. So many people whom I would never have dreamt of being in the same room with congratulated Adam on his fine and moving speech. Football hero Sir Bobby Charlton came over and asked if he could speak to Daniel, what could I say! He sat next to Dan and explained who he was and they spoke for a while. Richard Branson, whom we had spoken to earlier and I had cheekily given him one of Joe's band's CDs, and Piers Morgan thanked us for our contribution to the event, there is no way I could thank them enough for allowing us to be there. We had a long chat to Lisa Potts; what a beautiful young lady she is, broad smile, blonde hair, stunningly pretty and really nice with it. We promised to keep in touch and we have. She has been to our house for dinner since and included Dan in a book she wrote about heroes. Then we were introduced to Paul McCartney at his request; he looked very tired and drawn. I felt so sorry about his loss. He spoke very gently to Dan, introduced himself by putting his hands on his shoulders so Dan would have no doubt who he was speaking to. Paul congratulated Adam for having the nerve to stand up and speak and for having done it so well. That ranked highly amongst my proudest moments, my boys being praised by the great man himself. It was at this Pride of Britain ceremony that Sir Paul met Heather Mills, who was there to give support for her Limb Appeal, Heather had lost a leg herself which cut short her modelling career. Next Lennox Lewis and Chris Eubank who were delightful cornered us. They were giving Dan tips on how to handle himself next time, next time, heaven forbid! They made quite a double act.

I told Ronan Keating, who was with his young wife, that he was far too good looking and congratulated him on his new baby. He charmingly said that if his child turned out as well as Daniel he would be very pleased.

Chris Evans promised us a visit to *TFI Friday* if we in turn could promise that we could get drunk. He was another person who is very nice in person and Jules Barringer, his personal assistant told us, that if Chris said something he was always true to his word. We had been talking to Jules earlier and she was telling us about all the dreadful music tapes that they have to sift through every week and I told her that Joe was in a band called Krimo who were worth listening to. She spoke to Chris and he said to send a copy of Joe's tape; if it was any good maybe they might get on *TFI Friday* on the day we all went up.

Unfortunately it was by now 4.30 and we had a train to catch at 5.30. If it hadn't been reserved tickets we would have stayed a lot longer, we just didn't want the day to end. I tried to explain to Chris Evans that we had to go because we couldn't afford to just throw the train tickets away. I'm afraid we were back to the 'them and us' syndrome for a moment there.

Everywhere we turned there was another famous face actually wanting to speak to us, it was very strange. I am pleased to say that I had a chat with Doreen Lawrence, it was very enlightening. I rather thought I wouldn't like her as she seems rather formidable, but she was charming and I could have talked all evening to her, we do after all have quite a bit in common. We both have sons who were attacked by unpunished thugs and we both know who the assailants were, which makes it worse.

People reached out to shake Dan's hand as he passed. He was really quite overwhelmed by the whole event and I felt so sorry that so much had been lost on him because he couldn't see. We left the Dorchester on a real high. The car was waiting to take us to the station, we just had a moment to talk to a couple more famous faces before we were whisked away back to the real world.

We obviously couldn't stop talking about the day all the way home. Richard Branson had promised Dan and Adam a holiday along with the other award winners. They did not know where it would be or when.

The next day I had a call from the *This Morning* crew, Richard and Judy wanted Adam and Dan on their show the next Monday.

There was a lot of publicity in the *Mirror* about the Pride of Britain Awards and Piers told us that they were planning to televise the following year's event. Because of the publicity Dan was much in demand. Dan and I were asked by John Turner of Radio Bristol to talk about the awards which obviously we were pleased to do. He also gave a few brief interviews to the local papers.

The Richard and Judy Show

On Friday 21 May I went to work as usual and Dan slept in only to be woken by a phone call from Michelle Bowker of the *This Morning* crew asking if he and Adam could come back to London for the Richard and Judy Show the next Monday. Adam's speech and Dan's story had impressed the couple so much that they wanted to speak to my boys on air. Dan passed the phone number on to me to contact Michelle and make the arrangements.

Monday morning and Adam, Dan and I were off to catch the 6.30 a.m. train to London, having picked the tickets up the day before as arranged. Once again a man holding a plaque with Gallimore emblazoned on it greeted us at the station and we hopped into another limo and were swept away to the *This Morning* recording studios.

The studio looked to me like a large warehouse. We fought our way through props to the very large and very slow lift, which took us up just one floor. We were led through a labyrinth of narrow passages and deposited in the 'Green Room', which was surprisingly lacking in green and was more blue and yellow. There were croissants, fruit juice and coffee waiting for our arrival and several friendly faces ready to explain what was about to happen. Most of the programme was dedicated to Richard (Dickie) Attenborough and his favourite films, old and modern. The boys were due to be on at eleven o'clock as a sort of break from films. Why we had to get to the studio so early I cannot imagine if we were not wanted until eleven o'clock.

We sat watching the television in the corner of the room, following the Richard Attenborough interview. At some point, whilst a short fashion display was taking place, Richard Madely came into the Green Room for a quick word. I stayed quiet whilst Dan and Adam talked to 'mine host' about the show and answered a few questions thrown at them about the details surrounding Daniel's injuries.

Richard seemed genuinely annoyed about the outcome of the

trial and interested in general about the details of the case.

Adam and Dan were examined facially to see if it was necessary to ply them with make-up and it was decided that they would be fine with just a little powder to stop the shine. Then Dan was taken on the precarious journey through the studio, over enough wires to make Spaghetti Junction look tidy, to be sat on a settee so the producer could make a short trailer for his forthcoming interview.

I was surprised how small and cluttered everything was. Every corner of the room had a separate compact set in it. One was arranged like a cinema for the Dickie Attenborough session, there was a kitchen in another, and what looked like a very small sitting room housing Richard and Judy in a third.

Back we went to the Green Room to await the witching hour. 10.45 a.m. arrived and the three of us returned to the studio set, this time for the actual interview. I handed over an assortment of photographs that I had been asked to bring with me; one of Dan before the incident and some taken whilst he was in hospital.

I sat in the cinema section and watched my boys talking to Richard and Judy with admiration. Adam spoke with such clarity and confidence and Daniel surprised me with his repartee. Daniel got in a couple of very good points regarding how to approach someone with unclear eyesight. He mentioned how you should touch the person you are approaching on the shoulder to make it clear that you are talking to them and how you should never just walk away leaving them talking to thin air. Afterwards, they told me how easy it had been, how Richard and Judy had made them feel comfortable and actually feel as if they had been just talking casually in a sitting room. I had sat with one eye on the monitor and the other on the actual set and was so glad I had videoed the interview to watch when we got home as it was hard to really take everything in when so much was going on around you. I was impressed by the clever way that the camera crew cut the photos into the interview from time to time, bringing home the horror of the incident that had left Daniel blinded.

We just had a couple of moments to say our goodbyes to the stars of the show. I had a hug from Judy and then we went back to the Green Room for sandwiches. Richard Madely popped into the room and asked if there was anyone we wanted to meet or anything else he could do for us. Dan had mentioned the fact that I was writing a book about the incident that blinded him and I promised to get in touch if it ever got to print so we could all come back and talk about the book. We stayed another hour or so watching the rest of the show on the television then decided to go back to Bristol.

As usual there is always something that puts a damper on a good time. On this occasion it was the fact that my mother's sister, Aunt Evelyn, was in hospital in Bristol having had a funny turn the weekend before. It did not seem at first that there was anything to worry about but after a few days it became clear that life had become a chore to her and she did not want to fight to recover. I loved my aunt like a mother, she was my friend and confidante and I wanted to get back to Bristol to see that she was still there for me. My own mother, sweet as she was, was always a little vague. Eve was the opposite, she was bright, alive and vibrant. You could talk anything over with Eve and I did.

We were driven to the railway station, clutching messages from viewers that had either come by e-mail or over the phone. There was a message from a faith healer urging us to contact him, one from a university student who was doing a thesis on blindness and wanted some input from Daniel, and others from people asking all sorts of questions about the incident and how it had changed Dan's life. I made a point of contacting everyone who left a number to call.

We phoned on ahead and Joe met us at Bristol Parkway Station. I literally popped into my house for a second before hurrying off to the hospital to see my aunt. One of Eve's friends was sitting at her beside when I arrived and I could see that time was short for my dear aunt. She was in a very deep sleep and unable to be roused. I picked up her hand and knew it would probably be the last time I would have any physical contact with this wonderful lady. I didn't stay very long as I was tired and wanted to get back to Daniel, I didn't want to spoil his day.

Adam, Dan and I watched the video of the interview; unfortunately, it wasn't very clear. I think that the equipment wasn't quite tuned in correctly but we were all pleased with the content of the piece.

I drove Adam home and another exciting day was over. Unfortunately, the early hours of the morning brought the news that Evelyn had died and the Richard and Judy interview didn't seem quite so exciting after all.

The next couple of weeks were taken up with Evelyn's funeral, already booked, paid for and planned by her a few years earlier, and sorting out her flat.

A light spot was a call from Jules Barringer, Chris Evan's PA, to ask when she could expect Dan and his brothers for a visit to *TFI Friday*. Bearing in mind that the season only ran until the end of June, if they didn't go in June they would have to wait until September. So obviously they wanted to go up sooner rather than later and 18th June was the date agreed, the weekend before the Glastonbury festival. Joe's band, Krimo (later called Kreemo), was booked to play at Glastonbury.

Joe and the rest of Krimo were thrilled to be playing at Glastonbury. They had all been there the year before and despite the muddy experience were desperate to go back again. Joe had bumped into Ronnie Size whom he had gone to school with, having been born in the same road in Bristol. Ronnie was called Ryan Williams when we knew him in Sefton Park Road and I was quite surprised when he became famous. He was always a nice enough lad and Joe and him always got on well although Ronnie was a couple of years older than Joe.

Glastonbury is quite expensive when you have young children at home to consider. Happily though, actually playing at the event meant getting in for free and using the band enclosure, which also meant better toilets and better facilities in general. Needless to say Joe had a fantastic time at Glastonbury. Krimo played in the bandstand by the jazz area at 2 p.m. on the Saturday to quite a good size audience.

Dan chose not to go to Glastonbury much as he would like to have listened to Joe. It is just too complicated a set up for a blind person to cope with, all those tents and enormous crowds of people.

Joe has played at several festivals since including Ashton Court in Bristol, which was easier for Dan.

TFI Friday

Once Dan had made up his mind which Friday he wanted to go up to London for *TFI Friday*, I was on the phone to Ginger Productions to tell Jules. I had already decided not to go myself as I think I would have stuck out like a sore thumb at my age, much as I would actually have liked to have done. Dan asked if Joe, Kate and Adam could all go and the answer was positive. We could have asked several people but they would have been placed down in the audience instead of in the bar, which was the preferred place to be. Unfortunately Jules had not received the Krimo tape we sent as requested. She is so protected by the staff about her that she doesn't get to actually open her own mail. I should imagine that the studio must be inundated with tapes and video sent in by would-be stars and it would be very difficult to actually get any work done if your whole time was taken up by going through these every day.

So unfortunately the plan to have Joe's band play on the show was not going to happen at this time.

We didn't realise that Chris Evans had planned to arrange travel and a hotel for the travellers, although he did say at the Pride of Britain Awards that he would. Dan and his brothers were going to go to *TFI Friday* even if they had to arrange getting there themselves, luckily this problem did not arise.

Jules soon had everything arranged for 18th June. The morning post on the Tuesday brought a recorded delivery of train tickets, details of the hotel and a map of how to find Ginger Studios from the hotel along with a mad letter from Jules explaining the plans for Friday and Saturday. Dan and the others were so excited, Kate was the worst.

The four of them caught the 10.30 a.m. train from Temple Meads station on the morning of Friday 18th. It was good planning reserving the train seats because as the royal wedding of Edward and Sophie was set for the Saturday, people were flocking to London. People are very strange, why would anyone want to go to a stranger's wedding?

A car met Dan's party at Paddington Station and they were taken to a hotel near the Embankment. It was a lot different from the Checkers of Kensington but it was clean and close to their eventual destination. The youngsters were so grateful to have had a hotel booked and paid for that they would have happily stayed anywhere.

TFI Friday was recorded at 3.30 in the afternoon. It used to go out live but people spoilt that by swearing and Chris was in danger of having the show taken out of the six o'clock slot, so they started pre-recording and cutting out bits if necessary, putting them back in for the later viewing of the programme.

They got to the studio an hour before 'lift-off'. They went through the guests' entrance and were issued with a pass each that allowed them into any area in the studio. The studio was much smaller than it looked on the television.

Mel B of Spice Girl fame was there, complete with baby Phoenix, along with Courtney Love. The baby was with a minder in the garden and Kate said it was really bonnie.

Dan was hoping to speak to Mel as she had been one of the judges at the Pride of Britain but unfortunately it was not to be, she just swept on, did her bit and left.

Jules was absolutely charming to Dan and the others and Joe remembered to bring a copy of the Krimo CD to hand to her personally. Stools are not allowed in the bar normally but Chris insisted that Dan sat down, which was very kind but of course meant he was stuck in one spot. Incidentally, the drinks were real and free; however, if you looked miserable they threaten to charge you. Everyone was very friendly and there was a real party atmosphere. A good time was had by all. A young lady recognised Dan from the *Good Morning* programme and treated him like a film star, which amused him no end.

I watched them on the television and they all seemed to be grinning from ear to ear. There was an inquest after the show and whatever was said round the table upset Chris. Jules said that they had intended to go to the pub across the road as usual and on to a night club but as Chris was now in a bad mood they would let him go home. The crew took Dan, Joe, Adam and Kate across the road anyway and Jules was very embarrassed. She need not have been, the day had been all that the youngsters had expected and more. Chris had been great at the start and he is known to be temperamental, so you have to take your chances. Besides I would imagine he was tired, what with doing a breakfast radio show as early as he did and then *TFI Friday* in the day, I think he was entitled to get a little tetchy. Dan reckons he would go to *TFI* every Friday if he could, he enjoyed himself so much, mainly thanks to Jules.

Jules Barrington is the nicest woman you could ever meet and all of Chris's staff are totally clued up on blindness. The fact that Chris is the patron of Blind Golf is probably the reason. He has obviously taken an interest in how to interact with unsighted people and passed on his skills.

Joe and Kate went over to Forest Hill on the other side of London to see friends, leaving Dan and Adam with Jules and the crew. Jules very kindly invited Dan and Adam back to *TFI Friday* in September when the new season started, a date to be set later, with the plan that Dan would be on Chris's radio show in the morning first. She said she would arrange two nights in a hotel for them. I think Chris Evans had himself one hell of a PA there.

A great deal of alcohol was consumed that evening finished off by a meal in a nearby restaurant. Apparently Dan and Adam were up for breakfast at just after seven in the morning, hard to imagine, as they did not get up that early normally as a rule. Joe and Kate didn't make it for breakfast but they joined forces to catch the midday train home. London was heaving, what with Edward and Sophie's wedding and some sort of protest march that was taking place as well, it wasn't a comfortable place to hang about in that day.

Dan did, however, have other good weekends at *TFI Friday* thanks to Chris and his team. The best one being a longer weekend when he and Adam went to the Virgin Radio Station and sat in on the *Rock and Roll Football Programme*. They spent the majority of Saturday with Chris and Gale Porter who was lovely to them. They ate chicken and drank champagne and as you can imagine had a brilliant day. Chris's team are so clued up about blindness that it made life so easy for Dan. He wasn't treated like a halfwit as so often happens. Everyone was, however, careful and understanding about the difficulties that come with being poorly sighted.

I wrote and thanked Chris several times for his kindness and consideration. I only hope that he realises what a boost he had given to my son's confidence. I liked the fact that he never made

Life Goes On

I do not know long term what life will throw at Daniel but at this time he was on a roller coaster of events. He had been invited to speak at several schools in Bristol and he is a regular speaker at Cotham where we used to work. He talks about the dangers of alcohol and the streets of Bristol at night. He also talks about disabilities and how to treat people who are disabled for whatever reason, obviously scanning in on blindness mainly. He is trying to get the message over that unsighted people are not aliens and should not be treated as such. He explains how to approach an unsighted person and how to speak to them. He seems to go down quite well.

In October 1999 Dan and Adam went on holiday to Cala Santandria, compliments of Richard Branson, and had a great time. It was good to meet up with others from the Pride of Britain; Adam said it seemed as though they were on holiday with an extended family.

We were pleased to be visited by Lisa Potts, who wanted Dan to give her a hand with a project she was undertaking. Lisa is an absolutely delightful young woman, as brave as she is beautiful.

In the last week of October Richard and I took Dan away with a coach full of friends to Belgium. The trip was marred at the start by the sad news that Cilla Black's husband, Bobby Willis, had lost his fight for life against cancer. I felt it hard to believe that this extremely pleasant, unassuming man who had treated Dan with such kindness as short a time ago as May that year had died.

Now we had lost Helen Rollason who was absolutely delightful and so full of fun, as well as Bobby to this disgusting disease. Once again I felt privileged to have been able to meet such people if only briefly and also so glad that I had been given my son back.

We returned from Belgium to discover that once again burglars had visited us. These people were so determined to get into our house that when they found, having demolished the conservatory door, that they could not get any further into the house they simply got up on to our kitchen extension and smashed their way through the double-glazed bathroom window. Then they came downstairs and literally took the stable door into the conservatory off its hinges from the inside. They must have been on site ages and made one hell of a noise. Just what you need after a few days away! We had only just had the conservatory fitted and felt sure it would keep burglars out. We had already replaced the French doors damaged the year before with heavily reinforced doors.

Once again exactly the same items were stolen. They had not bothered to look in draws they had not found valuables in last time so obviously it was the same people. I had been so confident that we were burglar-proof, that I had left my last remaining valuable ring behind, my engagement ring and a pearl ring that was my Aunt Eve's twenty-first birthday present from my grandparents. She had given the ring to me just before she died aged eighty-six. So now I had nothing left at all of sentimental value. The police were as sure as I was that it was the same people who had burgled us before. It makes you very wary of leaving the house for more than a day.

Dan paid a high price to acquire an element of fame and I know he hopes to use his story to benefit others. He is concentrating on raising money mainly for the RNIB, abseiling over 200 feet down such tourist attractions as the Avon Gorge. He also is trying to organise starting up a charity of his own called 'Blind Aid'. He wants to raise money to help individual blind people recommended by others. Instead of just giving money to large established charities such as RNIB he wanted to seek out people who cannot afford to buy items that would make their lives easier, or organise and fund alterations to blind people's houses where necessary. We have met a great number of blind people in the past few years and realised that they usually only hold down ill-paid jobs. Being blind is an expensive business. There are so many wonderful electronic gadgets that you can get, such as the 'parrot', a hand-held device that stores phone numbers and, when held up to the phone handset, dials them for you. Talking software for computers, talking scanners all beyond the grasp of many because of the cost. Dan wants to try to even the balance and buy these type of items for individuals who would most benefit from them.

He does himself have all the latest equipment attached to his computer and has started to catch up with his own correspondence. All of a sudden, really from Christmas 1999, Dan seems to have come alive. In months before, occasionally the lights had come on but they seemed to flicker and go out again. Now at last they seemed to be staying on most of the time.

In May 2000 Dan and I were invited back to the Pride of Britain Awards. It was even stranger going as guests with so many famous faces. People who remembered Dan from the year before came up to say how well he was looking and to shake his hand. We were greeted like long lost friends by Paul Burrell, all the *Mirror* crowd, Judy Finnegan, Lisa, of course, and several others who remembered us from the year before, which was lovely. We spent quite a bit of time with William Roach (Ken of *Coronation Street*) and his wife. Bill was kind enough to say that he had wanted to speak to Dan the year before but didn't get the opportunity so he would make up for it then. He was really very nice and looks much younger than his age.

We were at the table with Chris Eubank and Dan had his back to Martine McCutcheon who was very sweet and friendly. We were on a table next to the outrageous Michael Barrymore. He was like a hyperactive child, he never sat still. I was also glad to be near Matthew Wright who is absolutely barmy, he never stops laughing.

The awards were great but I felt it lacked the spontaneity of the year before that had given it an extra something. Probably because it was televised and more poised and orderly. Carol Vorderman took centre stage again. I was talking to her mother later in the afternoon and she was such a nice down-to-earth lady. I even spoke to Christopher Lee briefly and he still seemed creepy even without the cloak and teeth.

Dan and I went on for a drink with the *Mirror* crowd after the awards and had a really good time. Everyone kept asking where Adam was. Because we had made our own way to the Hilton for the awards we were not rushed to get home. Dan was very bright and chatty and we spent most of the evening with Sue Carroll who is a lovely lady. I think that between us we managed to put the world to rights.

We had to go home and place our feet firmly back on terra firma and get ourselves prepared for the next stage in our lives which was to pursue the complaint against Southmead and Frenchay Hospital A & E Departments.

217

Preparing for Battle

I have learnt an incredible lot since my son's assault in 1996, some of which I wish I did not know. I now know that fighting the health authority is a difficult exercise and if you are involved in an incident or accident it is a good idea to be very careful where the ambulance takes you.

In my pursuit of justice I have learnt that so long as laid down procedures are carried out it is difficult to pinpoint accountability, and that these procedures differ in hospital authorities. So when you are picking your child's school based on good results and ethos maybe we should be given a list of hospitals and their priorities as well so we can make sure we are living in the best area for treatment.

I wanted simply to protest at the treatment that Sarah and I had at both Southmead and Frenchay A & E departments on that horrendous night in 1996. In the pursuit of this we acquired the medical records that related to Daniel's stay in Ward 2, the Serious Head Injuries Observation Unit. From these records we discovered that a scan of Dan's brain on 3rd June showed serious swelling but was subsequently ignored, or treated conservatively as they term it. This started our wonderful solicitor off on a tangent and we discovered that there were certain medical procedures that could have been administered that would have saved my son's sight. Had Daniel been at that stage artificially paralysed, intubated and ventilated, and the intra-cranial pressure monitored and aggressively treated he would not have suffered the degree of damage that he eventually sustained on 8th June when he arrested. The hospital were happy enough to admit this as fact but were adamant that no negligence resulted as it was not the policy of the hospital to use this procedure, as being ventilated for a long period can damage the vocal cords. Other reasons for not rushing into ventilation were that it upset families to see their loved ones in intensive care on life support. I would have hoped that the patient's welfare came well above the feelings of family in the priority stakes. The possible lack of beds in the ICU being a consideration I could relate to but it would not have been an issue in the particular hospital we were dealing with.

The Glasgow Coma Scale of the patient decides the whole plan of action in Head Injury Units. It seems that Daniel's Glasgow Coma Scale did not tally with the other danger signs, such as disorientation, pupils being sluggish, a right lower motor neurone palsy and the gag being reduced but the hospital had chosen to ignore the danger signs and stick with the Glasgow Coma Scale findings. He had actually arrived at A & E with a Glasgow Coma Scale of six which is dangerously low, but this was put down quite incorrectly to alcohol intake despite protests from Sarah.

Naturally we contacted other hospitals through our solicitor and there is a variation across the country as to the stated treatment of serious head injuries patients. I believe that Frenchay have actually changed their policy since my son's treatment, too late for him unfortunately.

Endless statements were gathered from different eminent specialists in different fields of medicine, logged and placed in different coloured ring binders ready for court. I had copies of most statements and was particularly disturbed by a report on possible neglect compiled by a consultant at the Emergency Unit at the University of Wales.

The report mentioned that a high level of alcohol intake was recorded as the reason for Daniel's level of consciousness at Southmead A & E Department on the night of 31st May. It was also noted that no attempt was made to measure the alcohol level. It was stated that although a high level of alcohol could alter the level of consciousness it should never be assumed that this is in fact the cause. If tests had been carried out and a low alcohol level discovered then it would have strongly indicated that a significantly depressed level of consciousness was as a result of a serious head injury. He was critical of the fact that no such tests were taken. He also noted that the A & E doctor recorded that there was no loss of consciousness, which he found difficult to understand because at the time Dan had a Glasgow Coma Scale of six, well below the 'coma' classification of eight. Added confusion comes from the fact that the ambulance records showed that Dan had a normal pulse and blood pressure but was 'not K'OD' (not knocked out). This I found strange, as he was unconscious when I arrived at the scene and the witnesses had placed Dan in the recovery position prior to the ambulance arriving because he was knocked out cold. The ambulance notes went on to state – eye opening, nil; verbal response, none; motor response, localising pain, that is, a total of six from fifteen on the Glasgow Coma Scale. So the ambulance crew wrote 'not knocked out' and then proceeded to register that Dan's Coma Scale was six which does indeed show that he was unconscious. The Glasgow Coma Scale measures the level of consciousness and a GCS of less than eight indicates 'coma', that is, deeply unconscious, and this contradicted the hand written notes of 'not KO'D'. I was beginning to despair; even the paramedics seemed to be having a bad day that day.

There was apparently also a record that Dan's oxygen saturation was only ninety-three per cent on arrival. This is a level of oxygenation of the bloodstream and normally this is ninety-nine to one hundred per cent. Any level below ninety-four per cent is significant and suggests a potentially serious lack of oxygen in the bloodstream.

Dan had a laceration to the scalp at the back of his head which was closed and stapled in Southmead A & E. It seems, however, that this laceration was not cleaned and it later became infected and bits of grit found to be present some days later. The report was very critical of this, of course. It was also critical of the time span between Dan being taken to Southmead in an ambulance, his transfer to Frenchay and the added delays once there before proper attention was given to Dan's injuries. It was not, however, felt that the treatment at both A & E Departments, although well below standard, had added to Daniel's injuries.

So Southmead and Frenchay A & E, although considered to be very shoddy and our treatment there considered below expectations, as the doctor and houseman concerned did not cause any actual damage to my son they cannot be called to book. So you can be treated in an obscenely rude manner by medical staff but so long as they only insult you and do not actually worsen your condition, it is acceptable. I do not think so, but that is what the law states.

As for the other and more serious matter, this we decided could not be swept under the carpet and Daniel and I reached the conclusion that we had to take on the NHS on a need to know basis. Dan wanted to know if Frenchay could have in fact saved his sight as suspected and why they chose not to.

Firstly Frenchay tried to blame Behçets for clouding the issue. This was disproved by experts and so it was back to the following written procedures ploy that does not advocate intubation and ventilation prior to neurological deterioration. Careful scrutiny of the medical notes showed that there was a marked neurological deterioration and the presence of the scan taken on 3rd June confirmed brain swell that could lead to brain stem dysfunction. This showed to our minds possible clinical negligence, not an easy thing to prove but we decided to try. We did not feel that Frenchay's policy of wait and see was right in a serious head injuries unit; we could see no benefit in a policy of only shutting the stable door after the horse has bolted. Frenchay's wait and see decision was a very costly decision, both in terms of Daniel's health and the expense to the health authority, considering how many weeks Dan languished in Intensive Care. I would like to state at this point that Frenchay Intensive Care is probably the best in the world, I have nothing but the highest of praise for everyone involved there. It was only Ward 2, the so-called Emergency Head Injuries Close Observation Ward, that we had had problems with.

Hector Stamboulieh took time and trouble to explain to Dan and me the problems connected to attempting to sue such a defendant as the NHS due to a little known law connected to medical negligence claims called the Bolam Clause. You have to actually prove that *no other* doctor in the land would have behaved as the medical staff did at Frenchay in the week of 31st May to 8th June. You only have to have one other health authority of the same stature that agrees with Daniel's treatment, regardless of your finding several who do not, and the case is lost. The whole thing leaves a very bad taste, but to my mind it just comes down to the fact that my son's sight would have been saved if he had come to grief in, say, Cambridge or London, which makes the National Health Service just another lottery and I found that fact disturbing.

The first obstacle was funding the case. Hector got in touch with the Legal Aid Board and they agreed to cover the cost of the proceedings, which was estimated to be around £30,000 at the start. So we decided to go ahead and pursue a claim for loss of earnings due to clinical negligence against the North Bristol NHS Trust. Southmead and Frenchay Hospitals had by now combined under one trust so we were really taking on the big boys.

There was a lot of work to be done, statements to be collected and endless discussions about that first week in hospital. I was very glad that I had kept such full notes of events, people thought me very strange at the time but it proved very useful.

It was towards the beginning of the year 2000 when we got our first possible date for a hearing. This was altered to the end of July and was due to take around five days. Once again the North Bristol NHS Trust managed to get a stay of execution by insisting that the hearing would need at least eight to ten days, which actually proved to be correct. Dan was being sent for meetings connected with case all over England and the likely costs were now around £50,000.

We went up to London to see a Behçets specialist who turned out to be the very doctor that we had been to see under the National Health as a referral from our GP in July 1995. This time we were there in the private sector and what a difference! When we had seen Professor Dorian Haskard previously at Hammersmith Hospital in London where he is an honorary consultant in rheumatology, we had waited in the general waiting area on one of the hard seats placed in rows and were shown into an adequate but simple examination room. This time as we were paying for this visit under the private sector it was a very different matter. Firstly you have to gain access into the private wing. Once inside the waiting area we were shown to one of the alcoves containing settees, a coffee table, magazines and we were offered tea or coffee. The décor was very chic and the whole atmosphere palatial; both Dan and I decided on the spot that private medicine was for us.

Professor Haskard greeted us like old friends and was clearly moved by Daniel's plight. It wasn't a long visit but the results were a seven-page report for the courts.

The report detailed Daniel's already complicated medical history. It explained how Daniel had been admitted to the Bristol Children's Hospital in 1983 for the first time at the age of eight with widespread lymphadenopathy and left lower lobe pneumonia. Whist in the ward he had developed penile ulcers, both externally and in the urethral meatus plus mycoplasma infection. The following year, aged nine, Dan had been admitted with a likewise list of ailments.

Then again in 1985, aged ten, Dan was admitted to the Children's Hospital in Bristol with progressive buccal ulceration to the point of being too painful to drink. He also had an intermittent fever and sore eyes. In May 1986 Daniel was admitted again and it was decided that Daniel had Steven-Johnson Syndrome. At this time he was having four full-blown attacks a year with oral and genital ulcerations, fevers, conjunctivitis and a severe cough. A Dr Williams, however, had apparently doubted the wisdom of the Steven-Johnson Syndrome as the problem and had suggested that maybe Behçets was the disease.

Daniel had not been admitted to hospital again until 1989. He was by now fifteen and he went to the Bristol Royal Infirmary for the first time because of vomiting and neck stiffness. This was thought to be viral meningitis.

Daniel continued to have almost perpetual headaches and suffered from severe fatigue. In 1992 Daniel was admitted to Southmead Hospital on two separate occasions under Dr Glover who now was thinking in terms of Behçets. By the end of 1992 Southmead Hospital was liaising with Bristol Royal Infirmary over the management of Daniel's putative Behçets Syndrome. Dan was back in hospital in 1993 with a history of malaise, photophobia, headache and oral ulcerations. 1994 and 1995 had both been difficult years for Daniel health wise. In 1995 Dan had been admitted to the BRI with fever, headache and a right upper lobe pneumonia.

Under the backcloth of all the previous medical evidence before him, Professor Haskard had to conclude as to whether he felt that Behçets had played any part in hindering Daniel's treatment at Frenchay in 1996 and he felt it had not. He only said that he felt Daniel's quality of life due to Behçets was now much diminished because of his blindness.

This court case was really a paper exercise. There were literally dozens of witness statements taken and submitted. The judge read them all, as did council of course. Some statements, my own as an example, were taken as read and their accuracy never questioned. Other statements needed closer inspection and the answers to a few questions. People submitting these statements would be asked to appear in court and answer questions about their statements. Professor Haskard was not asked to appear. All the statements were in the coloured ring binders previously mentioned, cross-referenced and the defence, judge and our team all had exactly the same information. There was everything possible, starting with Dan's medical records from birth to the present day.

Because so little importance is placed on the loss of sight in this country it was important to seek damages for future care and loss of earnings for Daniel. Daniel had to meet with Gwen Watkins, a state-registered occupational therapist, who wrote a rehabilitation cost report, Michael Charles, an employment consultant, who wrote a report on Daniel's employment potential, and a neuropsychologist called Frank Vingoe who was supposed to establish whether Daniel would have ever worked again after the incident had he not lost his sight. Dr Vingoe seemed to think that once Dan had recovered fully from his head injuries, had the relapse not occurred on 8th June 1996, he would have gone back to his previous employment. The NHS Trust didn't seem to like this report from Dr Vingoe so they brought another neuropsychologist into play called Dr RM. Now Dan and I had gone to Cardiff to meet Dr Vingoe but had never met Dr M. Dr M concluded that Dan would not have been mentally able to return to work even if he had not collapsed on 8th June. So the NHS Trust was trying to imply that even if Dan had not gone into a coma and subsequently lost his sight, he was unemployable due to the brain damage already caused by the original injuries, thus cutting costs owed if proved negligent. The bit that amused me about Dr M's report was the fact that the first half concentrated on the idea that he did not feel Dr Vingoe was qualified to make the original assessment and yet he used Vingoe's findings to make his own judgement. I was quite looking forwards to meeting this man in court and I think he would have felt very foolish once he actually met Dan and discovered that he is not a brain-dead zombie but in fact a very pleasant young man.

All these eminent people were obviously pushing up the potential costs of the case. Along with having to instruct a barrister, Mr Peter Barry, we were now talking in the region of £60,000.

It was now the beginning of the year 2000 and we still did not have a final date for the hearing and the payment was due from the Criminal Injuries Board which was going to complicate matters. Obviously we knew we would have to inform the Legal Aid Board as soon as a payment was received as a recipient of legal aid must have no more than £3,000 to his/her name to be eligible. An outdated amount of money. Being honest and above board we were not likely to be able to put into operation moves to hide money received. Still, we decided to worry about this pending problem when it arose.

As I have already stated, most of this hearing was to be a paper exercise so only a small group of people who had made statements were actually called to attend. One such unfortunate person was Sarah, Dan's ex-girlfriend. She willingly gave statements but the defence picked up one section of her statement and they wanted her on the stand.

In February 2000 Dan received a payment from the Criminal Injuries Board. We decided that the important thing for Daniel was to buy himself a house and we searched high and low until we found one that he felt comfortable with. He didn't want to live near where the incident had occurred; he wanted to start afresh. This I knew would obviously complicate all our lives as we, the family, would have to travel further to help Daniel. Anyway, Daniel fell for a house in the suburbs of Bristol and as it was really very cheap compared to inner Bristol, we all thought it was a good decision. Receiving the criminal injuries compensation pay-out meant that we had to inform the Legal Aid Board and this in turn would mean that they could withdraw their support.

A date was set aside for August for the hearing, we were all sighted up for that month. Somehow the NHS Trust managed to get a stay of execution and we were given a date in January 2001 instead. By this time Hector Stamboulieh, our solicitor, was beginning to think that we would need a QC to add weight to our cause. He chose a gentleman called Adrian Palmer who proved to be an excellent choice. However, the potential court costs rocketed to around a nerve racking £150,000. We had to sort out the financial aspect before we could continue. You have to prove you can afford to lose before they will allow you to go to court. Daniel had £60,000 to put in the kitty and we managed to organise the remaining money needed. We were willing to risk everything to get to the truth. Hector had obviously tried for an out of court settlement which was rejected by the trust so it was all systems go, let battle commence. I think we were all, despite the losses that could occur that we could ill-afford, hyped up and keen to face the opposition in the courtroom. I didn't want to be the underdog unable to pursue this point just because the NHS was so powerful. If we lost because we were wrong and had misjudged the situation, we were ready to accept that but we didn't want to have to drop out simply because we had been outflanked financially.

We had a good Christmas and tried to forget the forthcoming events of January. I had managed to get a bit stressed before

Christmas and took some time off work. By Christmas itself I was well rested and prepared for the coming battle. Dan, Richard and I went away for the New Year, something we had not done before. We went up to friends in Baldock, a market town, just outside Letchworth, and had a thoroughly good away from it all few days.

The NHS Court Case

15 January seemed to be upon us before we had time to catch our breath. The Monday was a day set aside for the judge, Justice Toulson, to catch up on last minute statements. Dan and I spent the day in a huddle with our legal beavers. Adam had the day off and came to chambers with us. The chambers were opposite the solicitors' offices in Corn Street in the centre of Bristol. The actual court was only just down a side road, literally two minutes from the solicitors as well. The pitfalls of the case were pointed out to Dan by his barrister and QC and we were asked if we wanted at this point to withdraw, which we did not, of course. We did not want to have come this far and not learn the truth.

Tuesday at 10.30 was the start of the case of Daniel Gallimore versus North Bristol NHS Trust. Richard had the day off to come and give Dan a bit of moral support. We decided to always go to the solicitors' office first and walked down to the court with him. The press were waiting outside and it brought back memories of the Crown Court case back in 1997. The trial was actually taking place in the same Crown Court building so it felt almost like déjà vu.

It was all very strange. We stood when the judge came into the room; anyone leaving the court had to walk out backwards and bow towards the judge as they left. Justice Toulson was a very tall, thin man. He looked at first as if he was not even listening, scribbling notes as everyone spoke. It was not very far into the proceedings, however, when it was quite apparent that this learned gentleman was very astute and totally on the ball. As the case proceeded his knowledge became more and more obvious and Dan and I were quite spellbound by this obviously very clever gentleman. A prison officer friend of mine, Jim Harris, explained a point to me later about judges. He said that they had to be sure that everyone in the court fully understood what was going on and sometimes asked what sounded like stupid questions such as the famous 'Who are the Beatles?' But that we should not be under the illusion that the judge was out of date; he knew exactly who was who and what was what, the questions were asked to clarify any points for anyone else.

All of the first morning was taken up with the opening addresses we broke for lunch around 1.15 arranging to return at 2.15 for Daniel to take the stand. Joe had promised to come in the afternoon to hear Dan and give him a little support as we all knew he was nervous about speaking in court. We had decided to let Dan speak to prove that he was not brain dead as suggested. We realised that Dan putting on a good show would go against him care allowance wise but we were into matters of principle now.

Sarah, Dan's ex-girlfriend, was due to give evidence on that day as well. The poor girl, her memories of Bristol must be almost entirely of court cases and dramas surrounding them. Geoff Warnock, the head of IT at Cotham, was due to speak that day as well about the likelihood of Dan having been able to return to work had he not list his sight.

We had arranged to meet up with Adam and his new fiancée, who is now his wife, every lunchtime at a nearby pub to relay the latest events. Dan's ex girlfriend Sarah, her mum, Sarah's boyfriend, Geoff Warnock, Richard, Dan and I all descended on the pub as arranged; even Joe managed to join us there so it was quite a gathering. It was strange to all be together again. We had all been through a lot together and had not met as a group for a long time, though it seemed like only yesterday once we all got talking. Adam has a wonderful way of breaking the ice and making everyone feel at ease. It was actually quite a pleasant lunch hour.

We all arrived back at the appointed time and Dan went straight on the stand. He was asked lots of questions about how he managed, how he spent his days, what his hopes for the future were. I felt he came over as a very good-natured young man and obviously the judge felt the same way as he made a point of saying that he felt Dan was an inspiration, which was very nice to hear.

Straight after Dan they called to the stand Geoff Warnock. Geoff explained the financial workings of Cotham and how they had even now not replaced Daniel with another information technology technician despite advertising twice a year. Geoff stated that Dan would definitely have had a position at Cotham had he not lost his sight. Geoff's input was to do with loss of potential earning though I could never quite grasp why such importance was put on whether Dan would or would not have returned to Cotham. As Dan had only been twenty-one at the time of the assault I felt he had not yet even scratched the surface of his earning potential.

Mr B, the NHS defence counsel, seemed to have a problem understanding the funding of a school and how, if a post was not filled, the money put aside had to be reallocated. It seemed very straightforward to me and the judge appeared to grasp the idea. I think it was just a matter of getting as many brownie points as possible though why so much time was wasted on a simple part of the proceedings, I do not know.

Mr B was about thirty-five to forty, with dark hair and a rakish-type style to his apparel. He wore his robe slightly off one shoulder and spoke very softly and monotone, almost mumbling, I found it very hard to follow what he said. Dan said he could not hear him properly either and his hearing has sharpened considerably since the incident. Our QC, Mr Adrian Palmer, had an older, more orderly appearance, he spoke clearly and I could understand him. They both amazed me how they could just pluck a statement out of the air and find the correct quote amongst the different coloured folders lined up on their tables in front of them. They must have phenomenal memories.

Geoff had been more than kind towards Dan both when he worked at Cotham and since his accident, and we were all very grateful to him.

Sarah was next to take the stand. She had changed very little physically since we had last met, her hair was a little shorter and she was a little taller. She was dressed very conservatively and stood very upright. She had been dragged all the way down from Birmingham because of a couple of words in her original statement that the defence felt they could make an issue out of. She had said that Dan had made a remarked improvement by the Friday, which is why she had gone home to Kings Winford for the weekend. Sarah had submitted a second statement explaining that she had only based the idea that Dan had improved on information given to her by the nursing staff, she herself had seen no improvement at all. She went on to add that when someone is only eighteen they put their faith in what they are told by the medical profession. A piece in the medical notes also said that Sarah had told the nurses that Dan was speaking appropriately on the Thursday of the first week. A lot was made of this statement by the defence. It amused me because I was there and I know that Dan didn't say anything sensible all that week. He was in a computer game unable to get off level two. He proposed to Sarah but called her Ann-Marie and thought that the present prime minister was a short man in a mac, probably Winston Churchill who I think he mistook name wise for Harold Wilson by the description. I do not think that this was a sign of coherent conversation at all. Had the powers that be in Ward 2 explained to the family the seriousness of Dan's injuries we would have taken care to monitor him ourselves but we were totally unaware until the court case how serious Dan's original injuries had been. At no time was anything explained to any of us. We knew that the nurses suctioned Dan from time to time when he seemed to make a gurgling sound. I did not know at that time that they were actually keeping him alive and his airway clear. We all, Sarah included, assumed that Dan would be fine in a few days and go home. We were never given to believe anything different, which I was finding very irritating. I believe that families should be given full knowledge of what is occurring to their loved ones. We could be used as very useful tools to watch for danger signs if better informed.

Sarah was articulate and precise as you would expect from her and that seemed to end that line of questioning. At this stage we did not know the significance of this line of questioning but it soon was made clear to us. Sarah slipped out of the court straight after making her speech as she was now on a hospital complaints committee near her home and there was a meeting that evening.

It was near to the end of the day but Mr P, chief neurosurgeon at Frenchay, took the stand. It was then that I realised for the first time the way the defence was heading. Mr P explained the procedures in the hospital. He gave details of the injuries Daniel entered hospital with – bruising to the front of the brain caused by the brain striking the front of the skull when Dan fell and a large blood clot at the base of the skull caused by the actual impact with the curb. There was also a fracture in the left occipital region, extending down as far as the foramen magnum.

Mr P then went on to explain how ward rounds operated at Frenchay. He said that at eight o'clock he did a total ward round of up to sixty beds and then in the afternoon his SHO wrote up the notes of all these patients. I found this fact a little frightening especially when the rounds only took one hour and the SHO was a trainee.

We were then told about a scan taken on 3rd June 1996 which showed a considerable amount of brain swell. It was this X-ray that we believed had been overlooked and not acted upon despite being asked for as a matter of urgency. We were told how X-rays were placed on a shelf with the radiographer and how he would sometimes type up a report about the X-ray that would eventually find its way to the ward, possibly three days later. It all sounded very slip shod to me. Mr P did mention that results of X-rays were discussed during operations or moments when the team members managed to catch each other. I always realised that surgeons, and in fact all doctors, were overworked but it seemed that there was not enough hours in this man's day to guarantee efficiency. I was sorry to see Mr P on the stand as he has saved many lives in Frenchay over the years. However, as he had been the one who insisted on fighting this case I felt he had brought it on himself, and at the end of the day the buck stopped with him, he was then and still is in charge. He went on to say that he had looked in his diary and thought he might have seen Dan on Monday possibly, or it might have been Wednesday, but he wasn't actually sure if it was either as he had no recollection. There was certainly nothing in the medical notes to say he had examined Dan at all after the initial weekend when he was admitted.

We finished that day at about five and that meant that we would have to start the next day with Mr P still under oath and in the witness box.

The next day and all subsequent days, it was just Dan and me attending court, the rest of the family caught up on the proceedings when we got home. Wednesday began with Mr P being questioned by both prosecution and defence lawyers. It is not at all like proceedings in a criminal court. When at a criminal court case the witnesses were asked specific questions and they strayed beyond a simple answer, they were stopped. In this sort of trial the witnesses ramble on and on and are never stopped. If they say something and then think about it, they then clarify what they meant. This tended to make each witness spend a lot of time clarifying his or her statements.

I thought that Mr P did not show the hospital in a very good light, maybe he had seen Dan in that first week, maybe he hadn't. Possibly the registrar who ordered a second scan because he was concerned over the other signs Dan was showing and the SHO actually picked up the wrong scan and thought nothing had changed from admittance. Maybe Dr TS should have actually looked in on Dan when asked. It was all very maybe and possibly, I felt that the real blame was being shifted towards the SHO – who as the judge pointed out was after all only in training at that stage – and poor organisational details within the hospital. We are living in a society when no one can simply say, 'Maybe I made a mistake and I am sorry for it.'

Mr P faced cross-examination by our QC, followed by the judge asking a few relevant questions and then he was allowed to step down.

Next to take the stand was Dr G, whom I did not recognise at all. I cannot remember ever seeing him at Ward 2 and yet I was there all the time. His statement was amazing. It was full of 'I think', 'maybe' and 'possibly', except one major paragraph, paragraph four. He actually said that he remembered Dan walking about Ward 2. Seeing as how he could remember very little else, this comment seemed mind-blowing to me. Dan never moved from his bed. The medical records referred to him as immobile so obviously anything else in that man's statement under interrogation was dismissed by our QC. He eventually said he may have made a mistake and maybe only saw Dan being helped on to a commode a couple of times. That did happen once actually and that was a nightmare operation that was not repeated. I did wonder why Sarah was asked if Dan had ever been out of bed in Ward 2.

I did think it strange that so much was said about what a Dr S and Dr TS did throughout this first week in Frenchay and yet they were not called as witnesses.

We broke for lunch and Dan and I wondered off to find Adam as planned. Adam was eager to hear how the morning had gone.

Next to take the stand was our expert medical witness, Mr K FRCS (SN), head of the Neurosurgery Department at Addenbrooks in Cambridge. Mr K is not an outwardly friendly man but he is undoubtedly a very knowledgeable one and one I would willingly trust with my life. I remembered taking Dan to see Mr K at Cambridge. We came away wondering what he thought as he said very little. His statement said it all, he backed one hundred per cent our thoughts that intubation had been delayed unnecessarily, resulting in the loss of Daniel's sight.

Mr K was an excellent witness. He was precise and clear using diagrams to explain how the brain swell would push down on to the windpipe, causing an obstruction and eventually respiratory collapse. Which, of course, happened in Dan's case on 8th June 1996.

Mr K's statement started with his quite impressive curriculum vitae and his own background. He went on to talk about Dan's past medical history, he gave a narrative history of the accident on 31 May 1996, Dan's progress, present situation and details of the examination he performed on Dan. His statement went on to mention the extensive medical notes that he had studied relating to this case, the reviewing of the medical records, and reviewing of medical correspondence prior to the accident. His statement then went on to the day of the incident and the time at Southmead, six hours, before transfer to Frenchay where the admitting doctor in A & E noted a swelling due to a collection of blood in the left occipital region under the scalp. The admitting doctor made a diagnosis of concussion due to alcohol. He did not identify any focal neurological deficits and the doctor stated, 'No indication for CT scan.' He (we have to call him 'he' because to this day I do not know his name) did mention the X-ray that we had brought from Southmead but it was dismissed as irrelevant. Luckily a further four hours later (bringing it to ten hours since the incident) a more senior doctor who I now learnt was called Dr Younge declared that Dan had a significant head injury and referred Dan to the neurosurgeons. All this seemed to be a rough outline of how I remember events of 31 May and 1 June 1996.

Mr K described the original CT scan taken around 1.30 on 1st June, which declared bilateral frontal contusions, no mass effect, occipital fracture with posterior fossa haematoma and blood in the sphenoid air sinus. He went on to state that on 4th June a medical entry declared that Dan had become disorientated to place and time, was unable to look to the left and there was mention of a right lower motor seventh nerve palsy. Dan's gag was also reduced on the right and left. The entry also mentioned secretions pooling in oral pharynx and a poor swallow effect, although the registrar had written 'not for CT scan'. Of course, Mr K went on to describe the events of 8th June as taken from the medical notes. They mentioned the development of a right lower motor neurone palsy of the seventh nerve, but amazingly this information was followed by an entry stating that there was a plan to discharge Dan back to

Southmead within forty-eight hours. That was the Friday and the day that Sarah and I had been told that Dan was improving and although we could see no evidence of this we obviously trusted the doctors' judgement on this. Sarah believed it enough to go home for the weekend. However, in the night the notes stated that vomiting became tonic, Dan was incontinent of urine, there was a deep sighing effect, no response to pain and his pupils were no longer reacting. In fact his Coma Score was logged as three. He had arrested and fallen into a coma.

When Mr K had submitted his first written statement he was not aware of the obvious deterioration recorded on a CT scan taken on 3rd June. This scan was originally missing but eventually after several requests from our legal team was uncovered and showed a very precarious situation for Dan that was certain to result in brain stem dysfunction. Mr K's opinion, even without the view of the 3rd June scan, was that Dan was already in a very dangerous situation and that he would have intubated Dan on arrival at Frenchay with his original injuries.

Commenting under oath on Dan's level of care at Frenchay, his main concerns were that Dan was treated conservatively in Frenchay Hospital despite significant abnormalities on the initial CT scan. Another concern related to the subsequent CT scan taken on 3rd June which showed significant swelling in both parts of the brain (both in the posterior fossa and supra tentorial compartments) with documented tonsillor herniation. In other words the brain had swollen to the cubic capacity of the hard shell called the skull. He drew a sketch to show the brain swell. There was no room left for swelling and Mr K felt that in his opinion there was no option but to paralyse Dan and intubate. He felt that although these manoeuvres were put into place after Dan had suffered respiratory arrest it was by now too late to save his sight. Mr K also noted that the significant deterioration was reported by the SHO on 4th June 1996 when Dan became disorientated and his pupils became sluggish. There were several other signs of possible brain stem compression. These signs were itemised by a relatively junior doctor who reported them to a more senior colleague, the registrar (another name that has never been disclosed and remains a mystery) who felt, without even attending Dan, that a further CT scan was unnecessary. Mr K felt that in view of the fact that there was no indication that the registrar reviewed Dan at that time, this was a major concern over Dan's level of care.

Mr K's diagnosis was that many of Daniel's problems especially the visual disability could have been avoided by timely intubation and ventilation prior to neurological deterioration.

I was amazed by the technical level of questions asked of our expert witness by Justice Toulson and the obvious level of understanding of the answers. Several diagrams were used to explain the problems surrounding the seventh nerve. I felt that every biology lesson I had ever attended at school was suddenly heaped into one day.

Dan found it very strange hearing people discuss his medical condition in detail and I would imagine it must have been very upsetting for him to learn that his sight had been lost needlessly.

The day ended there and Mr K returned the following day, Thursday, to take the stand immediately.

It always amused me every morning when the defence would come in with a copy of the *Western Daily Press* to scan it for an account of the court case. Every day carried a significant coverage in the local papers. The headlines ranged from 'Judge praises Hero', as indeed he did, to 'We did our best for Hero' based on Mr P's testimony.

The defence was not best pleased by the press coverage but as it was an open court there was nothing they could do about it.

Obviously Mr K was cross-examined by the defence attorney but he was totally immovable on all counts. Mr K was not allowed out of the stand until the end of that day. We had hoped to get Mr Brice, the defence expert on the stand but decided to cut the day a little short instead.

Mr K had put himself in a very difficult position for us. He knew a couple of the doctors involved and I admired the fact that he was willing to stand up for what he felt was right, despite the obvious pressures of the 'old boys' network'. I wanted to win this case very badly for him so it would be recognised that he was right to stand up and be counted.

When we arrived on Friday morning it was Mr Brice's turn to get the grilling. Mr Brice was a very talkative man in what looked like his eighties. He was retired and had been in private practice for a number of years. Obviously prior to that he had been a neurological specialist. I did wonder why he had been chosen to represent the 'other side' as I felt he might be a little out of touch.

Hector assured me that Mr Brice was a doctor who did give evidence in court quite often and that sometimes this could be an advantage. I could not imagine anyone being more laid back and yet totally convincing than our Mr K so I was not unduly concerned about any evidence that Mr Brice would give, regardless of him being an old hand at court.

It seemed that Mr Brice's original statement was based on there never having been a scan on 3rd June. He had never been shown it and had only seen the original scan and the one taken on 8th June after Dan's collapse. So his entire testimony was based on the fact that, although there were signs of deterioration, they were not verified by the all-important scan. Obviously the fact that the scan had been left out of the testimony had to be compensated for and it became obvious that the NHS were trying to suggest that the brain swell was not the worry in Dan's case, it was the haematoma at the base of his skull that was the result of the original assault. This was suggested as a possible danger and reason for not intubating sooner in case it ruptured. I have very little medical knowledge though it has increased considerably in the past five years and I remember very clearly what I was told on the Sunday after Dan went into the coma. I remember how Dr Chris Chandler had taken great pains to explain to the family that the brain swell was the thing that would kill Dan, if anything, and that we were to ignore blood clots they would disperse. Had I have realised what direction the NHS would take, I would have instructed Hector to get a statement from Dr Chandler. I was actually quite annoyed that I would not be able to stand up and shout that what was being said was rubbish. Unfortunately, at this stage it is not allowed to add to already presented statements even when you believe that what is being said is not correct. You can only speak if on the stand.

Mr Brice had stated how serious and complicated Dan's head injuries were and how they were outside the norm. He said that he felt that it was right to treat Daniel conservatively and not aggressively as Mr K suggested. Mr Brice tried to discredit Mr K's testimony but was not at all convincing in my opinion and it was obvious that we had won this round, especially when we moved on to the question of the problem with Daniel's gag mechanism which Mr Bruce tried to skirted over. The judge himself asked Mr Brice why he had said that the problem of the loss of gag would be a reason to respirate. Mr Brice said that he felt that the question of loss of gag had not been definitely qualified owing to the fact that the usual test of gag was a stick at the back of the throat and Dan had not been co-operative because of his level of consciousness. He seemed to be talking himself into a hole as far as I could see.

I must admit to feeling a little sorry for Mr Brice. He was a very nice man who was inclined towards talking a great deal. Our QC is a very clever man and he found it quite easy to fluster Mr Brice and get him to say a little more than he needed to for his own good. It didn't take Mr Palmer long to get Mr Brice to admit that he had not been shown 'the scan'. Subsequently Mr Brice admitted that in view of the scan he himself might have been inclined to intubate or at the least arrange an MRI scan. He did try to reclaim some ground by stating reasons why intubation is not always used. They were feeble reasons, lack of ICU beds (not appropriate in this case), the fact that the voice box can be damaged by long-term intubation. The most ridiculous reason I felt was because it upsets relatives to see patients on life support as I explained in the previous chapter. Mr P had already added another reason to keep out of the ICU, he had said on oath that they had lost three patients the week before in the ICU due to infections. Mr Palmer was quick to remind Mr Bruce of this.

Mr Bruce was a little flustered and we broke for lunch. Mr Brice was obviously still on oath and was not allowed to speak to anyone about the case but he did come back in the afternoon very composed. Dan and I had gone to lunch very pleased with the day so far.

Mr. Brice was back on the stand in the afternoon. We reached a common agreement that the second scan on 3rd June was dangerous. On 4th June nurses were concerned that Dan had not been able to swallow his own saliva for a number of hours and secretions were pooling. The judge made the suggestion that the nurses must have been clearing Dan's airway, which is, in fact, what they did do. The judge asked, if gag reflexes were deficient would that not be the moment when things should have swung towards intubation and Mr Brice said, 'Yes.' Mr Brice agreed that on 4th June there was a suggestion that something was going wrong in the brain stem. The judge then asked, 'If the registrar had known what we know – the brain swell, the loss of gag and so on, would he have had a choice over whether he came to examine Daniel or could he give a reasonable judgement over the phone?' Mr Brice replied that he hoped that the registrar would have thought, Oh dear, what is happening, is the blood clot causing trouble? And he hoped that the registrar would have discussed with Mr P the possibility of ventilation. The judge further asked Mr Brice if he thought that the registrar could have discounted the problems without actually looking himself at Daniel. The judge continued by saying that he felt that an unqualified SHO would not have a full spectrum of knowledge and would require a registrar to check on his findings. Justice Toulson pointed out and not for the first time that, after all, SHOs were only training and not qualified to make life or death decisions. Mr Brice agreed that the NCO should have looked himself but that it appeared that he had not done so. Mr Brice said that he felt something should have been done on 4th June.

The judge asked if the gag reflex was checked on 5th June and followed this by asking about the speech therapist who had attended Dan. He wanted to know if the speech therapist could check a patient's swallow accurately. Mr Brice replied that he felt that they were experts in this field. The judge then wanted to know at what stage the speech therapist would be called in to test the swallow reflex. Mr Brice seemed to think that this was an open area and that they could be called at any time. He was then asked if the speech therapist could suggest intubation. Mr Brice said that the speech therapist's input would be valued.

As we finished very early that day Mr Brice had to return on the Monday as well. I felt this would give the defence time to rethink their strategy. It seemed as though an over the weekend break would be an advantage to them.

It was a strange weekend; we were all in limbo and couldn't really settle. I know that Dan was eager to get back to court and finish the case.

Monday soon came round and we returned with Mr Brice on the stand. There were a couple of extra faces on the NHS team, both of whom I knew, which was strange. One was a woman who had been a long-term girlfriend of a friend of Richard's when we were a lot younger. I did say hello to her and wondered why she was there. The other face was a woman who used to live next door to me when I lived in the School House in Cotham. I knew that she worked for the publicity department at Frenchay. She totally blanked me and did so again a few days later when I saw her walking near the school. Very strange as it was nothing personal and I could not understand why she should act as though it was, but there is no accounting for folk. Mr K had gone back to Cambridge so we were without a medical expert. Obviously this moment was used to try to discredit a couple of points brought up by Mr K. Mr Brice suggested that it was possible, because Dan did not arrest until 8th June, that the brain swell had gone down in between 6th and 7th June. He did however concede that he would have wanted a further scan on the 6th just to put his mind at rest had Dan been his patient.

By 11.20 all questions had been asked and answered of Mr Brice and he stood down from the stand. As we had agreed quantum (the amount of damages) at the end of the previous week it was no longer necessary to call Doctor Vingoe or Doctor M, the neuropsychologists, so effectively the case was over. Had we not have agreed quantum, the judge himself would have had to decide what damages should be awarded. Our team had come up with one costing and the defence came up with a far lesser one so we went for a line somewhere near the middle. I would have to say that Dan took a lot of persuasion to settle on the figure we did and I was sympathetic as I felt it was not enough for the loss of sight and possible earnings for the rest of his life. Hector did not want Dan to take a chance that the judge might consider that the case was worth less. It was a case of should we or should we not gamble and at the end of the day it was down to Dan what we should do. I felt we had already gambled and it might be worth carrying on in that style but we were persuaded and I think, now having spoken to others who have been awarded damages, that we probably did the right thing. We had to take into account the fact that the CICA wanted all the criminal injuries compensation repaid, which didn't seem quite right to me and Dan would also have to pay back any social security payments he had received over the past five years. Obviously we wanted Dan to win enough money to have made this exercise worthwhile. We hadn't even got a result yet and the vultures were gathering already.

It was now down to the judge. It was decided that closing submissions would be put in writing and faxed to the judge that evening and a short discussion about these submissions would take place on the Tuesday morning.

Tuesday – second week of the trial and the last day. Dan and I arrived with Hector and his assistant, Louise, who is a pretty little young lady who barely looks old enough to be out of school but is studying law and doing a few weeks in practice with Foster and Partners.

The HTV camera crew were outside and several reporters from different newspapers inside. There had been reporters at every sitting for the past week and a piece in the *Bristol Evening Post* and *Western Daily* Press every day about the trial. On this day, however, there seemed to be a larger than usual press presence. I believe that the press were expecting a decision that day – if only!

Closing submissions had been faxed to the learned judge and he had obviously read them. Regardless of the fact that closing submissions were in writing, Adrian Palmer and Mr B still spoke for quite some time, emphasising and elaborating on points they had brought up in their closing submissions.

The defendant's counsel asked Mr Justice Toulson if they could have an early decision on this case. We were told that the judge can sometimes take a couple of weeks to read over all the information and come to a conclusion. We were obviously quite happy to allow the learned gentleman any length of time needed especially if it would help him see in our favour. Mr Justice Toulson said he would try to make an early decision and felt that Dan would also be keen to know the result. I thought the judge seemed a little peeved with the defence over this point. The judge said that he felt that a couple of days might be suffice to make a decision and that he would contact the solicitors concerned and confirm if, in fact, Thursday was going to be possible. The press were eager to get an overall view of how we felt the trial had gone but we were unable to comment for fear of prejudicing the case.

We had a phone call on Wednesday afternoon to say that we should be at Hector's office for 10.15 a.m. on Thursday morning. Thursday morning we had a further call to say that the judge had requested that the time be 1.30 p.m. for a 2.15 start. To say that Dan and I were nervous about this day would be an understatement. Wednesday had seemed a very long day and although we felt that we should win if life was fair, we also knew that life had been very unfair to Dan so far. Once we actually arrived at Hector's office I felt a lot better. Once again the cameras were out in force outside the court and we were filmed going in. The courtroom had a heavy press presence and a man from HTV stopped us before we entered to ask if he could interview us after the decision was announced.

Mr Justice Toulson came into the court. I didn't have a clue what to expect on that day. I assumed the judge would say who he found in favour of and then elaborate on why. This was vaguely right but he actually talked for nearly two hours about the case, reading from his own extensive notes and then gave his findings. I was amazed how accurate the judge's account was about the original incident and the terrible time we had getting Dan admitted, which he heavily criticised. He even made a point of mentioning that Dan had only drunk a small amount of alcohol because he was driving and the totally unacceptable attitude of the houseman on duty at Frenchay A & E that day. He went on to say that he felt the second scan taken on 3rd June must have been overlooked. He made reference to the amount of patients visited each ward round by the group of doctors at Frenchay and the way notes were written up by what amounted to a trainee doctor many hours later. He also pondered on the practices at the radiography department that allowed X-rays to be muddled and the length of time it seemed to take according to Mr P to get a written report on a scan, however urgent. He made it quite clear that he thought that too much pressure and responsibility was laid on the shoulders of the SHO who was, in fact, in training. He also felt that certain other members of the medical staff should have attended Dan when requested. He felt that it seemed to him that it was good nursing skills by the actual nurses in Ward 2 that had prevented Dan from arresting earlier by their persistent attempts to keep his airway open. He found no fault at all with the nursing staff at Frenchay or Southmead, which I totally concurred with. He dismissed the Bolam Clause as irrelevant in this case. He went on to say that he found Mr K's assessment of the case convincing and agreed with him that the treatment of Dan at Frenchay in his first week fell short of that which one should expect from a Serious Head Injuries Unit. Mr Justice Toulson then went on to praise Daniel and the way he had put his life back together and found in Daniel's favour. He spoke so softly at the end of his speech that I didn't catch what he said and had to ask Hector if we had actually won, which, of course, we had. I looked across at the 'other side' and could see that they were none too thrilled.

The NHS Trust barrister asked about costs and they were all awarded against them. The judge seemed pleased that we had reached a quantum on the amount of claim and our QC mentioned that we had suggested an out-of-court settlement that had been dismissed for far less. I actually think that if we had held out for the judge to decided the value of our case Dan would have got more, but that is purely academic now, so irrelevant.

I watched the defence solicitor leave the court and then their barrister ask leave to appeal against costs, which was denied. This was followed by a request to be allowed to appeal against the decision, having said the usual bit about having the greatest respect for Daniel. The judge said that he doubted the wisdom of such an action and the barrister, I felt rather rudely, said that maybe a different judge would put a different degree of importance on certain statements. The judge said that was as maybe and said they could have twenty-eight days to come up with reasonably grounds to appeal. Dan and I felt totally deflated at this point. We were so elated that we had won and then just two minutes later felt as though we had been shot down in flames by this move to appeal. I couldn't imagine what they could appeal about; the medical evidence would not change. Hector did explain later that it was a ruse to prevent us from talking to the press because an appeal was pending; the hope being that at the end of twenty-eight days all interest in the case would have been lost and forgotten.

The judge left the room and, although pleased, we wondered what the twenty-eight days to appeal would mean to the case. Hector said that, having won, now he felt the Legal Aid Board would cover the cost of an appeal if needs be but it could be eighteen months to two years hence and would be in London at the High Court. That really knocked the wind out of our sails. We were advised that we could not comment to the press. However, when we got outside the NHS solicitor was just finishing a very in-depth statement. Dan spoke briefly to the *Evening Post, Western Daily Press, Bristol Observer* reporters and the HTV cameramen and crew who had waited so patiently. I had prepared a wonderful speech if we won and I couldn't use it. We promised to keep everyone informed and let them know if an appeal was going ahead. If no appeal was forthcoming Dan agreed to any interviews being undertaken as soon as it was possible to do so.

So to put this chapter in a nut shell. I believe, and the judge agreed, if they had intubated my son at the first signs of trouble i.e. on admittance, enough oxygen would have reached his brain to prevent the swelling that subsequently led to his fitting, falling into a coma and consequentially losing his sight. If they had chosen to wait a while but looked at the second scan taken in the first week and together with the obvious other danger signs acted accordingly and intubated at that time, there was a second opportunity to possibly save Daniel's sight. Had Dan been in another part of the country in another hospital he could have probably walked out of hospital virtually intact. Life is definitely a lottery.

We could have made Daniel into a millionaire through capitalizing on his injuries had we pushed him around in a wheel chair for months after it was necessary and claimed that he was now agoraphobic and afraid of life. Psychological effects seem to carry a lot of weight these days. Months at counselling can add thousands to a claim. But Daniel thought, and quite rightly too, that he had lost enough of his young life. Financially it doesn't pay to be strong minded and truthful but money isn't everything, a clear conscience is worth more to me. Hopefully with good financial advice Daniel will be reasonably comfortable and able to build a new life. Money would not restore his sight, if it could we would obviously bankrupt ourselves to this end.

All our team were very pleased with themselves. Dan and I felt rather in limbo and just wanted to get everything over with. It was two weeks before we learnt that the appeal was not going to take place and we were very glad. Hector arranged a press conference, which seemed very strange. We used a room in a hotel in the centre of Bristol, a short walk from the solicitors' offices. All the local press and TV stations attended. Hector was excellent and gave a very good account of the proceedings and our feelings. We arranged to meet the HTV and BBC people separately later at Dan's house for a more in-depth interview. This happened and we had a very heavy local press coverage of the case both in the newspapers and on the actual news programmes.

I have chosen only to use initials instead of names for some people as regards the hospital negligence case. We should not loose sight of the fact that the medical staff, especially the more prominent ones, have saved many lives before and since the incident. I also believe that procedures have changed since Daniel was in hospital so as to avoid a similar incident occurring. Hopefully, something positive has come out of this very disturbing period in our lives.

So that's it, it's all over, and now we have to wait for the cheque, which could take several months. Court costs having to be worked out before payment and other expenses deducted. But at least we had won and Dan could start living again. Careful investing was to be looked into and hopefully an income for life could be organised for Daniel.

I myself felt as though there was now a bit of a void in my life. You get used to fighting in your corner after a while. Dan had a book about dreams called *Puzzled by Blind Dreams* published. Dan had experienced a re-occurring dream whilst coming out of his coma and had put it down on his tape recorder for me to type up for him. It made good reading so he decided to ask others who had been close to death like him if they had experienced such dreams. We gathered a selection of these together and they formed a book which he originally wanted entitled *Do You Dream in Black and White?* a question Dan is often asked. We found an interested publisher and the book went to print, all be it under a new name (Puzzled By Blind Dreams) as the publisher did not like Daniel's choice of title. Daniel also launched his own web site which is a blind awareness training scheme called 'Have Stick Will Travel'. Having given talks in several schools, he wanting to branch out into industry and commerce. The intention being to raise money to assist other blind people or groups through his web site, his first project provided the Avon Blind Sports Cricket Team with their cricket tops. Dan also completed the first part of a counseling course, as he is interested in helping trauma victims. Not bad for a brain-damaged, dyslexic blind Behçets sufferer!

My son was let down by the very people I had brought him up to respect and put his faith and trust in. Firstly the police, when the perpetrators of the original injuries walked free on a technicality and secondly by the medical profession, due I am sure to human error and we are human after all and possibly overworked and under funded.

Several people, mainly journalists for obvious reasons, tried to urge us to take MB and H to court privately. But at the end of the day, they are not famous and do not even have a reputation to protect. It would have been a painful and pointless exercise bringing unnecessary distress to innocent youngsters who had been brave enough to stand up when they thought the law was with them. Just to prove a point we could have taken them to court but there would be no custodial sentence so the whole exercise would have been pointless, tempting as it was. MB and H are not closet millionaires so there would not even be any financial gain for such an action. It would have cost my family a fortune that we would rather use making Daniel comfortable.

Dan works out regularly down the gym thanks to Paul Emsley, a new found friend and starting to get really fit and, more importantly, a new social life. Adam got married in August 2001 to a lovely young woman who we are all pleased to have as a new member of our family. Joe is still very involved with music, his new band is called Tin Dogs: he seems happy enough. Kate got married in 2003 and we were all happy for her. The family were all glad to hear that Dan's ex girlfriend Sarah was also about to get married. We moved from Muller Road to live near Dan. I was not sorry to leave that house, I liked the house structurally but it wasn't a lucky house. The last time we went away for a few days we weren't burgled but we did find our cat dead in the gutter when we got home, and I felt enough was enough, that house didn't like me and I didn't like it. We have very little information about the rest of the youngsters involved in the incident that inspired this book back in 1996, for them life has moved on as it must. Richard has gone back to working for himself. I left Cotham School and opened a web site that provides individual original poems for every and any occasion and I also run a small publishing company.

David Blunkett

One very encouraging visitor that Dan received at his home in 2002 was David Blunkett. Despite his obviously full life as home secretary he took the time to contact Dan when he was about to visit the West Country and ask if he could call in. Needless to say we at first thought this was someone messing about but soon confirmed that it was in fact Mr Blunkett himself and he did want to visit Dan in his home. He arrived in his red jaguar, with his driver, body guard and a following car that contained a further two gentlemen but no press and that we felt was wonderful. He stayed chatting casually to Daniel for an hour and a half, only leaving because he had an appointment at Highgrove with Prince Charles. Obviously Adam, his wife Sarah, Richard and I all gathered at the house to meet the great man, keeping his men fed and watered and looking after Lucy the guide dog whilst Mr. Blunkett spoke privately to Dan. Of all the people we have met over the years I can honestly say that David Blunkett was the warmest, and most charming of them all, an absolutely delightful man and an inspiration for anyone with a disability. He called his blindness a disadvantage and a challenge to overcome, and what an example he showed my son, for which I will be forever grateful. We all shook his hand warmly when he left. Politics aside that man is one in a million.

David B had also promised to keep in touch, which is something he has also done. He has a particular interest in Poetry and was kind enough to write a forward for a book of poems that I recently published to raise money for Shelter. It is called '*Sleeping Rough*'. I am only sorry that David's life has gone a bit off track because he really deserves to be happy, he is a good man.

The Lord Mayor's Medal.

On the 9th May 2002, Dan was presented with the Lord Mayor's Medal in the Bristol Council House by the right Honourable Lord Mayor of Bristol, Counsellor Brenda P. Huggitt. This was in recognition of his charity work and his courage in personal adversity.

Life has changed quite dramatically for all of us involved in this book. To say we have put the dramas of May 1996 behind us would not be strictly true, it was all too horrendous to ever forget completely, but as time goes by the memories are a little easier to live with. I am hoping that writing this book will prove a therapeutic exercise laying a few ghosts. I hope it might also encourage anyone who has had a similar experience to Daniel not to give up on life.

One thing that the assault on Dan and his subsequent blindness have taught us it that you never know what life is going to throw at you. You have to try to deal with life one day at a time as best you can and that is exactly what Dan has done. I am so proud of the way my youngest son has dealt with the hand he has been dealt. He really is 'The Wind Beneath my Wings.'

Thank You

At this point I would like to say a special thank you to all the youngsters who so bravely stood up and were counted at both the Magistrates' and Crown Court. It was a harrowing experience for them all and one I hope they never have to repeat.

I would like to add a special thanks to the girls who seeing my son's assault on the night of 31 May 1996 risked their own safety, Kate, Babe, Sarah and Rachel. I would add an even greater thank you to Kate and Isabelle for continuing to be there for my sons and to anyone who was not there on the fateful night but has been ever since, especially James Stokes and the members of the Somerville Club. Collette and Pierre. The new groups of friends at the Bristol Royal Society for the Blind, the Bristol Young Visually Impaired Club and the Avon Sports and Leisure Club for the Visually Impaired. Individual new friends especially Paul Elmsley and Andy, who are helping to get Dan fit and stimulate his mind. A friend in need and so forth.

Our brilliant legal team led by Hector Stamboulieh, what an inspired choice he was. Frenchay intensive care, who I can not praise enough.

Thanks also to my personal friends who have helped me come to terms with the past years and regain my sense of humour. Ted and the Rabble, Foxey and Margaret, Sima, Helena, Theresa and Pete, Julie, Eileen, Christine, Jim, my sister Judy, Paul, Alex and Michael, Richard's family, numerous Somerville club members (our extended family), and everyone still on my Christmas card list. The staff past and present of Cotham (Grammar) School in Bristol, especially Jim McKay, Geoff Warnock, Sylvia Aldis, the Forbes family, the Sleighs, Belinda Sully, mad Kim and John, Thelma, Elaine, John Heybeard and old administration friends. A special thank you to Neville Jones. Biddles Ltd for their patience and help. Many more that I hope will forgive me not mentioning them by name.

Lastly but most importantly my wonderful family - Joe, Emma, Adam, Sarah, Daniel, Dave, Ricki and my husband Richard.

Thank you all for your friendship and support.

The Behçets Syndrome Society
Registered Charity No. 326679
21, Conference Drive,
Locks Heath,
Southampton,
Hampshire.
SO31 6WP
Tel: 01488 71116

Honorary Secretary: Richard West

Daniel's web site can be accessed on www.havestickwilltravel.com
And also of interest www.poemstoorder.com
www.pomegranatebooks.co.uk
www.biddles.co.uk

I would also like to mention the friends that we have lost since this book started to take form.

Justin Lawrence (1973 – 2003)
A valued childhood friend of Daniel's (see page 15)

David Webb (1950 - 2002)
A gentleman in the full sense of the word.

Richard (Clive) Beckingham (1951 – 2004)
Always there giving support throughout the whole ordeal.

Always in our thoughts.

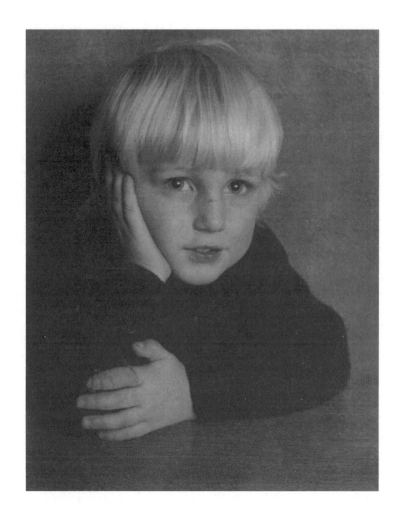

Dan at 18 months old.

Dan and I in 1976

Dan aged 14 when on the books for The Model
Trends Agency in 1989.

Top: Dan with the late, great Bobby Moore
Bottom: Joe, Adam and Dan in November 1990

Dan immediately prior to the incident in 1996

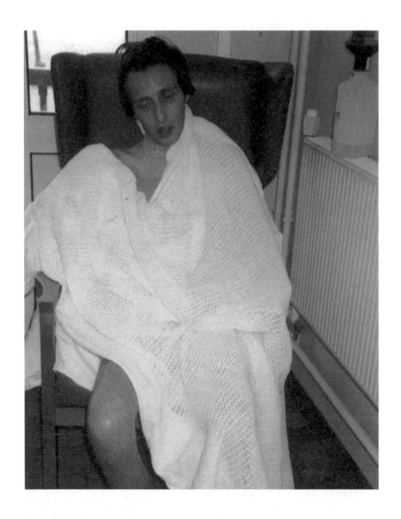

Dan at Southmead Hospital in August 1996 nearly 3
months after the assault.

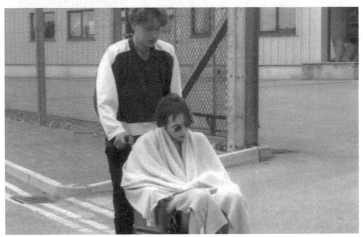

Top: Learning to walk
Bottom: Being pushed around the grounds of
Southmead by his brother Joseph in August 1996, 3
months after assault.

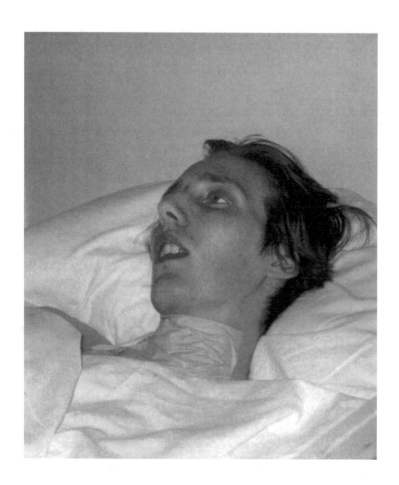

Dan 10 weeks after assault.

Dan as he is now.

Top: Dan with Robbie Fowler
Bottom: With Michael Owen

Adam and Dan with the Liverpool football team of 1998.

Top: Dan with Lennox Lewis and Chris Eubank at the
1999 Pride of Britain Awards.
Bottom: At same event with Sir Paul McCartney and
his brother Adam.

Dan with ex-Emmerdale and Bad Girls
actress Claire King at Pride of Britain 1999.

Top: Richard Branson and Dan at Pride of Britain 1999.
Bottom: (From right) Adam, Paul Burrell, myself and Dan at 1999 Pride of Britain awards.

Top: Lisa Potts Gm and Dan
Bottom: Babara Windsor and Dan at 1999 Pride of
Britain awards.

Top: Dan with William Roach and his wife at the
2000 Pride of Britain Awards.
Bottom: Dan, Adam and I with Cilla Black at the
1999 Pride of Britain Awards where Dan received
a bravery award

Dan with Martine McCutcheon at Pride of Britain
Awards 2000

Top: Barbara Windsor and I.
Bottom: Michael Greco with Dan at Pride of Britain 2000.

Top: David Blunkett with Dan in Dan's kitchen 2002.
Bottom: Dan recieving the lords Mayors medal in Bristol 2002.